A Practical Guide to Assessing Without Levels: Supporting and Safeguarding High Quality Achievement in Physical Education

ISBN: 978-1-909012-28-8

Author:
Andrew Frapwell

afPE appreciates the contributions in case studies or thinking and ideas to this resource made by:

Ben Hill – Physical Education and School Sport Consultant at Tower Hamlets Youth Sport Foundation, London

Iain Hunter – Physical Education Coordinator, Manorfield Primary School, Tower Hamlets, London

Mike James – Physical Education Teacher, Thomas Aveling School, Rochester, Kent

Dominic Limb – Education Consultant (PE and School Sports) at Derbyshire County Council

Mark Pearson – Head of Physical Education, St Margaret Ward Catholic Academy, Stoke-on-Trent, Staffordshire

Jim Preece, Head of Physical Education, Bishop Perowne CE College, Worcester

Jason Rhodes – Subject Inspector for Physical Education, Education Development Service, County Durham

Fiona Ryan – Physical Education Teacher, Wilmslow High School, Cheshire

Karen Shopland – Area Manager and School Games Coordinator, North East Derbyshire School Sport Partnership, Chesterfield, Derbyshire

Mark Tournier – Partnership Development Manager, Chesterfield School Sport Partnership, Brookfield Community School, Chesterfield, Derbyshire

Sue Trotman – Physical Education Consultant, Director, Dancedesk, Sandwell

Huw Williams – Head of Physical Education, Wilmslow High School, Cheshire

afPE project lead officer: Sue Wilkinson
Coachwise editor: Christopher Stanners
Coachwise designer: Saima Nazir
Photographs © Alan Edwards except where otherwise stated

While every effort has been made to trace and seek permission from copyright holders, the publishers, Coachwise Ltd, invite any unacknowledged copyright holders to email enquiries@coachwise.ltd.uk

It is the publisher's intent to fully credit any unacknowledged copyright holders at the earliest opportunity.

Published on behalf of afPE by

Association for Physical Education
Room 117
Bredon
University of Worcester
Henwick Grove
Worcester WR2 6AJ
Tel: 01905-855 584
Email: enquiries@afpe.org.uk
Website: www.afpe.org.uk

Coachwise Ltd
Chelsea Close
Off Amberley Road
Armley
Leeds LS12 4HP

Tel: 0113-231 1310
Email: enquiries@coachwise.ltd.uk
Website: www.coachwise.ltd.uk

91058

If a child can't learn the way we teach, maybe we should teach the way they learn.

Ignacio 'Nacho' Estrada

Education is not to reform students or amuse them or to make them expert technicians. It is to unsettle their minds, widen their horizons, inflame their intellects, teach them to think straight, if possible.

Robert M. Hutchins

The mediocre teacher tells. The good teacher explains. The superior teacher demonstrates. The great teacher inspires.

William A. Ward

Preface

About the Author

Andrew Frapwell is the Association for Physical Education (afPE) National Lead for Assessment. He is currently a registered Office of Qualifications and Examinations Regulation (Ofqual) subject expert, a physical education subject adviser for Hartpury University College and a company director. Internationally, Andrew has presented/run workshops in the United States, New Zealand, Switzerland, Greece, Germany, Finland and Kosovo; consulted on the production of teacher training materials in Saudi Arabia in 2012; and was the author of the physical education curriculum for Kosovo (January to June 2014) as part of a European Union donor project. In his capacity as a writer, he is widely published, has authored qualifications for the Qualifications and Credit Framework (QCF) and was co-editor of the afPE national journal *Physical Education Matters* 2010–2014.

Previously, Andrew worked as a senior teacher, assistant training manager and head of department in schools and subsequently at the University of Worcester (1996–2004), training teachers as a principal lecturer and curriculum leader for the Postgraduate Certificate in Education (PGCE) Secondary PE and PE undergraduate courses.

Andrew holds a Master of Science degree with distinction in Education Leadership and Management and is a fellow of the Higher Education Academy (HEA). He has three children, and is an avid skier and supporter of Everton FC.

About this Book

A fairy tale by Danish poet Hans Christian Andersen tells of an emperor who is promised the finest suit of clothes by two swindlers he has hired. They tell him that the beautiful cloth is invisible to anyone who is either stupid or unfit for his position. The emperor pretends that he can see the cloth for fear of appearing foolish, and his ministers do the same. On a procession through the capital, the emperor shows off his 'new clothes'. Only a small child has the candour to exclaim that the emperor has no clothes! The crowd realises the child is telling the truth. The emperor, however, holds his head high and continues the procession.

The phrase 'the emperor has no clothes' has become synonymous with a situation in which the majority of people are unwilling to state an obvious truth, out of fear of appearing unenlightened or perhaps out of political correctness. The rationale for not seeing the obvious truth becomes so ingrained that the majority do not even realise that they are perpetuating a falsehood. This was and, for some, is still true of the profession's assessment practice using levels in schools. In all summary reports since the Office for Standards in Education (Ofsted) was inaugurated in 1992, schools' use of assessment has consistently been criticised as something that 'does not sufficiently inform teaching and learning'. Is it time we listened to the little boy?

This book has been written specifically for the physical education profession who are working towards a future that involves assessing without levels. Understanding the principles of effective assessment and its primary purpose to improve learning, coupled with effective change management and a growth mindset, are essential to establishing and embedding effective assessment practice throughout the system. The book is structured in six sections. At the end of each section, there are reflective questions to enable deeper thinking about assessment, and references to aid research into relational aspects of education.

The first two sections of this book provide a history of the national curriculum and a policy context for the changes respectively. To that end, *A Practical Guide to Assessing Without Levels* not only presents background information for undergraduate studies at university, but also provides an insight into previous changes that have taken place, to enlighten new members of the profession who are too young to remember a previous world without levels. Section 2 in particular also looks at a practice context, why levels had to be removed from the system, the origin of data-driven practices and what will now replace them. Sections 3 and 4 begin to explore assessment as an integral necessity for the curriculum while examining the programme of study sections and the language used. Section 3 in particular focuses on the purpose, aims and values of the curriculum, highlighting implications for practice. Section 4 explores floor standards in the light of research into threshold concepts, and explores a framework for planning teaching and assessment based on the three learning domains: cognitive; psychomotor; and affective. For each learning domain, an insight into typical behaviours and appropriate verbs for the hierarchical layers or stages are provided. Assessment principles, strategies and methodologies that drive progressive and inclusive practice are examined in Section 5. Finally, Section 6 provides examples of practice from various schools that combine to create a holistic approach to assessment **of**, **as** and **for** learning. Specific examples develop constructive alignment through the structure of observed learning outcomes (SOLO) and illustrate how this might look when planning a unit of work.

I and afPE wish you well in your endeavours. Please enjoy your read, but if you do nothing else, do your utmost to ensure all children feel good about themselves, provide high quality opportunities for them to connect with physical education and school sport, and inspire them to go on to develop a lifelong love affair with physical activity and sport. This is not a quick fix, keep at it. Thank you.

> *Children don't care what you know until they know you care.*
> **John Maxwell**

Disclaimer

The contents of this book were factual at the time of publication. The transformational change agenda is ongoing, and readers are advised to check national policy updates and developments before using content to devise school policy and strategy for curriculum, assessment or pedagogy practice.

Contents

Section 1: The National Curriculum – Introduction and Background

To know that we know what we know, and that we do not know what we do not know, that is true knowledge.

Henry David Thoreau

Beware of false knowledge; it is more dangerous than ignorance.

George Bernard Shaw

Introduction

In 1986, I graduated as a qualified physical education teacher (with mathematics and science) following a four-year Bachelor of Education honours course. I felt fully prepared for teaching physical education. I was ready to be let loose. My first post was at a school in Solihull, near Birmingham. I remember my first day all too well for three key unrelated events.

The first was that it took me three attempts to bump-start my car, which I always had to park on a slope a distance from my home. There was no slope at or near the school. Already, I was concerned as to how I was going to start the car to return home.

The second, rather more astounding occurrence was being met by the head of maths, who was also the school's National Union of Teachers representative, to be informed that I was on strike! My first day in a new job at the start of my career, and I was already on strike. I just wanted to teach. This was what I had been prepared for. I was ready and keen, and now, I was being told I was not allowed to do my job. I felt confused. Having not followed the political narrative too closely at the time, I did not understand the reason why.

The third lasting memory I have from that day was meeting with one of the senior leadership team, who was to be my mentor, and being told to 'forget everything' I had learnt in teacher training as I was 'in the real world now'! There followed a one-way conversation about how the curriculum was implemented at the school and how I was required to put any elaborate ideas that I might have 'on ice' at least until I had gained 5–10 years of experience. This was a difficult message to receive and one I have heard on numerous occasions from trainee teachers reporting to me words of advice from their own mentors. Needless to say, I ignored the senior leader's advice and throughout my career have managed to consistently lobby effectively for physical education, contributing ideas about best practice, and improving my own and others' ways of doing things.

What have these events got to do with this book and the new national curriculum in England from 1 September 2014? Well, nothing really, except that they broadly reflect the current situation the profession finds itself in, and translate to three implications for practice.

Knowing What to Do When You Don't Know What to Do

The first message relates to my worry about the absence of a slope that was required to bump-start my car. I had become so reliant on a slope – and this became my major concern – that I didn't know what else I could do to start the car to return home. In our current climate, many teachers are experiencing the same situation. Levels have been removed, and because practice has become so focused and so reliant on the use of numbers to represent learning and progress, we have a whole generation of teachers who find it difficult to articulate the progress a learner might make in physical education to an attainment target without the use of a number or sub-level, and do not know what else to do.

The problem in my situation was in accepting the status quo and maintaining the practice of bump-starting my car, rather than sourcing a new battery and using a far more reliable way of starting the engine – with the turn of a key! This was not an efficient or effective way of conducting my travels, but one that I had become used to at the time for over a year. Even a police intervention while bump-starting my vehicle on a main road was insufficient to change my practice. In the same way, the profession's use of levels had become progressively so distant from their initial intended use, over a sustained 14-year period, that no one questioned their reliability and validity. No one was looking for the key to a more effective way of assessing, despite Ofsted's intervention in every single summary report since inauguration in 1992 stating that assessment did not sufficiently inform learning and teaching.

Interestingly, many schools actively promote learning to learn skills for pupils. A number use Guy Claxton's classification, which he has referred to as learning muscles. One of these four areas is termed 'resourcefulness', which he explains is about 'knowing what to do when you don't know what to do' (Frapwell and Caldecott, 2011). We need to become more resourceful.

Meaning Making

> *Rationale (noun) – Explanation of the logical reasons or principles employed in consciously arriving at a decision.*
>
> **Oxford English Dictionary**

The second message is one of understanding. If I had followed the political narrative at the time, I would have had a better understanding of the reason why I was required to strike. If I was provided with a rationale, then I would possibly have been more inclined to accept the decision or directive. This is the same for any individual or organisation involved in a change process, especially when there is a huge paradigm shift like the one teachers are being asked to make in system-wide transformation. A rational adoption of change where we question and attempt to understand is far more productive than instant, often negative reactions or instant agreement with something we don't really understand. The national curriculum has been pared down, programmes of study content has been stripped out, levels have been removed. These conditions allow the possibility of a more inclusive and progressive future. Let's attempt to understand why, think for ourselves and take informed action. Let's not wait to be spoon-fed.

Leadership and Management – Enablers or Blockers?

The final message is the potential influence that leadership and management can exert on any system, and this includes senior **and** middle leaders. Leadership and management can range from being enablers for change and improved practice to being blockers.

For my part, I was not going to forget everything I had learnt during teacher training just because I was being told to do so by a member of the senior leadership team. I was not going to disregard my beliefs about physical education and effective teaching overnight. I had an opinion.

I learn a great deal from teachers on courses, and although they have greeted the removal of levels with much acceptance, as they instinctively did not enjoy the ridiculous target-setting practice around numbers they were forced to employ in physical education, they are very pessimistic about actually implementing new ideas towards a world without levels. Largely, this is because head teachers have already informed them that they will be continuing to use levels. This in reality is a short-sighted and very limited approach that must be addressed. Teacher knowledge and understanding of the changes are essential to lobby senior leaders to develop a more reliable, valid and robust approach for assessment that is fit for purpose for learners and their progress in learning in physical education.

And so the battle lines are drawn. The scene is set. Let's ensure common sense prevails. To that end, the common sense guidance in this book is a text to support the physical education profession, but especially teachers, to develop:

- a more reliable and valid approach to assessment without the use of levels
- a robust system where the changes, especially for assessment, are understood, quality assured and fit for purpose
- a system where a broad and balanced curriculum and assessment for learning strategies that promote inclusive practice and drive higher standards are understood.

Background

As well as a landmark change for me from trainee teacher to teacher, and from student to professional, the start of my career was also marked by a period of significant transformational change. There were already major reforms being debated and developed, and these were manifested in the 1988 Education Reform Act, which is widely regarded as the most important single piece of education legislation (in England, Wales and Northern Ireland at that time) since the Butler Education Act in 1944. The Act heralded changes that included the introduction of a national curriculum. This was significant for physical education because, under the Butler Education Act, schools were only required to provide facilities for physical education.

With the 1988 Education Reform Act (often called the Baker Act after the minister who was in post), physical education became a foundation subject. For the first time in the history of physical education, it was now a compulsory subject on the curriculum.

What I found interesting, reflecting on this period, was that we moved from an era where we had freedom to develop our own programmes for physical education to an era where we have been required to follow various degrees of prescribed national curriculum content. Even more interesting was that little change was required to much of the profession's practice in terms of the activities followed. What had already widely been accepted by practitioners as a broad and balanced physical education programme was largely in place.

I also recall that, before the new programmes of study were finalised, dance was drafted as a compulsory activity. When the programmes of study were released, it became compulsory at Key Stages (KS) 1 and 2, but at KS3, schools were allowed to follow either gymnastics and/or dance.

What did change, however, and had a profound impact on the way national curriculum subjects were taught and assessed, was a focus on the processes of education. This process was known as plan, perform and evaluate in physical education. The standards for each component of plan, perform and evaluate were originally drafted as three separate attainment targets, but were finally documented as one attainment target that included all three aspects of the process.

These beginnings had huge implications for teaching, learning and assessment. The profession was now accountable in law to ensure standards, in the form of a national curriculum programme of study, and process standards, in the form of an attainment target. This was an entitlement for all pupils. Since 1988, the curriculum has been subject to a number of major reviews and revisions, never more so than now. To help understand the current changes, a brief factual review of the national curriculum timeline and changes since its inception is outlined here.

History of the National Curriculum with a Physical Education Focus

(adapted and developed from afPE, 2011)

Legislation/Year	Legislation: Key Changes to the Physical Education Programmes of Study and Attainment Targets
1987	The Department of Education and Science (DES) issued a consultation document that set out the rationale for a national curriculum and identified four broad underlying principles and intentions: 1 establishing an entitlement to a broad and balanced curriculum 2 improving school accountability 3 improving curricular coherence 4 aiding 'public understanding' of schools.
The Education Reform Act 1988	• The national curriculum legislation was produced. • KS were introduced in schools. • Physical education was introduced as a foundation subject. Prior to that, the 1944 Education Act only required schools to provide facilities for physical education. • Four KS were introduced: – KS1, typically covering years 1–2 (ages 5–7) – KS2, years 3–6 (ages 7–11) – KS3, years 7–9 (ages 11–14) – KS4, years 10–11 (ages 14–16). • For each KS, a number of educational objectives were listed.

1989	• The national curriculum was introduced to primary schools, with phased implementation continuing into the mid-1990s.
1992	• For each subject, a programme of study was produced, which included an attainment target or targets outlining the knowledge, skills and understanding to be assessed, and a breadth of study. • The formulation of the national curriculum physical education (NCPE) programme of study was achieved in 1992 (DES, 1992). • Physical education had one attainment target, which included planning, performing and evaluating. • The breadth of study included six activity areas: – games activities – gymnastics activities – dance activities – swimming activities and water safety – outdoor and adventurous activities – athletic activities.
1993	• A review of the national curriculum was undertaken by Sir Ron Dearing in response to teachers' observations that the curriculum was 'unwieldy'.
The Education (National Curriculum) Order 1995	• A revised national curriculum was introduced in 1995 with less prescribed content and changes to testing arrangements. The main changes for physical education were: – apart from games, all activity areas were slimmed down into what were termed 'half units' – an end of KS description (EKSD) making up the attainment target for physical education was produced for each of the four KS; this was to allow greater access for all learners and aid assessment of progress.
1996	• Two pilot support projects in numeracy and literacy were introduced. These projects were carried forward as the National Literacy and National Numeracy Strategies by the incoming Labour government.
The Education (National Curriculum) Order 1999	• A major review of the national curriculum was overseen by the Qualifications and Curriculum Authority (QCA), resulting in further slimming down of prescribed content, and the introduction of an explicit statement of overarching aims and purposes for the national curriculum. • Overarching statements were made with regard to inclusion and equal opportunities in the national curriculum. • National expectations were also set for the attainment of levels by the end of the various KS. Pupils were expected to work across a range of levels, with a stated expectation for the majority of pupils by the end of the KS: KS1, 1–3, target = 2; KS2, 2–5, target = 4; KS3, 3–7, target = 5/6.

	The main changes for physical education were: • the knowledge, skills and understanding expected were outlined as four processes or 'aspects' as they were documented, which developed the previous concepts of plan, perform, evaluate: – acquiring and developing skills – selecting and applying skills, tactics and compositional ideas – evaluating and improving performance – knowledge and understanding of fitness and health • the inclusion of an attainment target that incorporated eight level descriptors and an exceptional performance descriptor. Schools were asked to judge the level descriptor that 'best described' a pupil's performance in physical education at the end of a KS. The phrase 'best fit' was born, although teacher practice that evolved changed this to a 'best average'.
2005	• A review of the secondary national curriculum was carried out by QCA, with CfBT Education Trust and subject associations – including afPE – contributing to materials and resources to support implementation. • Again, the aim of the review was to slim down prescribed content. It was also influenced to a large degree by the Children Act (2004), which was manifested in the Every Child Matters (ECM) policy and greater prominence of child-centred systems. This resulted in more emphasis on cross-curricular themes, personal learning and thinking skills, and personalised learning.
The Education (National Curriculum) Order 2007	Only the **secondary** national curriculum was revised (KS3 and 4), which was statutory from September 2008. For physical education, this meant: • a revision of the national curriculum aims • the introduction of an importance statement • the introduction of four key concepts: – competence – performance – creativity – healthy active lifestyles • a change from four aspects to five key processes: – developing skills in physical activity – making and applying decisions – developing physical and mental capacity – evaluating and improving – making informed choices about healthy active lifestyles • a change in the range and content to allow greater flexibility of choice for learners: – outwitting opponents – accurate replication

	– exploring and communicating ideas and emotions – performing at maximum levels – identifying and solving problems – exercising safely and effectively • a slight change in the wording of the level descriptors (4–8 plus the exceptional performance level) to reflect the five key processes • a combined attainment target for levels 1–3 from the 1999 order and levels 4–8 plus the exceptional performance descriptor from the 2007 order.
2007–2009	• What was termed a 'root and branch' review of the primary national curriculum was announced by the Labour government. This was subsequently undertaken by Sir Jim Rose from 2008, and the findings were published in April 2009. The primary curriculum unfortunately did not become a Bill of Parliament as a third reading on it was never completed due to the announcement of a general election in 2010.
2010	• Shortly after coming to office in May 2010, a coalition government of the Conservative party and the Liberal Democrats announced it intended to review the entire national curriculum. • In November 2010, the government published the schools White Paper *The Importance of Teaching*. Chapter four of the White Paper contained proposals on the curriculum, qualifications and school accountability. It stated the government's intention to review and reform the whole of the national curriculum, with key aims again being to slim down content and reduce the bureaucratic burden on schools. This was so that the national curriculum would serve as a 'benchmark and not a straitjacket': *4.1 The National Curriculum should set out only the essential knowledge and understanding that all children should acquire and leave teachers to decide how to teach this most effectively.* • The White Paper also highlighted a reform of assessment and qualifications. • Physical education was mentioned specifically in relation to a compulsory subject and a focus on competition.
2011	• A national curriculum review was formally announced on 20 January 2011. The stated aims of the review were: – to ensure that the new national curriculum embodies rigour and high standards, and creates coherence in what is taught in schools – to ensure that all pupils are taught the essential knowledge in the key subject disciplines – beyond that core, to allow teachers greater freedom to use their professionalism and expertise to help all pupils realise their potential. The review was influenced in part by England's slide down the Programme for

	International Student Assessment (PISA) international league tables in English, maths and science. Our performance hadn't got worse, it had flatlined. It was just that other countries had improved beyond our performance. • The government also decided to change the timetable for the review. It announced that instead of new curricula for English, maths, science and physical education being introduced from 2013, and the remainder in 2014, the new curriculum for all subjects would instead be introduced in 2014. The intention from the outset was that core physical education would be compulsory throughout KS1–4. • An expert panel led by Professor Tim Oates produced its report on 19 December 2011. From research of high-performing jurisdictions around the world, the panel's report made suggestions based on evidence it had gathered about practice that had led to an improvement in standards. A slimming down of prescriptive content, an aim of all previous national curriculum reviews, was again proposed, but this time focused on the principle of less content but more depth. Key skills and essential knowledge and concepts in each subject would be taught in greater depth. Aligned to this change in principle, as opposed to the incremental change previously prescribed, was a need to change our view of assessment. To this end, the removal of levels was proposed.
2012	• Michael Gove MP responded to the expert panel proposals in June 2012. He accepted many proposals and rejected others. The proposal with regard to the removal of assessment was accepted with the statement: 'levels will be removed and not be replaced'. • On the same date, the government published draft programmes of study for the core subjects of English, maths and science at KS1 and KS2. The drafts were described as a 'starting point' for discussion with key stakeholders. Major changes were summarised, which included: – the introduction of 'more demanding' programmes of study in English, maths and science to better align England with other high-performing jurisdictions – 'raised standards' in basics, including reading, grammar, fractions and scientific concepts. • The government also suggested that the programmes of study for other foundation subjects would contain far less detail than those for English, maths and science, meaning that schools would have greater freedom to teach what they saw as appropriate in their local contexts.
2013	• On 7 February 2013, the Department for Education (DfE) published further draft programmes of study, this time for formal consultation, in a draft national curriculum framework document. • A consultation on the programmes of study ran from 7 February to 16 April 2013 and generated a very large number of responses. It also asked for views on a number of other issues, including implementation of the changes, assessment arrangements, and the planned disapplication of certain curriculum requirements during the transition year 2013–2014.

- Draft programmes of study for the core subjects of English, maths and science at KS4 were published on 19 February 2013, but these were not included in the formal consultation.
- On 10 July 2013, the DfE published a summary report of responses received during the consultation. In response to the consultation outcome, the government made further changes to the programmes of study, and launched a further final, short consultation, which ended in August 2013.
- On 17 July 2013, the government also published final proposals for primary assessment and accountability arrangements under the new curriculum, for consultation.
- Plans to remove the 1999/2007 national curriculum attainment target level descriptors, and not replace them, were confirmed. The document explained the rationale behind this move, which was based around the following principles:
  - The national curriculum is designed to give schools genuine opportunities to take ownership of the curriculum.
  - The new programmes of study set out the essential skills, knowledge and concepts that pupils should be taught by the end of each KS (DfE, 2013a).
  - Teachers will be able to develop a school curriculum that delivers the core content in a way that is challenging and relevant for their pupils.
  - Imposing a single system for ongoing assessment, in the way that national curriculum levels are built into the current curriculum and prescribe a detailed sequence for what pupils should be taught, is incompatible with the notion of curriculum freedom.
  - How schools teach their curriculum and track the progress pupils make against it will be for them to decide.
- The document restated the government's intention to continue with national curriculum tests at the end of KS1 and 2 (SATs). These have had to be modified to reflect the content of the new curriculum. The first tests based on the new national curriculum are scheduled in the summer of 2016.
- The document also proposed significant changes to the way that the outcomes of the tests are reported – against a 'scaled score' where the national cohort would be divided into 'deciles' (10 'bands'), and parents would be told which band their child fell into. The consultation on the assessment and accountability arrangements ran from 7 June to 11 October 2013.
- On 5 September 2013, the government produced legislation in the form of Statutory Instrument 2232, which introduced a new national curriculum and programmes of study, and revoked the use of levels. This was laid before Parliament on 11 September 2013, with effect from 1 September 2014 for all maintained schools. The national curriculum for year two, year four and KS4 English, maths and science becomes legislative for all maintained state schools from September 2015 (Statutory Instruments, 2013).

Whatever our views, due regard has been paid to the views of afPE, subject experts and teachers, and to the findings of international best-practice comparisons in developing a reformed national curriculum from 2014. This national curriculum is statutory for all maintained state schools and was introduced from 1 September 2014. As is the case currently, there will be no requirement for academies, free schools or independent schools to follow the national curriculum, although they may do so if they wish. The national curriculum does however provide a benchmark and a reference point for a 'broad and balanced curriculum', and this is the legal requirement for the aforementioned type of school, including for academies meeting any other curriculum conditions specified in the academy trust's funding agreement with the secretary of state.

Although maintained schools must teach the national curriculum and deliver other elements of the statutory curriculum, generally speaking, they are free to organise teaching and the school day in the way they see fit. Maintained mainstream schools in England can still disapply from the national curriculum either in its entirety or in respect of particular pupils, but disapplications are usually only sought in particular circumstances – for example, in the case of individual children with statements of special educational needs (SEN) or in respect of a particular cohort to enable curriculum development or experimentation.

Independent schools do not have to teach the national curriculum. Like academies, they must offer a 'broad and balanced' curriculum, and meet the curricular requirements laid out in the Education (Independent School Standards) (England) Regulations 2010, as amended.

A Summary of the National Curriculum, Aims, Structure and Subjects

Sourced, adapted and used under the terms of the Open Government Licence

National Curriculum

2.1 Every state-funded school must offer a curriculum that is balanced and broadly based, and that:
- promotes the spiritual, moral, cultural, mental and physical development of pupils at the school and of society
- prepares pupils at the school for the opportunities, responsibilities and experiences of later life.

2.2 The school curriculum comprises all learning and other experiences that each school plans for its pupils. The national curriculum forms one part of the school curriculum.

2.3 All state schools are also required to make provision for a daily act of collective worship and must teach religious education to pupils at every KS, and sex and relationship education to pupils in secondary education.

2.4 Maintained schools in England are legally required to follow the statutory national curriculum, which sets out in programmes of study, on the basis of KS, subject content for those subjects that should be taught to all pupils. All schools must publish their school curriculum by subject and academic year online.

2.5 All schools should make provision for personal, social, health and economic education (PSHE), drawing on good practice. Schools are also free to include other subjects or topics of their choice in planning and designing their own programme of education.

Aims

3.1 The national curriculum provides pupils with an introduction to the essential knowledge that they need to be educated citizens. It introduces pupils to the best that has been thought and said, and helps engender an appreciation of human creativity and achievement.

3.2 The national curriculum is just one element in the education of every child. There is time and space in the school day, and in each week, term and year, to range beyond the national curriculum specifications. The national curriculum provides an outline of core knowledge around which teachers can develop exciting and stimulating lessons to promote the development of pupils' knowledge, understanding and skills as part of the wider school curriculum.

3.3 Pupils of compulsory school age in community and foundation schools, including community special schools and foundation special schools, and in voluntary aided and voluntary controlled schools, must follow the national curriculum. It is organised on the basis of four KS and 12 subjects, classified in legal terms as 'core' and 'other foundation' subjects.

3.4 The Secretary of State for Education is required to publish programmes of study for each national curriculum subject, setting out the 'matters, skills and processes' to be taught at each KS. Schools are free to choose how they organise their school day as long as the content of the national curriculum programmes of study is taught to all pupils.

Since the introduction of the national curriculum in 1988, the same structure has broadly been retained:

- 'core' subjects – English, maths and science
- additional 'foundation' subjects.

The national curriculum review and legislation with effect from September 2014 made two major changes to the national curriculum structure:

- languages will become part of KS2
- information and communication technology (ICT) will be replaced with computing.

The table overleaf is adapted from the DfE's National Curriculum Framework and used under the terms of the Open Government Licence. It gives an overview of the subjects that are included in the national curriculum at primary and secondary from September 2014.

National curriculum subjects from September 2014 (DfE, 2013b)

KS	Primary – KS1 and 2	Secondary – KS3	Secondary – KS4
Subject	Ages 5–7; 7–11	Age 11–14	Age 14–16
Maths	✔	✔	✔
English	✔	✔	✔
Science	✔	✔	✔
Physical Education	✔	✔	✔
History	✔	✔	✘
Geography	✔	✔	✘
Art and Design	✔	✔	✘
Music	✔	✔	✘
Languages	✔ (KS2 only)	✔	✘
Computing	✔	✔	✔
Design and Technology	✔	✔	✘
Citizenship Education	✘	✔	✔

Notes

- For maintained schools, several subjects outside the national curriculum are compulsory. Sex and relationship education is compulsory during the secondary phase of education, and religious education must be provided to all registered pupils at all stages. Schools are also expected to provide PSHE.
- For each national curriculum subject, there is an associated statutory **programme of study**, outlining the minimum subject content and essential skills, knowledge and concepts that should be taught.

Reflection

Successful 'knowledge managers' have an ability to communicate and network at all levels in their schools, and especially laterally across departments, hierarchically within the organisation and between organisations.

- ✔ **How do we keep up to date with knowledge developments in our subject and the narrative in education?**
- ✔ **How do we filter out the nonsense from the accurate so that our thinking about curriculum developments is informed and leads to effective practice?**
- ✔ **Are we sufficiently informed about curriculum developments in our subject to effectively make a case for physical education in schools with our colleagues, line managers or senior leaders?**
- ✔ **What do we do when we don't know what to do?**

References

afPE (2011) *L2CSLPESS Tutor Support Pack*. Worcester: afPE.

DES (1992) *National Curriculum Physical Education*. London: DES.

DfE (2013a) *Physical Education Programmes of Study: Key Stages 1 and 2, Key Stages 3 and 4: National Curriculum in England*. London: DfE.

DfE (2013b) *The National Curriculum in England: Framework Document*. London: DfE.

Department for Education and Employment (1999) *Physical Education: The National Curriculum for England*. London: DfE.

Department for Children, Schools and Families (DCSF) (2007) *Physical Education: Programme of Study for Key Stage 3 and Attainment Target*. London: DCSF/QCA.

Frapwell, A. and Caldecott, S. (2011) *In Deep: Learning to Learn*. Leeds: Coachwise Ltd/afPE. ISBN: 978-1-905540-57-0.

Gove, M. (2012) 'National curriculum review proposals response: Open letter to Tim Oates, Director of Research and Assessment, Cambridge Assessment, chair of the expert panel'. London: DfE.

Statutory Instruments (2013) *No. 2232 Education, England: The Education (National Curriculum) (Attainment Targets and Programmes of Study) (England) Order 2013*. Norwich: The Stationery Office. ISBN: 978-0-111103-66-1.

Section 2: A Practice and Policy Context

We are searching for some kind of harmony between two intangibles: a form which we have not yet designed and a context which we cannot properly describe.

Christopher Alexander

The frame, the definition, is a type of context. And context, as we said before, determines the meaning of things. There is no such thing as the view from nowhere, or from everywhere for that matter. Our point of view biases our observation, consciously and unconsciously. You cannot understand the view without the point of view.

Shpancer (2010)

A Practice Context

During my professional career, I have become familiar with the stress and additional workload created by successive government reform initiatives, either as a practitioner or a consultant supporting curriculum implementation. An era of teacher accountability, signified by the advent of the 1988 Education Reform Act, and typified by successive national curriculum and assessment changes, has resulted in one undeniable fact – accountability has, unfortunately, been viewed as synonymous with 'proving' greater progress and higher standards. For many, this has resulted in more frequent measuring or testing, additional procedures and an increase in paperwork or electronic records. This is the fundamental change as a result of our many reform initiatives – a greater workload.

To address issues such as our greater workload, a workforce reform policy, which sought to transform our professional practice, was developed. This reform began in the late 1990s and is ongoing. Work-life balance for teachers was a key aspect, and among the many changes, reported comprehensively in the tabloid press in the mid- to late 2000s, there emerged, for example, a list of administrative tasks that a secondary teacher should have completed for them by support staff, and planning, preparation and assessment (PPA) time created in the school day for primary teachers.

Incredibly, measures that were introduced to raise standards through school accountability, such as attainment targets, national tests, performance indicators and the comparison of the results of testing using school league tables, had created a need for more time allocation within the school organisation to effectively administer. The resulting culture and practice that evolved during this era of accountability, which included a plethora of administrative meetings and paperwork, I believe, was retrogressive. It encouraged a content-driven teach-to-the-test approach, and this quite typical practice actually reduced the amount of time available for learning. Schools scheduled meetings into academic calendars that parents, and often pupils in many institutions, were required to attend to receive information about SATs testing or GCSE examinations and how to help improve potential test scores.

Worse still, physical education lessons would be cancelled in primary schools to make way for practice test sessions, or pupils (including my own son) forced to attend revision sessions after school instead of attending after-school sports clubs. Secondary schools began using indicative GCSE target grades throughout year groups to report whether pupils were on track to achieve their targets as a result of sitting a national test in KS2. The introduction of, and appointment to, a new school role – that of 'data manager' – became prevalent, and 'flight paths' to track progress were extensively used.

The system was driven by the use of data derived from Fischer Family Trust (FFT) statistics. Unfortunately, guidance around the use of its data relating to the indication of a starting point and estimation was either largely ignored or widely misunderstood and misused. The more that the quantitative measure, based on levels of progress, became used for decision-making about schools and subjects (including Ofsted ratings, the amount of local authority support provided, examination choices and, in particular, parental choice), the more it became subject to superficial teaching and learning, and the more it became subject to corruption pressures that actually distorted the measure it was intended to determine in the first place.

By this, I mean the inflation, lowering or making up of student grades that went on in schools in order to 'demonstrate' greater progress in the stage of learning for which they were responsible. This 'grade creep' or the manipulation of data to prove that learners were on track became almost commonplace. It was a game that was being played by schools, and this form of 'fixing' was tolerated. The assessment tail was wagging the learning and teaching dog. What should have been a **means** of gauging pupil progress and attainment became the main **end** of education, and teaching methodologies were distorted as a result of this.

It is in the light of this distorted practice that I personally welcomed the legislative changes to the system and will attempt to explain in the following section the need for change in relation to the practice that had evolved in a physical education context.

The Problem with Levels

While working on the national curriculum in Kosovo in May 2014, it was put to me in a conversation I had with Kirsi Lindroos, an education reformist from Finland, that 'schools change reforms as much as reforms change schools'. In many situations, this can be productive, and when teachers understand the reforms, and the reforms allow for flexibility, there can be some useful adaptation by schools.

In the context of the use of attainment target level descriptors, however, the reverse happened. Schools changed the reforms and used attainment target level descriptors in a way that was never intended. The best analogy I can think of is one of watching a play at the theatre. The scenes that the audience watch lead to successive decisions being made. In the penultimate scene, these decisions have led to the vicar in the play dropping his trousers in all innocence. To the audience, it appears plausible that this event has taken place as they have understood and followed the narrative of the play. To the female who enters the room stage left and views the scene, it appears shocking and ridiculous.

In a similar way, individuals, schools and local authorities have made decisions that have incrementally changed the use of levels and data. They made these decisions in the best interests of system improvement. Over time, however, the profession has dropped its trousers. The use of levels had become unfit for purpose. When the rest of Europe observes our practice, or 'enters our room' (to continue the analogy), and observes our approach to levelling, they perceive this as a nonsense. They believe we test too much and are obsessed with managing data, rather than managing learning. This is illustrated by my attendance in 2012 on a two-day RAISEonline course. Two days to train people to interpret data; data that was derived from everyday teacher assessment practice in the first place. Data that is then broken down into its individual component parts relating to individual pupils!

The Problem with Levels: Estimated Grades Prior to the New Progress 8 and Attainment 8 Measure

Physical education was the final subject to have an attainment target structured in the form of eight level descriptors plus an exceptional performance descriptor. When the 1999 national curriculum was published for implementation in September 2000, all subjects had an attainment target. In 2001, a company called FFT sent a letter to chief education officers (CEOs) in local authorities (LAs), asking them to participate in a project intended to make use of performance data related to attainment and levels.

The project began with 55 LAs in July 2001, and by 2004, FFT was working with all LAs in England and Wales. The majority of LA members came on board following feedback they received from colleagues in neighbouring LAs who were already part of the project. The use of data-driven practices was born.

In January 2006, FFT was one of the members of a consortium of companies that included Forvus, RM and SERAP (part of the University of Bath) to be awarded a major data services contract by the then Department for Education and Skills (DfES). The contract was for processing the data for the National Pupil Database/ Achievement and Attainment Tables (Performance Tables). Previously, FFT, Forvus and SERAP had been responsible for delivering separate parts of the Performance Tables process, but by joining forces, they provided a single, more joined up service.

Under the 'levelling' system, baseline data was previously used by FFT to provide schools with an estimate of pupil performance. FFT used the word 'estimate' to provide a starting point for discussion about potential future performance. Estimates were not targets. They provided information for discussion that led to the setting of targets.

This was unfortunately not the way schools often used the information. There were too many variables to use the word 'prediction', yet this is how the data was used, and it was employed by a great many schools. The information FFT provided took into account pupils' prior attainment, gender and age, and the progress made by pupils with similar characteristics nationally. Estimated grades provided an indication of the most likely grade in each subject group.

FFT was keen to highlight the following information when using estimated grades:

- There was likely to be variation around that grade.
- Pupils' interest and aptitude in the subject has a significant impact.
- There were variations within subject groups (eg between different sciences).
- The amount of variation was more for some subjects.

In subjects such as English and maths, the percentage of pupils that attained within one grade of the estimate tended to be quite high. Since the 'project' began, this figure has been in excess of 90%. This would be expected because the test is in English and maths. In most other subject groups, the figure during this period has been in excess of 80% of pupils attaining within one grade of the estimate.

In subjects such as art and design, creative arts and, in particular, physical education, however, the pupils attaining within one grade of the estimate has only been just over 70%. In other words, the estimate was almost 30% inaccurate. Any mathematician or statistician will tell you that working with data that is 30% inaccurate is unproductive.

Even in our own lives, legislation – in the form of the Data Protection Act 1998 fourth principle – requires that personal data held must be 'accurate'. If it is not, then the individual concerned has a right to apply to the court for an order to rectify, block, erase or destroy the inaccurate information. The inaccurate data that schools developed, especially in the context of physical education, was unfortunately still used.

Many head teachers I spoke to about the changes and assessing without levels said they would continue to use levels and data as there was nothing else to replace it. Yes, there was and is – it is called teacher assessment.

In 2009, schools that afPE worked with that were using their own teacher assessment or teacher judgement (albeit using levels) for pupils in year nine had greater correlated estimates for GCSE physical education grades than any FFT estimates using national baseline tests. This small-scale project with secondary schools highlighted that teacher assessment in physical education was far more reliable and valid than using estimates derived largely from national tests in English and maths.

In January 2009, Sue Hackman, Chief Advisor on School Standards at the DCSF, addressed a letter to all head teachers and school leaders, highlighting the removal of the statutory KS3 tests in 2008. Schools were asked to use teacher assessment and internally moderate, rather than be held to account for statutory test scores.

As part of the National Assessment for Learning Strategy, the DCSF provided £150million for a three-year period (2008–2011) in support of an approach called Assessing Pupils' Progress (APP), which provided a criterion-referenced tool for making sound judgements against national standards. A National Physical Education Group, of which I was a member, led by QCA, developed APP for physical education, and afPE (2010) also commissioned me to produce support materials and a poster outlining the process.

Despite these advances, what happened? Schools decided to stick with data-driven practices and commissioned FFT to provide data from KS2 SATs as a replacement for the 'missing' data at KS3. Organisations and individuals in the system were addicted to levels, and many felt unable to even start the withdrawal process, despite a government-funded programme providing the means.

The Problem with Levels: Levelling Activities or Individual Pieces of Work

In 2004, the Physical Education Association of the United Kingdom (PEA UK) produced guidance to the profession stating that language such as 'level 4 games or level 2 dance should not be used'. At the same time, the QCA asserted on each subject's attainment target website page that 'levels for individual pieces of work should not be used'. Prior to these instances, national guidance had always been positive. For the first time, the profession received guidance that affirmed 'you should not'. Rather than curb teachers' malpractice around the (mis)use of levels, it appears that it had the opposite effect.

What is worth remembering is that level descriptors, as part of an attainment target, were intended to be used to determine an individual's performance against a national benchmark standard **at the end of a KS**. Teachers were originally required to make an informed judgement as to the descriptor that 'best described' an individual's attainment – a 'best-fit' judgement. This was required at the end of a KS, not at the end of a lesson or unit, or in six data points during the year, but **at the end** of a KS. The only time the profession was statutorily required to report a level was at the end of KS3.

In physical education, schools that used attainment target descriptors to level a pupil's performance in individual activities, usually every half-term, rather than making a best-fit judgement, actually disadvantaged many pupils. The following examples seek to explain this malpractice and contribute to our understanding of the rationale for change.

Levelling Performance in Sports Versus Levelling Attainment in Physical Education

From September 2000 (DfES/QCA, 1999), the language in the level descriptors for KS1–4 reflected four aspects of physical education: acquiring and developing skills; selecting and applying skills, tactics and compositional ideas; knowledge and understanding of fitness and health; and evaluating and improving. From September 2008 (QCA, 2007), this changed to five key processes for secondary: developing skill; making and applying decisions; developing physical and mental capacity; making informed choices about healthy active lifestyles; and evaluating and improving. On being asked what a level 4 gymnast meant (or a level 5 netball player or a level 7 footballer), more often than not, teachers would provide information almost solely related to a pupil's physical skill performance. Not many teachers ever articulated an individual's ability to evaluate and improve their own or other's performance, or an ability to compose a sequence, or select an appropriate attacking or defending strategy. A 'level' in these schools had become synonymous with skill performance.

The minority of schools that were able to articulate performance in physical education beyond just the skill would also give a level for each of the aspects or processes, but would then attach a heavier weighting in the overall level for the activity in favour of the skill performance (it was always designed to be an even weighting).

This approach, coupled with the absence of department moderation to standardise a level 4 for hockey and a level 4 for football for example, became even more of a nonsense when reputable companies, convinced they were producing something worthwhile, began to develop resources that rewrote the level descriptors for different sports. Not only was this very poorly attempted (and I made this known to such companies at the time with email correspondence), but for schools that used this type of resource, it led to the creation of a huge bank of statements and increased administration for teachers yet again.

The following is a summary of the various (mis)uses of the descriptors that formed the attainment target:

- Skill performance was often the sole judgement employed, and pupils were labelled for this performance while the remaining physical education aspects or processes were ignored.
- Aspects or key processes, if considered, were weighted differently, rather than equally.
- The need for moderation within departments was disregarded. Incompatible practice in levelling individuals, groups and cohorts within and between schools became widespread.
- The act of levelling was employed too frequently – in some schools, as often as every three weeks.

The Link Between 'Curriculum and Assessment', 'Best Fit' and 'Average'

The (mal)practice of levelling each activity and then averaging a level score took on a greater importance when considered in relation to the school's curriculum provision. This was regardless of whether the level number related to skill performance or each of the aspects or processes.

From experience, the majority of secondary schools between 2008 and 2014 followed a KS3 curriculum that **on average** consisted of:

- seven outwitting activities or games (although Ofsted [2014] recently indicated this number averaged 10)
- one accurate replication activity (usually gymnastics)
- one maximal performance activity (usually athletics)
- one problem-solving activity (usually orienteering).

If the school had a swimming pool, then swimming would also form part of the physical education provision – usually as a maximal performance activity. Dance or trampolining would be included in the provision for the minority of schools as an 'expressing emotion' or 'accurate replication' activity respectively.

If schools employed a practice that labelled or levelled each activity, then pupils who preferred games (outwitting) and were good at games would be favoured by an assessment system that judged performance in a games-dominated curriculum. Contrast this with a pupil who preferred accurate replication type activities and was good at them, but who was assessed only in one activity – gymnastics. The importance of the link between curriculum opportunity and assessment is even more apparent when the impact on 'performance grades' is illustrated, as in the tables overleaf.

Pupil A

Outwitting	Level	Accurate Replication	Level	Maximal Performance	Level	Problem Solving	Level
Football	5	Gymnastics	4	Athletics	5	Orienteering	4
Rugby/hockey	6						
Basketball/netball	6						
Badminton	5						
Volleyball	5						
Tennis	5						
Cricket/rounders	5						

Total score: 5 + 6 + 6 + 5 + 5 + 5 + 5 + 4 + 5 + 4 = 50

Average: 50 ÷ 10 = 5.0

Pupil B

Outwitting	Level	Accurate Replication	Level	Maximal Performance	Level	Problem Solving	Level
Football	4	Gymnastics	6	Athletics	6	Orienteering	6
Rugby/hockey	5						
Basketball/netball	4						
Badminton	4						
Volleyball	4						
Tennis	4						
Cricket/rounders	4						

Total score: 4 + 5 + 4 + 4 + 4 + 4 + 4 + 6 + 6 + 6 = 47

Average: 47 ÷ 10 = 4.7

The examples serve to highlight the imbalance created due to the method of assessment (levelling activities) between a pupil with a games background and a games interest (Pupil A), and a pupil with a gymnastic background and a gymnastic interest (Pupil B). In the Pupil B example, we have also increased the level for maximal performance and problem solving, yet the method utilised weighs heavily in favour of the pupil with a games interest and ability. The overall level is drastically altered depending on the number of preferred activities followed.

It also becomes noticeable, however, that if the pupil with an accurate replication interest were to be offered the opportunity to follow more activities aligned to their interests and abilities in the accurate replication area, such as Olympic gymnastics, rhythmic gymnastics, sports-acro and trampoline (given sufficient trampolines) and the number of outwitting activities was reduced, then Pupil B would have the higher score. The inequity of the assessment methodology due to curriculum imbalance is further underlined when we consider that it is taught by a majority of teachers with a games-based interest and ability, to a majority of children who also have a games-based interest and ability.

If we now calculate an overall level based on the range of content areas in physical education, then a best fit for Pupil A would be a level 4 or a level 5 depending on the attainment target language that best described the overall performance in the four areas followed. Pupil B has three areas that were deemed to be commensurate with a level 6 so the best-fit descriptor is likely to be a level 5 or level 6.

This example serves to illustrate that 'average' and 'best fit' methodology do not necessarily result in the same attainment. The methodologies of the two are different. Teachers in schools that used an average methodology therefore skewed overall level judgement in favour of the games player and disadvantaged pupils with a more aesthetic interest when compared to their counterparts in schools who employed a best-fit approach.

A few years ago, a school I was working with countered that they had addressed this issue by giving an overall average level for 'outwitting opponents' then added this to the average of the remaining range of content scores. Another school said they averaged the outwitting, then averaged the remaining activities, and totalled these averages before finally dividing by two for an overall average. Another school informed me that they used the three best outwitting 'scores' from the 1999 national curriculum categories of invasion, net/wall and striking and fielding, averaged this score and then totalled this with the remaining three areas before dividing by four to average overall. Using the 'scores' from the previous tables, all of these methods result in a different 'score' or overall level.

Sub-levels

Sub-levels were initially introduced in response to the profession's request for greater clarity with regard to performance in the SATs. Teachers wished to know whether a pupil's test results were **just** a level 3, for example, a secure level 3 or nearly a level 4. The letters c, b, a were used to specify this attainment. This 'sub-levelling', in terms of c-b-a, was originally developed, therefore, as an indicator of raw mathematical data falling in a particular range of marks as a result of sitting a test.

The issue arose when the reform was reformed (again), and decision-makers, who confused the difference between scores on a test and teacher assessment, advised schools and/or teachers to label pupil performance c-b-a as a result of their teacher assessment. Raw test scores indicating a level and sub-level were not the same as using teacher assessment to judge attainment.

Take for example the sentence in the old level 5 descriptor of the physical education attainment target that stated:

When performing in different physical activities, they (pupils) consistently show precision, control and fluency.

The contrast in language from a level 4 to a level 5 in the previous sentence is the words *consistently* and *in different physical activities*. The word *consistently* is defined as 'a majority of the time'. In numerical terms, a shooting performance that scores 5 out of 10 would therefore be inconsistent and a score of 6 out of 10 would be consistent. This begs the question – 'What is c-b-a of consistency?' The language of the level also clearly stated *in different physical activities*. How could pupils possibly be levelled a 5 for netball, for example, when they would need to demonstrate performance commensurate with the characteristics of a level 5 over a range of activities over time (*in different physical activities*)?

To make matters worse, a number of schools then converted c-b-a into numbers and labelled pupils 5.2, 5.5 or 5.7. One particular school in the Midlands stands out in my memory, where a spreadsheet of pupil scores was displayed in the corridor outside the changing rooms and sports hall. 'Performances' were levelled, sub-levelled and then averaged. When I asked the question about the difference in performance between one pupil who was a 4.467 and another pupil who was 4.647, the reply I received was '0.18'!

Hitting the Target, Missing the Point

These measures of performance, however they were arrived at, were then used to indicate progress. Statements such as '80% of pupils have made two levels of progress across the KS' abounded. What did this actually mean? What did it mean for pupils, standards and standardisation when primary school judgements in physical education were largely ignored and secondary schools conducted their own baseline assessments? What did it mean for reliability and validity when the claimed progress and attainment across the various KS did not lead to a similar increase in percentages of pupils achieving A*–C grades? What did it mean for accountability when national surveys indicated a strikingly low percentage of pupils engaging in recommended physical activity levels?

In whatever way we reflect on the use of levels in previous practice, schools found it difficult to apply them consistently and fairly because of varying methodology used to calculate an overall level. Teachers used levels in a way they were never intended for, and this reform of the reform led to different decisions being made about how to weight a huge array of factors. Levels have detracted from the main purpose of assessment – that of assessment information being used to feed back to improve learning. The practice of 'assessment' was very much one of teachers feeling they had to prove to senior leaders that assessment was taking place, that a pupil's progress was on numerical track, judging, averaging and labelling. This resulted in a plethora of paperwork that actually got in the way of teaching and learning.

Whether we like it or not, there is a whole generation of pupils who have gone through this system having been unfairly labelled. The challenge as part of the transformation agenda is to develop an assessment system that is fair, valid and reliable, and continuously strives to improve learning and drive up standards. In other words, an assessment system that is 'fit for purpose'.

A Policy Context

The national curriculum review and consultation took place in the context of other ongoing reforms to public examinations, school organisation, testing and accountability systems. Key developments were driven by:

- a re-emphasis on teacher assessment
- assessment methodology that matched what is to be assessed subject by subject, rather than an overall rule for all subjects
- the link to the essential skills, knowledge and concepts in the national curriculum programmes of study
- accountability measures that married to qualifications
- a focus on progress over time.

Some of the changes are outlined below.

1 **A review of KS2 assessment arrangements** and the role of SATs (2011) – one of the key points reported in the review led by Lord Bew concluded that both summative teacher assessment and external forms of assessment had important roles to play. Although KS2 tests were not scrapped, as the KS3 tests had been in 2009, the review team advocated that at least as much weighting should be given to progress as is given to attainment in assessments of the quality of education a school is providing. Lord Bew's recommendations were accepted by the government in full, and this led to the following changes:

   - **More teacher assessment has been incorporated** in an attempt to promote creativity and avoid teaching to the test. More teacher assessment should not be viewed as synonymous with more testing or more administration. A test is but one method of assessment.
   - **Secondary schools are provided with the results of teacher assessment** and more information on pupils' performance before the test results are published, allowing greater time for schools to prepare and plan for year seven teaching and learning.
   - **Testing is aligned to essential skills and knowledge**. In other words, the new national tests from 2016 have been mapped to the programme of study essential skills, knowledge and concepts of the 2014 national curriculum: a curriculum that focuses on less content in greater depth for all subjects. In a physical education subject context, this means that the assessment method the teacher uses should be mapped to the key skills, essential knowledge and concepts, and vital behaviours (attitudes and healthy active lifestyles displayed) that are outlined in the programme of study. This alignment also has obvious implications for planning and teaching.
   - **A greater emphasis on progress made by pupils is promoted**. Progress has been a focus for several years and is a key focus for Ofsted, as outlined in the 2012 inspection framework. With the advent of new legislation in September 2013 (Statutory Instrument 2232 implemented in September 2014), however, the progress required is for all children to meet the floor standard expected for each KS. This new standard, or in old language 'attainment target', was not framed in the form of level descriptors as per the previous attainment target legislation. Levels had been removed from the system.
   - **Data is summarised over a three-year rolling period**. The phrase that the profession uses to describe the inspection element of this aspect is 'work scrutiny', and it typically focuses on progress over a three-year period, although this focus might be over a shorter period such as one or two years due to school development timescales, for example.

2 **Changes to the 'floor standards'** that primary schools are expected to meet – the term floor standard is being used to describe the minimum standards of attainment expected in the national tests in relation to the essential skills, knowledge and concepts in English, maths and science. The attainment target for all subjects, integral to each KS, is the floor standard expected. The previous expectation was to reach level 4 by the end of KS2. The reasons for change were numerous. One central reason was that previous figures indicated only 47% of pupils who achieved a level 4 but did not achieve a level 4b or above in both English and maths at KS2 went on to achieve five A*–C GCSE grades (including English and maths) in 2012. However, 72% of pupils who achieved at least a level 4b in both English and maths at KS2 went on to achieve five A*–C GCSE grades (including English and maths) in 2012. The overall percentage of children that attained a level 4 on the old SATs was approximately 67%. The coalition government believed this figure to be too low. From September 2016, the new benchmark or **floor target** in relation to the **floor standards** is expected to be set at 85%. The challenge, however, is to ensure high quality provision (curriculum, assessment and pedagogy) so that all learners reach the standard. Schools must also demonstrate that the percentage of pupils making the progress expected between KS1 and KS2 is at or above the national median. This progress measure has become the way the government will hold schools to account.

3 **The introduction of a new reception baseline assessment from September 2016 onwards** – pupils are to be assessed using a new baseline assessment when they start reception, and the Early Years Foundation Stage (EYFS) Profile will no longer be compulsory. The baseline will be used to assess children starting reception in September 2016 and beyond, but schools will be able to introduce the assessments from September 2015. For schools that do not use the baseline assessment in 2015, progress will only be measured from KS1 to KS2. Teachers will be able to choose from a range of assessment approaches, and the check will be carried out by reception teachers. Schools will be able to opt out of the baseline check, however, and instead be judged on whether children's attainment meets the minimum floor standard at the end of KS2.

4 **Changes to the inspection framework for schools** – a new framework, used by Ofsted during routine inspections, came into force in September 2012. This was accompanied by significant changes to the process of intervention when schools are underperforming, which included the potential removal of a school's governing body. The supplementary subject inspection frameworks were also adapted in April 2014. In the physical education supplementary inspection framework, the minimum expectation of two hours' high quality physical education throughout KS1–4 remained. Significantly, the Ofsted notes to inspectors, released on 1 July 2014, for inspections in the academic year 2014–2015 reminded schools of their legal obligation, including the requirement for all schools, including academies and free schools, to publish for each academic year the content of the school's curriculum for each subject with details of how additional curriculum information may be obtained. They also reminded schools that national curriculum levels had been removed. Significantly, this Ofsted publication also replaced the term 'data' with 'assessment information' and focused inspectors and schools on considering how this assessment information was to be used for teaching and learning, especially to identify pupils who are falling behind in their learning or who require additional support to reach their full potential, including the most able. In other words, assessment information is not required to be in data or statistical form, and it is to be used to drive inclusive practice, increase progress and raise standards.

5 **Major changes to the system of public examinations at KS4 and beyond** – in September 2012, the secretary of state announced that the government intended to abolish GCSEs and replace them with new English Baccalaureate Certificates (EBCs). On 7 February 2013, the government, in responding to consultative feedback, confirmed it did not intend to proceed with this, but would instead reform existing GCSEs. The reformed qualifications are linear in structure, with assessment undertaken at the end of the course and graded 9–1. Grade 9 is the highest score and 1 the lowest. Grade 5 is internationally benchmarked, broadly equivalent to half to two thirds of a grade higher than that required for a current grade C. In physical education, the July 2014 consultation proposed a shift in assessment weighting from 60% non-examination (practical) assessment and 40% examination (theory) assessment to 30% non-examination assessment and 70% examination assessment. The consultation resulted in a final decision for 40% non-examination (practical) assessment and 60% examination (theory) assessment.

6 **The introduction of a new secondary school accountability system** termed Progress 8, which included Attainment 8 – Progress 8 will be introduced for all schools in 2016. The performance tables based on 2016 exam results, to be published in late 2016/early 2017, will show the Progress 8 results. Progress 8 will also be used for floor standards from 2016. The 'expected levels of progress' measure will no longer appear in performance tables from 2016. The system of levels that underpins this measure has been removed, and this measure is being phased out. It is also intended that the performance tables will show the amount of progress made in each school in the component parts of the Progress 8 measure. Separate progress measures will be listed for English, maths, the group of English Baccalaureate subjects overall, the group of other GCSEs and AS levels overall, and the group of approved vocational qualifications overall. This will help demonstrate a school's strengths and of course areas for improvement. Physical education can contribute to scores for the group of 'other GCSEs and AS levels overall'. The new measure should also promote greater inclusive practice. Schools can gain 'worth' for ensuring all pupils achieve higher scores, and this will prevent the previous misguided and overriding focus of energies on candidates who were C/D borderline and move to an inclusive approach that focuses on pupils' learning and achievement in key skills and essential knowledge, and concepts that ultimately should improve scores.

7 **The roll-out of the academies and free schools programme** – the government has encouraged high-performing primary and secondary schools to voluntarily convert to academy status. Other schools can convert with the help of a sponsor or as part of an academy chain. Schools that are deemed to be underperforming and 'eligible for intervention' can be required to convert to academy status.

Contextualising Change: Connecting Curriculum, Assessment and Pedagogy

The changes and the context for change outlined in these first two sections provide a template to ensure that education is fit for purpose. The challenges for the profession have been summarised in terms of the system and implications for curriculum, assessment and pedagogy in the following table:

System	Curriculum	Assessment	Pedagogy
Transformational change – higher expectations – the combination of effective leadership and high quality teaching is essential to success	Higher expectations. Each school has the freedom to develop its own 'local' curriculum, which must be broad and balanced. A return to a focus on subject disciplines, including: • a purpose and aims • essential knowledge, skills and concepts.	Higher expectations. Effective use of assessment information to: • identify pupils who need additional support, including those falling behind or the more able • improve teaching • raise achievement.	Higher expectations. Innovative and effective approaches to teaching and learning based on a secure knowledge and understanding of child development.
New schools (academies and free schools)	The national curriculum (which provides a reference point for all schools, including the standard against which academies and free schools can benchmark their curricula, where they choose to develop their own) versus the school curriculum.	Assessment that is fit for purpose. Schools to develop their own formative assessment (assessment for learning – AfL) methodologies, which need to match what is to be assessed in each subject, rather than an overall rule for all subjects.	Understanding key knowledge, skills and concepts and the transitional notion of learning (learning and progress aren't always linear).
Changing Ofsted framework and requirements	Broad and balanced (all schools). A requirement for all schools to publish – in relation to each academic year – the content of the curriculum for each subject.	Assessment without levels – a focus on the effective use of assessment information (a future without the obsessive use of data).	Differentiation to allow inclusive access to learning – a focus on learning outcomes/success criteria and all pupils making excellent progress.
Greater reference to international measures	New floor standards (threshold standards).	New floor target – 85% (threshold target – 'next stage ready').	Inclusive teaching and learning in greater depth.

National tests, Progress 8 and Attainment 8	Inclusive curriculum approach devised to meet learners' needs.	National tests, terminal examinations and system measures devised to prevent teaching to the test/exam.	Inclusive teaching and learning – no child left behind.
Qualifications	Linked to new programmes of study – a focus on a knowledge-based curriculum. Linear structure – no modules, no coursework.	Written exam is the default method. Non-examination assessment has a lesser weighting in physical education. 9–1 scale and U, extended writing and fewer bite-sized questions.	Focus on progress for all learners – not just A*–C and C/D borderline.
SEN – the new code of practice	Remove barriers to participation – all pupils have multiple opportunities to learn.	Ensure pupils participate in (gain access to) assessment tasks and have an opportunity to demonstrate the extent of their learning.	Focus on ability, rather than disability – learning experiences are equitable, rather than exclusive.
Performance-related pay	Supporting excellence – excellent curriculum?	Supporting excellence – excellent assessment?	Supporting excellence – excellent pedagogy?
Physical education and sport premium	Increased opportunity and participation. Requirement to list the curriculum provision and how additional monies are being effectively spent.	Improved outcomes for all pupils. Evidence of impact mapped to national curriculum standards and assessment. Accountability highlighted in Ofsted leadership and management category.	Increased teacher confidence, and practice that promotes an inclusive, enjoyable and sustainable approach.

Reflection

Change can be an elusive concept. It is inevitable and yet, paradoxically, it depends on the will and actions of individuals. A system that many professionals have used unquestioningly, and invested time and effort in creating, embeds beliefs and practices that are very difficult to influence. A response continuum results from people who embrace change to those who fiercely resist it. Individuals, groups, organisations and parties structure social movements, political campaigns and business strategies around the need for change, yet there are many who hardly understand how it works. Understanding context is essential for understanding change.

- ✔ **What is our response to change, and how do we go about understanding not only the need for change but how change should be led and managed?**
- ✔ **How is transformational change different to incremental change?**
- ✔ **How has transformational change, with the advent of assessment without levels, manifested itself in a change to our thinking, approach and practice?**
- ✔ **What have we done to find out about current thinking?**
- ✔ **What is our local context? Who are the go-to people who listen, rationalise and will help drive change? Who are the blockers?**

References

DCSF (2008a) *The Assessment for Learning Strategy*. Nottingham: DCSF. ISBN: 978-1-847751-47-8.

DfE (2011) *Independent Review of Key Stage 2 Testing, Assessment and Accountability: Government Response*. Norwich: The Stationery Office. ISBN: 978-0-101814-42-3.

DfE (2014a) 'National curriculum and assessment: information for schools', www.gov.uk/government/publications/national-curriculum-and-assessment-information-for-schools

DfE (2014b) 'Progress 8 measure in 2016: Technical guide for maintained secondary schools, academies and free schools', www.gov.uk/government/uploads/system/uploads/attachment_data/file/314294/Progress_8_measure_in_2016.pdf

DfES/QCA (1999) *Physical Education: The National Curriculum for England*. London: DfES/QCA.

Fischer Family Trust (FFT), www.fft.org.uk

Frapwell, A. (2010) *Assessment for Learning with Assessing Pupils' Progress in Physical Education*. London: DCMS and DCSF, afPE, sports coach UK and Youth Sport Trust.

Ofqual (2014) 'GCSE and A level reform consultation', http://webarchive.nationalarchives.gov.uk/20141031163546/http://ofqual.gov.uk/news/gcse-level-reform-consultation/

Ofsted (2014a) 'The framework for school inspection: The framework for inspecting schools in England under section 5 of the Education Act 2005 (as amended)'. Manchester: Ofsted.

Ofsted (2014b) 'Note for inspectors: use of assessment information during inspections in 2014/15'. Manchester: Ofsted.

Ofsted (2014c) 'Physical education survey visits: Supplementary subject-specific guidance for inspectors on making judgements during visits to schools', www.ofsted.gov.uk/resources/20100015

PEA UK (2004) *Assessment in Physical Education*. Reading: PEA UK.

QCA (2007a) 'Physical education: Programme of study for key stage 3 and attainment target', in QCA (2007) *The National Curriculum*. London: QCA.

QCA (2007b) 'Physical education: Programme of study for key stage 4', in QCA (2007) *The National Curriculum*. London: QCA.

Shpancer, N. (2010) *The Good Psychologist*. New York: Henry Holt and Co. ISBN: 978-0-349123-25-7.

Statutory Instruments (2013) *No. 2232 Education, England: The Education (National Curriculum)(Attainment Targets and Programmes of Study)(England) Order 2013*. Norwich: The Stationery Office. ISBN: 978-0-111103-66-1.

Section 3: Curriculum Coherence – Values, Purposes and Aims

> *Securing 'curriculum coherence' is a vital objective in refining the national curriculum.*
>
> **Oates, 2010**

Curriculum

There are three facets of curriculum that are generally accepted (Bauersfeld, 1979):

- intended
- implemented
- achieved/enacted.

At the intended level, **curriculum is that which is planned.** At the implemented level**, curriculum is that which is taught.** At the achieved level, **curriculum is that which is learnt**. The alignment of these three curriculum components is therefore essential to curriculum coherence.

What unites these components is assessment. Assessment **of** learning provides information as to the extent that the curriculum has been learnt or achieved, and also becomes a baseline measure for the next stage of the curriculum. Assessment **as** learning ensures that which is to be learnt and assessed is planned for. Assessment **for** learning is a process that uses information from learners and their learning in order to make changes to our teaching. The interaction of curriculum and assessment is therefore a vitally important matter. Assessment can either drive our practice favourably and raise standards, or if poorly designed and disassociated from curriculum, it can impact adversely on learning, progress and standards.

A vision for securing curriculum coherence and higher standards for all also involves meeting the needs and circumstances of individual pupils. The delivery of an inclusive curriculum requires expert teaching and assessment that builds a picture of what each child already knows and how they learn, and that helps them understand how to progress to fulfil their learning potential. These beliefs firmly place all pupils and their needs at the centre of planning and teaching, resulting in a personalised curriculum that carefully aligns curriculum, pedagogy (teaching and learning) and assessment.

Understanding these essential elements of our professional practice and their interrelationship **becomes** our professional learning – it develops us professionally. This is essential for making sense of the challenges and implications resulting from the transformational change we face. The paradigm shift that we have been asked to make in removing the operational burden of levelling practice from our system is part of a bigger shift to raise expectations and standards, especially in comparison to international standards, and ensure learning is engaging and enjoyable.

Assessment cannot be viewed in isolation. To do so would be like building a house with no foundations. The key components are depicted in diagrammatic form on the next page and clearly place learners and their learning at the heart of the process. The visual analogy is that the more integral and coherent our curriculum, assessment and pedagogy practice, the more learners' needs are met, increasing opportunity for progress and attainment.

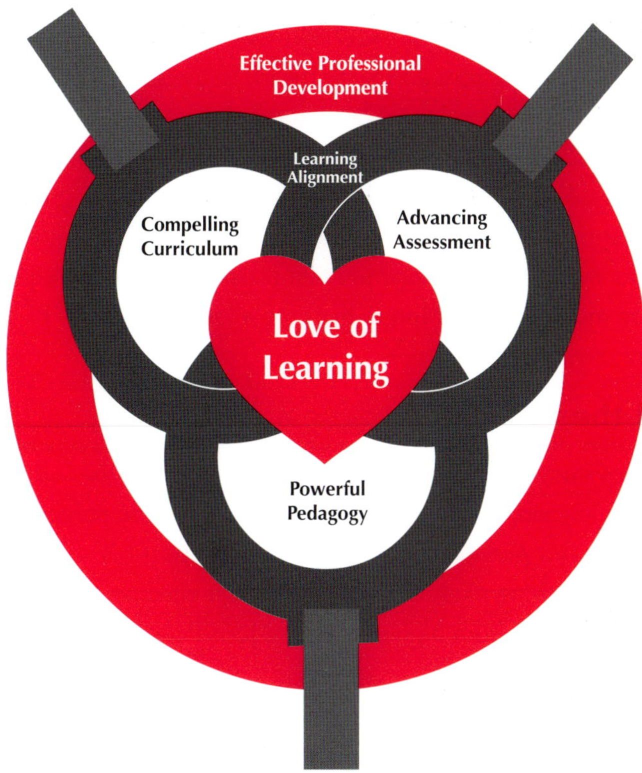

Diagram adapted from Frapwell (2010)

Curriculum Coherence in Practice

When we plan, we must have a clear idea of what we want students to be able to do at the end of the programme (long term), at the end of a unit (medium term) or at the end of a lesson (short term). We share intended learning with pupils so they are clear on the expectations, and assessment criteria give more detail of the learning expected.

We know from research that assessment has a very powerful influence on pupils' learning behaviours. Children will make sense of their learning by structuring and ordering engagement in order to optimise their assessment performance. We must therefore make sure that the assessment very obviously does measure the intended learning we want pupils to achieve. In other words, the learning intended, the learning activities planned, the assessment criteria and the assessment methods employed must all be aligned. When we have this alignment, we must teach well, and this goes beyond simply 'knowing about' something, but also 'knowing how to'. This has implications for how we view improving 'subject knowledge' to teach well.

> *Teachers need pedagogical content knowledge – knowledge about how to teach in particular disciplines – rather than only knowledge about a particular subject matter.*
>
> **Bransford et al, 2000**

To teach something well is integral to curriculum coherence. Assessment information about learners and their learning is continuously used to evolve our curriculum practice and inform or change the way we teach to ensure the key components are always aligned. The curriculum includes, but is not limited to, the statutory national curriculum programme of study for physical education.

The Programme of Study

Some teachers have requested clarification from afPE with regard to the status of the programme of study. Reportedly, certain organisations have informed teachers that the document is only 'statutory guidance' so it does not need to be followed (because it says in some elements 'should' and not 'must'). This is incorrect. The DfE unequivocally states that schools are **required by law** to follow the statutory guidance that applies to them. Core physical education is statutory throughout KS1–4. Specifically, there is a programme of study to be followed at KS4, and this cannot be replaced by examination physical education (eg GCSE, BTEC). Any examination physical education **must be in addition** to the time allocated for core PE at KS4 (for which the guidance stipulates a minimum of two hours).

Purposes and Aims of the Curriculum

In developing the programmes of study for each subject, the DfE (2011) and the subject stakeholder groups ensured aims and purposes were aligned. It is essential to be clear about the purposes and aims that the curriculum is expected to serve, as this provides the basis for the best possible selection of curriculum content, context, assessment activities and teaching methods, and is the most effective way of establishing and maintaining coherent provision. Learning from high-performing jurisdictions around the world resulted in three layers of aims.

Layer 1: System-wide Educational Aims for a National Curriculum and School Curricula

The DfE (2011) believed that previous versions of the national curriculum had gone beyond the original remit, that of a **minimum** entitlement, providing a national benchmark and reference point. The following two overarching aims for the national curriculum were legislated:

- The national curriculum provides pupils with an introduction to the essential knowledge that they need to be educated citizens. It introduces pupils to the best that has been thought and said, and helps engender an appreciation of human creativity and achievement.
- The national curriculum is just one element in the education of every child. There is time and space in the school day and in each week, term and year to range beyond the national curriculum specifications. The national curriculum provides an outline of core knowledge around which teachers can develop exciting and stimulating lessons to promote the development of pupils' knowledge, understanding and skills as part of the wider school curriculum.

For state-funded schools (**and** for academies – with reference to the Academies Act 2010), the requirement is a curriculum offer that:

- is 'balanced and broadly based'
- promotes the spiritual, moral, cultural, mental and physical development of pupils at the school and of society
- prepares pupils at the school for the opportunities, responsibilities and experiences of later life.

These are the aims and purposes legislated as part of our education system. The sole practice of reporting progress against target GCSE grades in secondary schools, therefore, is staid, stuck in the previous system, misaligned and ill-informed. School leadership and management should ensure the assessment system (including reporting) is aligned to the national curriculum and the school's curriculum, and assessment information should be used to improve teaching and the curriculum provision for all pupils to achieve these aims.

Layer 2: Clear School Purposes and Aims for Their Curricula

All school leaders are expected to develop a vision and mission statement for their school. Most schools have a motto, and all schools also have their own aims. These aims can often be rather numerous and wide-ranging.

As a chair of governors at a West Midlands school, I remember working with a new head teacher to develop a vision and aims for the school. As a starting point, we revisited the existing vision and aims, and asked a working group, which included teachers, parents, governors and pupils, to list any related language, phrase or focus. The response was limited. Some groups couldn't list a single aim. All too often, a school's vision and aims can be developed and unfortunately overlooked.

What has evolved over the last decade is the notion of a values-driven education. Schools have the opportunity to:

- revisit their vision, mission statement, motto and aims
- ensure these are aligned to the system-wide purpose and aims
- develop a focus that potentially sets them apart from other local schools.

Value-laden language in writing this layer should permeate or influence everything a school does. A school's values – commitment, respect, achievement, honesty, praise etc – should be demonstrated in actions, attitudes, behaviours and approaches each day.

Layer 3: Purposes and Aims for the Programmes of Study

For the first time since the Education Reform Act 1988 legislated a national curriculum, subjects have had purposes and aims specified for their respective programmes of study. The importance and relevance of this struck me when I was in discussion with my eldest boy on his transfer to high school. I asked him to reflect on his 'PE' at his first and middle schools. The conversation led to the question of what 'PE' stood for. He didn't know. 'PE is PE, Dad. What are you on about?' He didn't know that 'PE' stood for physical education, and he didn't know why he was participating in physical education. No one had ever explained to him the purpose and relevance of the subject for him personally, or his education for life and employment. I also felt somewhat personally responsible for not having this conversation with him earlier in his schooling!

In building understanding of assessment that is fit for purpose, it is essential that the new purpose and aims of physical education are considered in greater detail. If there are a new purpose and aims for physical education, then what and how we assess **has** to be adjusted, or in this case transformed, from what went previously. The national curriculum programme of study for physical education is reproduced in full in Section 4 on pages 45–47. The purpose and aims are addressed here.

Physical Education Purpose of Study

> *A high-quality physical education curriculum inspires all pupils to succeed and excel in competitive sport and other physically demanding activities. It should provide opportunities for pupils to become physically confident in a way which supports their health and fitness. Opportunities to compete in sport and other activities build character and help to embed values such as fairness and respect.*

The physical education purpose of study is analysed here in terms of the three sentences of which it consists, the language used and the meaning conveyed.

> *A high-quality physical education curriculum inspires all pupils to succeed and excel in competitive sport and other physically demanding activities.*

A high-quality physical education curriculum is not anything new when considered in terms of previous government national physical education and school sport strategy and expectations. The (re)emphasis in this national curriculum, however, is inclusive practice, in that *all pupils* are expected to succeed and excel, and they must do this in relation to *competitive sport* and *other physically demanding activities.*

Breadth and balance are a legislative requirement for all schools, and those that offer a curriculum that is heavily weighted in favour of games do not necessarily meet the needs of all pupils. My daughter, for example, would prefer a curriculum offer heavily weighted in favour of more aesthetic activities such as gymnastics or dance, whereas my two boys are happy to follow a more traditional games-based programme. This is a dilemma that faces all teachers.

Staff expertise, equipment, facilities and timetabling all play their part in decision-making about the nature and content of the curriculum. The overriding influence, however, should be learner needs. There are more than 120 recognised sports and activities. We cannot include them all.

Of high importance in developing a coherent curriculum that meets the needs of the learner is an understanding of lateral transfer. This can be lateral transfer of knowledge, concepts, behaviours or skills. A major reason, for example, why rounders is deemed 'easy' is the amount of exposure to 'hand-eye-implement coordination' activities a pupil undertakes. Boys may not follow rounders during secondary school but often do well in this activity in their GCSE practical assessment. This is because it involves key skills and essential concepts (game tactics and strategies) that boys may well have developed through cricket, badminton and tennis, and the essential knowledge and key skills are easily transferred.

The same is true for a pupil who has played a lot of basketball, and is given the opportunity to play netball. The rules of the game are different, but essential knowledge of invasion games, key sending and receiving skills, and understanding outwitting concepts are all readily transferable. A classic example illustrates this. History informs us that basketball was introduced/invented as a close season game for American football players to retain their fitness and skill levels without the heavy impact of tackling.

Understanding lateral transfer in relation to a broad and balanced curriculum turns out to be a focus on the range of key skills, and essential knowledge and concepts to be learnt, rather than a concern for a range of activities. The activity of handball, for example, could be a competitive games focus offered in curriculum time that allows lateral transfer to the pursuit of netball and basketball in after-school clubs.

The inclusion of a number of activities in curriculum time that all develop the same key hand-eye-implement coordination skills and key games strategies can lead to a curriculum that overemphasises handling skills and team game concepts to the detriment of kicking skills, individual competitive games, individual pursuits or aesthetic activities.

A keyword in understanding the meaning of this first purpose of study sentence is *inspires*. A national curriculum physical education programme of study is the minimum entitlement for pupils. It is an outline of the content, and the knowledge, skills, concepts, behaviours and processes that are required to be taught and mastered. It is the teacher who ultimately selects the learning, context and content for pupils to learn and engage with. It is also the teacher and the way they communicate the curriculum content that will bring this subject matter to life. What is better – a poor curriculum taught inspiringly well or a broad, balanced and coherent curriculum taught poorly? The quality of teaching wins hands down. It is the teaching, therefore, that will **inspire** *all pupils to succeed and excel.*

The words that teachers get hung up on, however, are contained in the phrase *succeed and excel.* Everything we know from research into childhood growth and development indicates that all children, unless they have a special educational need or are disabled, can be successful and excel in relation to the national curriculum attainment or floor standard expected.

All pupils should experience some kind of *success* – accomplishment or triumph in competitive sport or other physically demanding activities. All pupils can *excel* or do well in relation to surpassing individual expectations linked to threshold or floor standards. What is essential once more is the ability of the teacher to select appropriate opportunities and present these in a way that maximises all pupils' understanding, facilitates a commitment and engagement with the subject, and promotes a 'can-do' orientation. We need to raise our expectations.

> *It should provide opportunities for pupils to become physically confident in a way which supports their health and fitness.*

Providing *opportunities* in the second sentence is also integrally linked to language in the first sentence. The *opportunities* provided must be high quality, based on pupils' needs, and presented or taught in a way that is inclusive so all pupils can gain access to understanding in order to feel successful and excel. This positive orientation promotes self-esteem, and this in turn leads to confidence.

A curriculum that provides opportunities to develop and deepen a range of skills, knowledge and concepts (breadth and balance) also develops physical competence, which in turn leads to greater confidence. Understanding the relationship of the three Cs in physical education – **competence** that helps develop **confidence** to **continue** in a competitive game or physically demanding activity – is important to pupils actively engaging in a healthy active lifestyle that *supports their health and fitness.*

The importance of opportunity can be illustrated using the example of children learning to walk. The bell curve of distribution for this essential action suggests that the majority of children will walk between the ages of 10 and 14 months.

If a young child has been offered a lot more opportunity to 'practise' or 'weight bear', if colourful and noisy toys are placed on couches, armchairs or window sills, to encourage children to use the furniture to pull themselves up and balance on their legs, then this activity will help to 'make ready' or strengthen muscles. If maturationally a child's nervous pathways are appropriately developed, then it is likely they will walk before 10 months because of the increased opportunity to weight bear.

If, however, a child is constantly strapped in a pushchair and lives in a high-rise block of flats, then they will still eventually walk, but it is likely to be later than 14 months because of the lack of opportunity provided by their environment.

Nature and nurture both have their part to play. Interestingly, in the first example, no one has 'taught' the child to walk, the child has just been provided with the opportunity. In a school context, when children gain language and begin to make meaning or sense of their worlds, the quality of opportunity can also be improved by effective communication or teaching.

> *Opportunities to compete in sport and other activities build character and help to embed values such as fairness and respect.*

In the last decade, there has been a move to a values-driven education. In this context, a person's character consists of the values they espouse. *Opportunities to compete in sport and other activities* are again the responsibility of the school and department. The way the competition and activities are structured and 'transmitted' to pupils is essential for embedding values. All schools have a vision statement derived from value-laden words and statements. Ofsted expects leadership to revisit their vision on a 'regular basis'.

In a physical education context, the examples given are *fairness and respect*, but these are only examples, and schools have the opportunity to align programmes of study with the aims and vision of the school. Embedding values isn't something that just happens by default. It is part of a comprehensive and consistent strategic approach that permeates everything we do.

My children are at an age where they go to friends' houses for tea or sleepovers. It is a very proud moment when other parents comment on their behaviour, in the phrase 'they are a credit to you as their parents'. When I was head of a physical education department, it was also a very proud moment, when visiting or hosting other schools in fixtures, when teachers commented on the attitudes and behaviour of the pupils as being 'a credit to the school'.

Competitive sport and other activities therefore become vehicles for developing appropriate behaviours in terms of how we act in different situations and circumstances. It is very difficult at an early age to cope with losing or not performing as well as one would have liked, or indeed coping with winning. In each situation, values such as respect and dignity can be promoted and become a social learning experience.

It is important, therefore, that all pupils have the opportunity to participate in *competitive sport and other activities* in order to experience real situations where they can develop these values and champion them through their behaviours. This doesn't simply mean experiencing formal inter-school fixtures or performances, but also experiencing competition in intra-school contests or displays and in timetabled lessons.

Viewing competition in this way should prevent the overuse of competition as an extrinsic motivating factor in performances, or the results of competition becoming an overriding focus that can have a negative effect on the way young people feel about themselves and can in turn inhibit inclusive practice.

If facilitated appropriately, competition can be a vehicle that is used to promote educative and respectful social values, rather than just a winning-losing mindset.

The importance of ensuring values are an integral part of a whole curriculum experience, including timetabled, after-school and club experiences, is highlighted in the following two contrasting examples.

In 2013–2014, I was contracted to work with football community coaches who were themselves contracted by primary schools to provide their 'expertise' in supporting the delivery of physical education and school sport. Part of the contract involved progressing coaches' knowledge of the 2014 national curriculum. Coaches found it difficult to articulate how they even introduced, let alone embedded, the value of respect in their teaching. This was despite the vast promotion of a 'respect' campaign in football at the time. Values that influence socially acceptable behaviours therefore need to be planned for, they don't just happen by chance.

The second example is from the summer of 2014. I delivered an afPE keynote on assessing without levels at Millfield School. What struck me about every person I met associated with Millfield was their politeness, respectfulness and willingness to offer help. A values-driven approach can have a profound effect on behaviours and how individuals and organisations are perceived.

In a physical education and sporting context, we do not need to look further than the Olympic and Paralympic Games for values. One of the main purposes of The London 2012 Olympic and Paralympic Games was to 'reach young people all around the world' and 'connect them with the inspirational power of the Games'. Values, when observed in action, can be incredibly inspirational. One only has to remember the determination of athletes to face the pressure and realise a winning ambition, the courage of athletes in overcoming adversity, or the friendship displayed after races and during the closing ceremony.

Olympic Values	Paralympic Values
• Friendship	• Courage
• Excellence	• Determination
• Respect	• Equality
	• Inspiration

Aims of Physical Education

The national curriculum for physical education aims to ensure that all pupils:

- develop competence to excel in a broad range of physical activities
- are physically active for sustained periods of time
- engage in competitive sports and activities
- lead healthy active lives.

Aim 1: Develop Competence to Excel in a Broad Range of Physical Activities

This layer of aims aligns with the overarching curriculum requirement for breadth and balance. Competence in this context, and in the context of the purpose of study and the programme of study content, refers not only to skill, but aptitude, conceptual knowledge, capability, fitness and behaviours etc that are required to excel in a broad range of physical activities.

Aim 2: Are Physically Active for Sustained Periods of Time

When the national curriculum was published, a number of colleagues made representation to me that the reason that this aim is included as part of the physical education programme of study was due to the Ofsted (2013) report for physical education (2008–2012) entitled 'Beyond 2012 – outstanding physical education for all'.

This summary report highlighted the common overemphasis on evaluating and improving tasks, which resulted in pupils standing around in lessons. The national press had a field day, especially with it being Olympic year, with headlines such as 'not enough "physical" in physical education' and 'put the pens away'.

The inclusion of this aim, it is argued, is political. Whether this is true or not, research informs us that if children are regularly physically active at a young age, they are more likely to engage in healthy active lifestyles, **and** their motor proficiency is improved. This is the stronger argument for the inclusion of this physical education aim and should be particularly noted when instilling good habits and routines, and developing fundamental movement skills.

Several teachers have asked afPE how long, as a percentage of the lesson, children should be physically active in lessons. Beware of people who actually give you a figure for this. Tasks we set for young people should be both physically challenging and educational. There are ways of ensuring lessons are both physically active and develop a learning momentum, with the nature of the physical demands being congruent with the nature of the activity and what is being learnt.

A brief illustration using a gymnastic activity might involve pupils working collaboratively, developing a headstand or a handstand balance, and incorporating this into a short sequence focusing on the fluency of movement into and out of the balance. Pupils can work alternately with a partner on this task and carry out an evaluative feedback role for each other. Such an approach throughout the lesson would lead to pupils being physically active for 50% of the time. This amount of time would be wholly appropriate due to the physical (strength) demands of the weight-bearing balances and sequence.

In order to ensure feedback is effective and implemented, a rest is required before further attempts in order to at least maintain, or improve, the quality of movement for performance. As pupils gain strength and strength endurance, they should be expected to execute increasingly difficult series of movements, more complex sequences and overall more physically demanding performances.

Pupils in a competitive games activity, learning about tactical awareness of players who play in the middle of the field/playing area, can be frequently stopped and questioned or given evaluative feedback by their teacher. Game time of at least three or four minutes, organised with small numbers in a team covering a spacious area to maximise participation with effective intervention not longer than one minute emulates the physical demands commensurate with the midfield role in an actual game.

Alternate periods of low intensity (rest, walking, jogging) and high intensity (running, sprinting) can result in an effect similar to interval or fartlek training. The heart rate will be kept 'in the training zone'. Again, this would be wholly appropriate physical activity for the activity and context linked to learning and may result in as much as 60–70% physical activity time if sustained for the duration of the lesson. Lengthy intervention by the teacher combined with shorter periods of activity would of course be inappropriate.

Another suggestion often made is to use physical indicators such as heavy breathing and sweating. Please also be aware, however, that young children, boys especially, have a lower sweat rate than adults, and since the sweat glands of children are closer together, their sweat droplets are more likely to evaporate quickly and so not be noticeable.

Aim 3: Engage in Competitive Sports and Activities

Competition was initially discussed when addressing the purpose of study earlier in this section. I wish to examine competition further with reference to goal orientation theory as understanding this area is also vitally important for understanding the implications for our teaching and educational outcomes, and of course assessment.

Goal orientation theory originated early in the 20th century but became a particularly important theoretical framework in the study of academic motivation after 1985. Although goal orientation theory is predominantly studied in the domain of education, it has also been used in studies in the domains of sports psychology, health psychology and social psychology. Such studies (Pintrich, 2000) indicate that learners tend to fall into two major groups – those who are mastery-oriented and those who are performance-oriented.

Mastery-oriented is when a goal is to understand or master a specific task. Pupils are interested in self-improvement and tend to compare their current level of achievement to their own prior achievement. This type of goal orientation might also be referred to as 'competition against self'.

In contrast, performance-oriented is when the goal is to demonstrate ability compared to others. Such learners are interested in or motivated by competition, where their competence can be demonstrated in competition by outperforming others. These learners use other pupils as points of comparison, rather than themselves.

Interestingly, learners **can** hold multiple goals simultaneously so it is possible for a pupil to be both mastery-approach oriented and performance-oriented. The pupil wants to learn and master the specific task but is also concerned with appearing more competent than others. These types of goals are examples of personal goals. Teachers and schools, however, can also give emphasis to these types of orientations and promote a mastery or a performance goal culture as perceived by pupils.

Much research has been conducted as to which approach is better, but this is inconclusive. Several studies indicate that performance-oriented goals are related to higher achievement, with very few studies indicating a direct relationship between mastery-oriented goals and achievement. Other studies indicate that pupils who think they can increase their intelligence tend to adopt mastery goals, whereas those who believe intelligence is fixed tend to adopt performance goals.

Some researchers (eg Anderman and Johnston, 1998) also refer to performance goals as 'extrinsic goals' where pupils engage in tasks to earn a reward, such as praise or acceptance from the teacher, or to avoid a punishment. Avoiding punishment, such as press-ups or even ridicule, can be a negative of competition or performance-avoidance-oriented goals.

In another series of studies, Elliot et al (2005) divided students into groups of performance-approach, performance-avoidance or mastery conditions. They found that when learners believed their work would result in future opportunities to reap rewards, the performance-approach group out-achieved those in the mastery group. When they thought there were no future 'rewards', they performed no worse. In other words, there appeared to be benefits from being in an environment that encouraged a performance approach.

The argument against a performance-oriented approach was that of labelling. If learners are always given grades and judged against others and against standards, then inevitably, there will be individuals who experience failure and tend to avoid engaging fully in academic or physical tasks.

In contrast, in other studies where mastery goals such as critical thinking, communication skills and participation were the focus, learners who adopted a performance-oriented approach achieved higher grades, but had less interest than the mastery-oriented learners by the end of the unit of work. The importance of interest from a physical education perspective is that mastery-oriented learners adapt their behaviours according to their amount of interest. This is vital for leading healthy active lifestyles. Such studies (eg Barron and Harackiewicz, 2003) suggest that performance **and** mastery serve two ends – achievement **and** interest, and both are important for the learner.

In England, over the last 20 years, schools have evolved a performance-oriented culture – one that promoted an obsessive, almost unhealthy focus on high test scores, levels and examination grades. This effect is compounded by parents who can also influence pupils' goal orientations. One of the basic beliefs of goal-oriented culture, however, is that goal structure can be changed, and this will depend on the teacher's management of the context and environment. Teachers' planning focus and assessment methods can therefore influence this enormously.

Aim 4: Lead Healthy Active Lives

Since 1999 and the Bologna agreement – a joint declaration by European ministers of education – countries have considered education as an area that not only impacts on economic development, but also contributes to greater social returns. From a physical education perspective, this means a physically educated workforce is a workforce that is healthier and fitter, and a workforce that is more economically productive, both in terms of turning up for work and being more productive. It also means a population that is potentially less of a burden on the National Health Service (in England).

Internationally, in the last three decades, physical education has embraced education processes and sports science. The subject has evolved from a performance-sports-oriented discipline that emphasised the development of motor skills to an educative process and a more comprehensive health-related curriculum, motivating students and contributing to psychomotor, cognitive and affective overall development.

Physical education teaching at schools in Europe and most developed countries today is not limited to just the teaching of physical skills, tactical and bodily awareness, and it has more than just a recreational dimension. Internationally, learning outcomes for physical education today include a focus on learning and practising skills that enhance lifelong healthy active lifestyles, fitness, and social and emotional values. By involvement in physical education during early and later childhood and youth, pupils should improve their knowledge, but even more importantly, their competence and skills to enhance health-related physical fitness, and to understand the value of these activities for improving or maintaining health later in life.

At the same time, teaching of the subject has had to provide the opportunity for pupils to improve understanding of social principles and concepts such as fair play and respect, social awareness linked to personal interaction, team effort and social inclusion. These societal values of physical education and sport have been expressed in various documents by the European Commission (White Paper on Sport, EC, 2007; EU Guidelines on Health Enhancing Physical Activity, EU Working Group 'Sport and Health', 2008; Physical Education and Sport at School in Europe, EC, 2013).

A focus on health and fitness has always been an integral part of the national curriculum, referenced, for example, in the end of KS descriptions (EKSDs) in the mid-1990s. In 1999, it became one of the four aspects of physical education as 'knowledge and understanding of fitness and health'. This aspect was incorporated into the level descriptors of the attainment target for physical education, yet despite guidance, it was never something that became important enough in a teacher's practice to contribute with an equal weighting to a pupil's overall level of attainment.

Much of the consideration was given to the acquiring and developing of skills aspect, and the selecting and combining of skills, tactics and compositional ideas. A level 3 or a level 5 in most teachers' language gave meaning to the ability to perform a skill or employ a tactic or compositional principle as part of performance.

This was borne out by a small-scale research project I carried out for the QCA in 2007–2008. The response across the age range from case study schools suggested that knowledge and understanding of fitness and health rarely moved beyond communicative practice that concentrated on how to warm up and how to cool down. The same warm-up and cool-down question was repeatedly asked by teachers of year two pupils through to year 11 pupils.

In secondary schools, knowledge and understanding of fitness and health became synonymous with circuit training. Pupils **did** fitness, but more often than not, it was not health-related, nor did the activity deepen knowledge and understanding of essential knowledge and concepts of the area.

In 2007, the secondary curriculum was revised, and the four aspects of physical education evolved into five key processes. The aspect 'knowledge and understanding of fitness and health' became two key processes – 'developing physical and mental capacity' and 'making informed decisions about healthy active lifestyles'.

This change reflected both the accepted practice in schools with regard to fitness training, which a large majority of pupils enjoyed, and the move to a better informed and healthier young population who made informed decisions about healthy active lifestyles. If these behaviours were embedded, then they would ultimately lead to lifestyle habits continuing after leaving school and provide the economic and social returns government anticipated.

Unfortunately, what happened was that the practice of 'levelling' and attaching importance to performance outcomes was so far ingrained in the profession's practice that revised processes, a greater emphasis on informed decisions for health and revised wording of the level descriptors had no impact on assessment practices. A huge rhetoric-reality gap had transpired. This is not to say that there was not good practice in the system; unfortunately, it was only a minority.

The evidence became available following the British Heart Foundation (BHF) survey in 2012. This national survey, which included England, Scotland, Northern Ireland and Wales, gathered evidence from thousands of young people of school age in each country. A lot of information was collated, and much statistical information resulted.

The standout statistic for me, however, was that for England, the percentage of 5–15-year-olds who engaged in the weekly recommended physical activity levels was 21% for boys and 14% for girls. By the age of 13–15 – an age when the system really ought to be having an impact on a pupil's health behaviours – the percentage actually drops to 14% for boys and 8% for girls. In other words, 86% of boys and 92% of girls aged 13–15 did not participate in the recommended physical activity levels per week.

Intriguingly, one of the areas attributed to inhibiting participation was psychological. Both boys and girls, but especially girls, cited one of the main reasons for not engaging was that physical education lowered their self-esteem. For the purposes of driving home the point, 89% of young children in schools claim to have been bullied at some stage in their school lifetime. A majority of children state that bullying lowers their self-esteem. The only facet of school life that lowers a pupil's self-esteem more than physical education and school sport from the information available, therefore, is bullying.

This is the legacy of over a quarter of a century of national curriculum physical education. Engagement in physical activity has not improved one iota, and the headline healthy active lifestyle figures for adults have remained largely unchanged.

The DfE (2013) national curriculum legislative change, however, has created the prospect of making a difference to our practice, and impacting on increased participation and improved outcomes for children:

- firstly, because physical education has a clearly defined purpose
- secondly, because level descriptors and therefore the skewed practice of only 'measuring' skill performance in activities have been removed
- thirdly, because we have learnt from high-performing jurisdictions that we can have our cake and eat it. In other words, learning can be enjoyable, we can focus on increased economic and social returns as part of a world view (in particular healthy active lifestyles), and we can achieve higher performance standards.

Reinforcing aims throughout the system will help to ensure congruence and coherence. We must not lose sight of these. This is vital for curriculum coherence.

Research confirms that almost all pupils can engage in higher-order learning given effective curriculum coherence, and that all pupils can make progress with sufficient time and support (Assessment Reform Group [ARG] and Teaching and Learning Research Programme [TLRP], 2009). It is the schools and particularly teachers who make a difference, and Ofsted reports have consistently demonstrated the capacity of good schools and good teaching to make a positive difference to improved outcomes for all pupils.

- ✔ **How do we currently ensure curriculum coherence?**
- ✔ **How are the purposes and aims of the national curriculum aligned with our school vision, values and aims?**
- ✔ **How do we align the purposes and aims in our planning and teaching?**
- ✔ **How are we set up to realise the four aims of physical education?**
- ✔ **Is our practice truly inclusive?**
- ✔ **What are the implications for our professional development and practice?**

References

Anderman, E.M. and Johnston, J. (1998) 'Television news in the classroom: What are adolescents learning?', *Journal of Adolescent Research*, 13 (1): 73–100.

ARG and TLRP (2009) *Assessment in Schools: Fit for Purpose?* London: TLRP. ISBN: 978-0-854738-92-2.

Barron, K.E. and Harackiewicz, J.M. (2003) 'Revisiting the benefits of performance-approach goals in the college classroom: Exploring the role of goals in advanced college courses', *International Journal of Education Research*, 39: 357–374.

Bauersfeld, H. (1979) 'Research related to the mathematical learning process', in International Commission on Mathematical Instruction (ed) *New Trends in Mathematics Teaching*. Paris, France: UNESCO. ISBN: 978-9-231015-46-5. pp. 199-213.

Bransford, J., Brown, A. and Cocking, R. (2000) *How People Learn: Brain, Mind, Experience and School*. Washington: National Research Council, National Academy Press. ISBN: 978-0-309070-36-2.

British Heart Foundation National Centre for Physical Activity and Health (BHFNC) (2012) *Physical Activity for Children and Young People*. Loughborough: BHFNC.

Commission of the European Communities (2007) *White Paper On Sport*. Brussels: EC.

DfE (2011) *The Framework for the National Curriculum: A Report by the Expert Panel for the National Curriculum Review*. London: DfE.

Elliot, A.J., Shell, M.M., Bouas Henry, K. and Maier, M.A. (2005) 'Achievement goals, performance contingencies, and performance attainment: An experimental test', *Journal of Educational Psychology*, 97 (4): 630–640.

European Commission (2008) *EU Physical Activity Guidelines: Recommended Policy Actions in Support of Health Enhancing Activity*. Brussels: EU.

European Commission/EACEA/Eurydice (2013) *Physical Education and Sport at School in Europe: Eurydice Report.* Luxembourg: Publications Office of the European Union.

Frapwell, A. (2010) 'Assessment for learning with assessing pupils' progress in physical education'. London: DCMS and DCSF, afPE, sports coach UK and Youth Sport Trust.

HM Government (1988) 'Education Reform Act 1988', www.legislation.gov.uk/ukpga/1988/40/contents

HM Government (2010) 'Academies Act 2010', www.legislation.gov.uk/ukpga/2010/32

Oates, T. (2010) 'Could do better: Using international comparisons to refine the national curriculum in England'. Cambridge: Cambridge Assessment.

Ofsted (2013) 'Beyond 2012 – outstanding physical education for all: Physical education in schools 2008–12'. Manchester: Ofsted.

Pintrich, P.R. (2000) 'An achievement goal theory perspective on issues in motivation terminology, theory, and research', *Contemporary Educational Psychology*, 25 (1): 92–104.

Section 4: The Programme of Study and Floor Standards – New Understandings

> *Nothing in life is to be feared, it is only to be understood. Now is the time to understand more, so that we may fear less.*
>
> **Marie Curie**

A criticism by the DfE (2011) highlighted the disconnect between 'that which is to be taught' (the programme of study) and 'that which is to be assessed' (the attainment target). This fact was highlighted in Section 2 when I illustrated the disparate practice employed by a majority of schools and in Section 3 in the discussion of curriculum coherence.

In reality, previous teaching omitted aspects of the programme of study content because it was not specified in the level descriptors of the attainment target. The best example of this was the previous (2007) KS3 programme of study requirement for pupils to 'recognise hazards and make decisions about how to control any risks to themselves and others'. Or the KS4 programme of study requirement for pupils to 'organise and manage the environment they are working in to ensure the health, safety and well-being of themselves and others'.This is further illustration of assessment practice that was not aligned to the curriculum.

To aid coherence, the attainment target for the 2014 national curriculum was written as an integral part of the programme of study for each KS. It is explained in the phrase: 'By the end of each KS, pupils are expected to know, apply and understand the matters, skills and processes specified in the relevant programme of study' (DfE, 2013). The programme of study includes the attainment target, and the attainment target includes the programme of study. They have been combined. Each KS is organised with a paragraph statement followed by a series of bullet points. The language used refers to both the content and the context **and** standards.
The programme of study consisting of all four KS is replicated in full over the next two pages.

Physical Education Programme of Study

Purpose of Study

A high-quality physical education curriculum inspires all pupils to succeed and excel in competitive sport and other physically demanding activities. It should provide opportunities for pupils to become physically confident in a way that supports their health and fitness. Opportunities to compete in sport and other activities build character and help to embed values such as fairness and respect.

Aims

The national curriculum for physical education aims to ensure that all pupils:

- develop competence to excel in a broad range of physical activities
- are physically active for sustained periods of time
- engage in competitive sports and activities
- lead healthy active lives.

Attainment Targets

By the end of each KS, pupils are expected to know, apply and understand the matters, skills and processes specified in the relevant programme of study.

Schools are not required by law to teach the example content in [square brackets].

Subject Content

KS1

Pupils should develop fundamental movement skills, become increasingly competent and confident, and access a broad range of opportunities to extend their agility, balance and coordination, individually and with others. They should be able to engage in competitive (both against self and against others) and cooperative physical activities, in a range of increasingly challenging situations.

Pupils should be taught to:

- master basic movements, including running, jumping, throwing and catching, as well as developing balance, agility and coordination, and begin to apply these in a range of activities
- participate in team games, developing simple tactics for attacking and defending
- perform dances using simple movement patterns.

KS2

Pupils should continue to apply and develop a broader range of skills, learning how to use them in different ways and to link them to make actions and sequences of movement. They should enjoy communicating, collaborating and competing with each other. They should develop an understanding of how to improve in different physical activities and sports, and learn how to evaluate and recognise their own success.

Pupils should be taught to:

- use running, jumping, throwing and catching in isolation and in combination
- play competitive games, modified where appropriate [for example, badminton, basketball, cricket, football, hockey, netball, rounders and tennis], and apply basic principles suitable for attacking and defending
- develop flexibility, strength, technique, control and balance [for example, through athletics and gymnastics]
- perform dances using a range of movement patterns
- take part in outdoor and adventurous activity challenges both individually and within a team
- compare their performances with previous ones and demonstrate improvement to achieve their personal best.

Swimming and Water Safety

All schools must provide swimming instruction either in KS1 or KS2.

In particular, pupils should be taught to:

- swim competently, confidently and proficiently over a distance of at least 25 metres
- use a range of strokes effectively [for example, front crawl, backstroke and breaststroke]
- perform safe self-rescue in different water-based situations.

KS3

Pupils should build on and embed the physical development and skills learnt in KS1 and 2, become more competent, confident and expert in their techniques, and apply them across different sports and physical activities. They should understand what makes a performance effective and how to apply these principles to their own and others' work. They should develop the confidence and interest to get involved in exercise, sports and activities out of school and in later life, and understand and apply the long-term health benefits of physical activity.

Pupils should be taught to:

- use a range of tactics and strategies to overcome opponents in direct competition through team and individual games [for example, badminton, basketball, cricket, football, hockey, netball, rounders, rugby and tennis]
- develop their technique and improve their performance in other competitive sports [for example, athletics and gymnastics]
- perform dances using advanced dance techniques within a range of dance styles and forms
- take part in outdoor and adventurous activities that present intellectual and physical challenges, and be encouraged to work in a team, building on trust and developing skills to solve problems, either individually or as a group
- analyse their performances compared to previous ones and demonstrate improvement to achieve their personal best
- take part in competitive sports and activities outside school through community links or sports clubs.

KS4

Pupils should tackle complex and demanding physical activities. They should get involved in a range of activities that develops personal fitness and promotes an active, healthy lifestyle.

Pupils should be taught to:

- use and develop a variety of tactics and strategies to overcome opponents in team and individual games [for example, badminton, basketball, cricket, football, hockey, netball, rounders, rugby and tennis]
- develop their technique and improve their performance in other competitive sports [for example, athletics and gymnastics] or other physical activities [for example, dance]
- take part in further outdoor and adventurous activities in a range of environments that present intellectual and physical challenges and that encourage pupils to work in a team, building on trust and developing skills to solve problems, either individually or as a group
- evaluate their performances compared to previous ones and demonstrate improvement across a range of physical activities to achieve their personal best
- continue to take part regularly in competitive sports and activities outside school through community links or sports clubs.

What has Changed?

There is a purpose, and there are aims listed for physical education. This is the first time since the 1988 Education Reform Act that subject disciplines have had a purpose of study and stated aims. The categorisation of areas of activity (primary) or range of content (secondary) have been removed. Dance is statutory in KS1–3. Outdoor and adventurous activities are statutory in KS2–4, while games are statutory throughout all KS. Swimming retains its place as a statutory component in KS1 or 2.

While there is still a strong content steer in terms of meeting learners' needs, there is increased flexibility as the activities listed in square brackets are all examples and therefore non-statutory. There are no four aspects (primary) or five key processes (secondary). However, processes are still evident – for example, application of skill, and analysis and evaluation with the emphasis on recognising success. These processes remain inextricably linked to improving performance but also focused on developing competence to increase confidence in order to participate in physical activities or sports.

Expectations have been increased as it is expected that **all** pupils will attain key skills, essential knowledge and concepts, and vital behaviours. These 'essential learning standards' or 'floor' standards form the attainment target that is written as an integral part of the programme of study. These expected standards are no longer organised in the form of level descriptors.

Previously, when approaching the design of a curriculum to incorporate new statutory requirements, it had become common practice for schools and departments to identify the key differences to that which existed before and make modifications to incorporate these changes. Where the change had been incremental, this was perhaps adequate because it represented small alterations in an already accepted framework. Incremental changes are small changes to that which already exists. In terms of practice, this often manifested itself in additional boxes or columns added to a department's unit of work or lesson plan templates. We might have demonstrated that we were compliant with statutory changes, but this would be immersed into what we had always done. There is a limit to how much impact this approach will have on improved outcomes for pupils.

Meta-cognitive learning is the next stage in understanding change, and this approach to change can result in increased returns because it is essentially thinking about thinking or learning about learning. In embracing and attempting to understand change, it is our thinking about what is happening in the change process itself that helps us reorder our values and beliefs. This helps us to 'see the world differently', and we are more likely to change our practice as a result. Where the change required is transformational or 'epistemic', the aforementioned approaches are insufficient. Sterling (2010–2011), drawing on the work of O'Sullivan (2002) and Bateson (1972) about learning and change, explained epistemic learning and change as moving from seeing our world view to seeing **with** our world view so that we can be more open to, and draw on, other views and possibilities:

> *The case for transformative learning is that learning within paradigm does not change the paradigm, whereas learning that facilitates a fundamental recognition of paradigm and enables paradigmatic reconstruction is by definition transformative.*

In summary, epistemic learning occurs when an expansion of consciousness and a more relational way of seeing arises, inspiring different sets of values and practices. This is the learning and change required of many of us with the removal of levels. Our worlds have been challenged. We are being asked to remove an assessment practice that many employed without question for 14 years. What is crucial in this change environment, in going through this process, is not only understanding the rationale for change but our understanding of the conceptual underpinnings for this change. We are the people who make up the system, and we are the people who make it work. This is the attribute that is fundamental to understand the new floor standards.

The Programme of Study Floor Standards

To support the commitment to higher standards and inclusive and progressive practice, the DfE (2013) has set a common expectation for each KS and for all state schools to use in planning their curriculum. This common expectation is termed a **floor standard** and is in essence the **essential learning standard** that is expected to be attained by all pupils in each KS for physical education.

The standards are based on the fundamental principle that all pupils are entitled to an education that includes the essential knowledge and concepts, key skills and vital behaviours that are of enduring value and underpin learning in physical education. All pupils, unless they have SEN or a disability that inhibits access to this learning, should be able to reach these floor standards. It is our challenge to ensure all pupils are so included or enabled.

The floor standards provide a challenging threshold, rather than a minimum standard of competence, and are intended to stretch pupils in their learning. Higher expectations, such as developing agility, balance, coordination and fundamental movement skills at KS1, understanding how to improve at KS2, analysis of performance at KS3 and actually engaging in a range of activities that lead to healthy active lifestyles at KS4, have all raised the bar from previous expectations for national standards. The floor standards are intended as benchmarks that serve as the starting points for designing units of work as part of a scheme of work for physical education.

Subject leaders should co-construct appropriate physical education programmes that ensure the essential standards are achieved, in ways that reflect the resources and expertise available, and the particular needs and interests of the school community. Implementation of the standards therefore requires a departmental response integral to school and community practice. There is, however, no single approach, no right or wrong way, although there may be more effective ways of approaching this. Teachers have responsibility for, and control over, the programme they develop to enable their pupils to achieve the standards.

The Concept of Floor Standards

A floor standard in England has been used to refer to a percentage target for the number of pupils achieving a median score for progress in English and maths. A floor standard is calculated from the progress and attainment pupils make. Previously, this was against levels of attainment.

In a physical education context, and for the purposes of this book, we are therefore using the term floor standard to refer to the essential learning standards set out in the national curriculum programme of study for physical education that all pupils are expected to make progress to and attain. Over the past decade, this approach to thinking about learning has been embraced by many countries across many disciplines.

The research has focused on the understanding of a 'threshold concept'. This understanding has been seen as a valuable tool, not only in facilitating learners' understanding of their subject, but in aiding the rational development of curricula in rapidly expanding circumstances where there has been a strong tendency to overload the curriculum (Cousin, 2006 and 2008). In a physical education context, this overloading was true of departments that designed curricula around a multitude of activities, often teaching the same concept repeatedly or not focusing on conceptual learning due to an overriding concern with skill. At worst, activities were constantly changed every two or three weeks. At best, they continued for a six-week block or 12 hours spent learning an activity.

Understanding threshold concepts became part of the solution to the problem reported by the DfE (2011) of the national curriculum becoming too prescriptive and going beyond its original intention of a benchmark document delineating a minimum entitlement. In a physical education context, the focus on designing curricula around content and activities, and assessing pupils' performance in those activities ignored the fact that learners were insufficiently engaged in the essential learning in the subject discipline.

This is best illustrated with the figures indicating the percentage of pupils participating in the recommended physical activity levels outlined in Section 3 – they have not improved in 26 years of schools in the state system following a national curriculum. Tim Oates, chair of the expert panel, maintains that, to be effective, learning has to 'leave a trace'. In other words, it has to be transformative or have an impact.

Using engagement in healthy active lifestyles to illustrate this, it is the difference between knowing the benefit of a healthy and active lifestyle, possibly even attending a school club for a short period of time, and the regular engagement that demonstrates a change in behaviour that is consistent and maintained. It becomes 'the way of doing things', it becomes part of our everyday life, it becomes seeing with our world view. This transformative feature is the first of eight features that have been developed through research, and the characteristics of each feature are summarised in the following table:

The Feature Characteristics of a Threshold Concept

Feature	Characteristics
Transformative	Once understood, a threshold concept changes the way in which learners view the discipline. It represents a previously inaccessible way of thinking about something without which the learner cannot progress (Meyer and Land, 2003). When mastered, a learner begins to think and act like a 'professional', using appropriate vocabulary. In other words, they think, talk and act like someone who is 'physically educated', using language of learning in the discipline. This will be quite different to a scientist or historian – for example, engaging in regular physical activity, recognising space to exploit in a games context or space to explore in a dance context. This transformation involves not only grasping a concept, but also consistently applying it in practice or 'living the change'.
Troublesome	Threshold concepts are likely to be troublesome, difficult or frustrating for the learner. Knowledge can be troublesome, such as when it is counter-intuitive, alien or seemingly incoherent – for example, passing away from the goal or target in a game in order to create and exploit space, comprehending the unfamiliar concept of running forward and passing back in a rugby context, or overcoming the sense of vertigo when staying upright or perpendicular to your skis on a steep mountainous descent.

Irreversible	Given their transformative potential, threshold concepts are also likely to be irreversible. In other words, they are difficult to unlearn. Many of you may be able to remember when you first learnt to ride a bike or have children who have just learnt to ride. A lot of practice on stabilisers, moving in and out of balance, is undertaken often prior to a shorter time spent wobbling and falling/crashing before success in balancing on two wheels is achieved. Adults who have not ridden for decades can take to a bike and are able to balance in order to cycle. Balance is an attribute that, when learnt, is difficult to unlearn.
Integrative	Threshold concepts, once learnt, are likely to bring together different aspects of the subject that previously did not appear, to the learner, to be related – sending and receiving skills (control and accuracy); attacking and defending strategies; movement into space in games, dance and gymnastics; and athletics/gymnastic skills that are integral to game play. These are all examples of essential knowledge and concepts that can be transferred and promote relational or integrative learning.
Bounded	A threshold concept will most likely 'reside in' a particular conceptual space, serving a specific and limited purpose. In terms of subject disciplines, it is the knowledge that is endemic to English, for example, contrasted to the subject matter in another subject such as maths. Within the physical education discipline context, examples also include the conceptual language of dance versus the conceptual language of competitive games or the language associated with outdoor and adventurous activities.
Discursive	The crossing of a threshold will include a better and extended use of language. Conceptually, learners 'enter a new world', and new associated language creates the means to access and develop new conceptual frameworks. Once learners have had the opportunity to work with others to recognise success and begin to make improvements in their own or others' performance, then this discursive, thinking process helps provide access to becoming analytical, evaluative or creative depending on their stage of learning.
Reconstitutive	Understanding a threshold concept may often bring about a shift in learner subjectivity. This involves the features of both transformative and discursive aspects. Such reconstitution is more likely to be recognised initially by the teacher or peers and will, by its very nature, take place over time. Pupils' opinions on physical activity, healthy behaviours, tactics or composition will evolve over time. It is important, therefore, to give learners a voice and ask their opinion.
Liminality	A learner's conscious awareness of the process of mastering a concept is the point at which they enter what has been termed a 'liminal space'. There is no simple route in learning across this space. It does not go from 'easy' to 'difficult'. The mastery of a threshold concept often involves messy journeys back and forth across conceptual terrain (Cousin, 2006). One week, learners may appear to have grasped a concept or key skill; another week, they might struggle.

The Implications for Practice of Threshold Concepts

There are three major implications for our practice from understanding floor standards in the light of threshold concept research.

The first is teaching and the difficulties teachers have in retracing the journey they are creating for pupils back to their own days of inexperience, when understanding of threshold concepts escaped them in the early stages of their own learning. This can be frustrating for teachers, especially when pupils appear to have grasped a concept such as space finding, offside or expressing emotion one week only to seemingly 'forget it' the next.

This also has implications for planning. Teachers must embrace and plan for the 'messy' journeys that Cousin (2006) and Land, Meyer and Baillie (2010) speak of. The acquisition of threshold concepts often involves regression and fluctuation. Learning is not and will never be linear. This understanding brings a whole new meaning to the phrase 'progression in learning', especially with regard to the ultimate implication for practice, that of assessment. This is not a new phenomenon for physical education teachers as skill learning follows a similar pattern. New skills or new technique can often lead to an initial 'dip' in performance as can skills applied in a new context, whether a new game or a more complex activity.

Previous use of levels to indicate progression in learning created an anomaly. Learning is transient. While formative assessment (or assessment employed to inform teacher communication with the learner in everyday lessons to help them progress) is ongoing, summative teacher assessment needs to be based on many observations of an individual pupil's performance, across a range of activities and over time. To frequently make summative judgements and, worse still, constantly record them as a grade or level, before sufficient assessment information linked to the floor standards is collated, is a misuse of time.

In a parallel learning way, assessment practice itself becomes a teacher's own threshold concept to master. It is possible, however, to transform practice and strengthen the comparability and credibility of a teacher's own assessments by focusing on the processes of internal (to the school) and external moderation (ARG and British Educational Research Association [BERA], 2013). This is something that happens for GCSE or A Level moderation, but certainly didn't happen with levels for a majority of physical education departments. Although these processes take time to develop and embed, and also take time to implement on an ongoing basis, moderation activities constitute some of the very best professional development. They provide unique opportunities for teachers to discuss and continually refine their understanding of standards of quality and progression of essential learning within learning domains. These understandings are fundamental aspects of pedagogical content knowledge (how we teach our subject), crucial for effective teaching and for understanding what constitutes high expectations – and appropriate cognitive demand in physical education – so that it becomes the basis for effective assessment.

In summary, the threshold concept approach focuses on the identification of what is fundamental to the grasp of a subject and is essentially a transactional curriculum enquiry requiring a partnership between the relevant subject experts, teachers and learners (Cousin, 2009 and 2010).

A Way of Framing the Curriculum

The floor standards for physical education can be framed into the three broad categories or domains that learning and development are generally divided into:

- physical development (psychomotor domain)
- cognitive development (cognitive domain)
- social/emotional development (affective domain) (Bloom, 1956).

Physical development addresses any change in the body, including how children grow, move and perceive their environment. Cognitive development pertains to the mental processes (eg language, memory, problem solving) that children use to acquire and utilise knowledge. Emotional and social development addresses how children handle relationships with others, as well as an understanding of their own experiences and feelings.

A positive experience or positive 'affect' is vitally important for a positive 'effect' – especially in terms of a vital behavioural effect required in physical education – that of leading a healthy active lifestyle. While we know that there are certain aspects of our maturation that develop only according to what we have programmed in our genes, the importance of environmental factors has come to the forefront of the long-running nature/nurture debate. What **is** known is that a number of characteristics, especially behaviour, are tied to environmental influences. How a person behaves can be linked to social factors such as parental and school (parent or carer, teacher and pupil) influence and associated emotional 'affects'. In physical education, a child can learn to lead a healthy active lifestyle from social constructs leading to such behaviours, combined with positive emotional experiences influenced by goal orientation and feeling successful.

A less embellished way of looking at the three domains is to term them the 'thinking' physical being (cognitive domain – head), the 'feeling' physical being (affective domain – heart) and the 'doing' physical being (psychomotor domain – hands) **'head-heart-hands'** (see diagram overleaf). As a result of **doing** and **thinking** in physical education, we want pupils to feel good about themselves and their relationship with the subject and go on to **lead healthy active lifestyles**.

Head-Heart-Hands

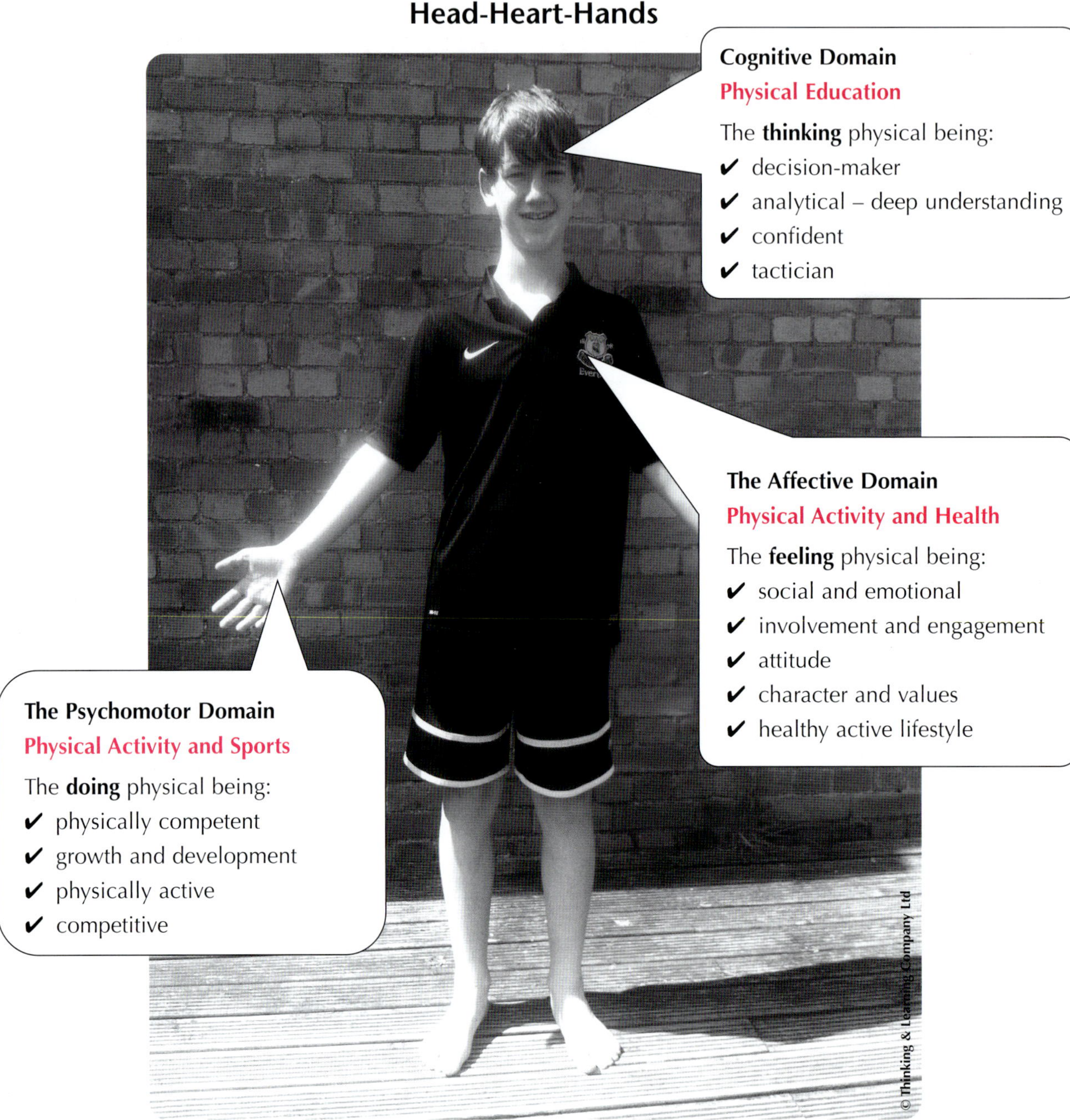

Understanding childhood learning and development also contributes to how teachers can teach to enable pupils to learn and progress. The flexible opportunity is provided for us to plan localised and bespoke curriculum programmes. The floor standards act as a starting point in the design of the curriculum, and help us to align the planning of assessment criteria through the writing of intended learning and success criteria, and the planning of learning activities. Consideration should also be given to school priorities and pupil learning needs.

The table that follows is a synthesis of the national curriculum programme of study requirements for physical education as three domains. Although these are in three separate columns representing each of the learning domains, they should be seen as three interwoven categories reflecting the integrative or relational nature of learning and progress.

KS1 Doing – Hands	KS1 Thinking – Head	KS1 Feeling – Heart
• Develop fundamental movement skills (specifically master basic movements, including running, jumping, throwing and catching) • Develop competence • Develop agility, balance and coordination • Perform dances using simple movement patterns	• Apply skills • Develop simple tactics for attacking and defending • Develop competence • Develop confidence	• Work individually and with others • Develop competence • Develop confidence
Contexts: Team games; dance; a range of physical activities (individual and cooperative); competitive situations (against self and others); possibly swimming; increasingly challenging		
KS2 Doing – Hands	**KS2 Thinking – Head**	**KS2 Feeling – Heart**
• Develop a broader range of skills (specifically running, jumping, throwing and catching in isolation and in combination) • Perform dances using a range of movement patterns • Develop flexibility, strength, technique, control and balance	• Apply a broader range of skills (specifically running, jumping, throwing and catching in isolation and in combination) • Link skills to make actions and sequences of movement • Learn how to evaluate and recognise their own success • Compare and improve performances with previous ones • Apply basic principles suitable for attacking and defending	• Enjoy communicating, collaborating and competing with each other • Develop flexibility, strength, technique, control and balance
Contexts: Competitive games; dance; outdoor and adventurous activity challenges; different physical activities and sports; individual and team; swimming (if not scheduled in KS1)		
All schools must provide swimming instruction either in KS1 or KS2. In particular, pupils should be taught to: • swim competently, confidently and proficiently over a distance of at least 25 metres • use a range of strokes effectively, such as front crawl, backstroke and breaststroke • perform safe self-rescue in different water-based situations.		

KS3 Doing – Hands	KS3 Thinking – Head	KS3 Feeling – Heart
• Develop expert technique to improve performance • Perform dances using advanced dance techniques in a range of dance styles and forms	• Apply techniques across different sports and physical activities • Apply principles of effective performance to their own and others' work • Use a range of tactics and strategies to overcome opponents • Develop skills to solve problems • Analyse and improve performances compared to previous ones	• Participate in exercise, sports and activities (out of school) • Understand and apply the long-term health benefits of physical activity • Build trust • Develop skills to solve problems
Contexts: Outdoor and adventurous activities (team, individual, group); direct competition through team and individual games; participate outside school through community links or sports clubs; other competitive sports; challenging		

KS4 Doing – Hands	KS4 Thinking – Head	KS4 Feeling – Heart
• Develop technique and improve performance	• Develop a variety of tactics and strategies to overcome opponents • Develop skills to solve problems • Evaluate and improve performances compared to previous ones	• Develop personal fitness • Engage in an active, healthy lifestyle • Take part regularly in competitive sports and activities (outside school) • Build trust • Develop skills to solve problems
Contexts: Outdoor and adventurous activities in a range of environments; in other competitive sports or other physical activities; team and individual games; participate outside school through community links or sports clubs; complex and demanding		

Notes

1 The non-statutory reference to specific activities [listed in square brackets on the reproduced programme of study at the start of this section] has been removed.

2 The purposes and aims of physical education are aligned in terms of the language utilised in the programme of study. Words such as competence, confidence and being physically active, especially in an out of school context, appear in the KS floor standards.

3 The prose of the programme of study has been adapted so that it is written to convey the floor standards as succinct KS headline learning intentions. This helps align our assessment practice.

4 The statutory context for performance and/or participation is listed separately. Schools can devise programmes using combinations of context and content, according to their locality and to ensure it meets learners' needs.

5 By adjoining the four KS, progressive pathways for each learning domain begin to emerge.

6 The programme of study provides a start point – the key skills, essential knowledge and concepts, and vital behaviours expected in physical education. It is the minimum entitlement.

The Psychomotor Domain Pathway

KS1

In teaching and supporting the development of children and young people, three attributes are essential to help pupils learn, progress and understand – agility, balance and coordination. These are often termed **the ABCs of movement**. These key components of movement underpin our ability to master fundamental movement skills, but are also improved by performing skills in isolation and in combination. Already in England, there is much input in this area, with courses supporting the teaching and development of these component skills. This is because fundamental movement skills are very important in the physical development of a child.

KS2

Pupils need to master fundamental movement skills if they are to enjoy the wide range of physical activities, sports and outdoor pursuits on offer. Necessary for this mastery is the development of physical abilities such as strength, flexibility and stamina. When a child is competent and confident with these fundamental skills, both individually and in combination, they become 'secondary ready' or KS3 ready.

KS3

When competent in their learning and confident about themselves, pupils can develop more sport-specific technique and advanced learnt movement. This in turn can lead to further improvement in performance. The difference between fundamental movement skills and advanced learnt movement or sport-specific technique is illustrated in the following examples. The skill of sending an implement in a majority of performance involves generating momentum from back foot to front foot and transferring this momentum to the arms or arms plus an implement when passing, throwing or striking. This basic movement therefore becomes fundamental to any activity that involves sending an implement. Technique refers to the fine motor movement when performing a skill. The skill of striking, for example, becomes the skill of batting when using a cricket bat, and different batting techniques employed define different shots. Forward defensive, forward drive and lofted drive all use different techniques.

KS4

Pupils should further develop complex movement skills that also allow them to continue to enjoy sport and physical activity. There is nothing worse than feeling incompetent in front of peers, at a time when young people are the most self-conscious they'll ever be in their lives, to negatively influence seeking more opportunity to participate in that activity. Having a firm grasp of the fundamental movement skills and being physically active will be more likely to lead to pupils engaging in regular healthy activity for life.

The Importance of Movement

There is much research and classification of fundamental movement skills, and even questions as to whether the term is entirely appropriate. The word 'fundamental', for example, suggests that the skills are somehow essential to every sport or activity we undertake, which clearly they are not. Care needs to be taken, therefore, when designing curriculum that the fundamental skills developed are fit for purpose and appropriate for the curriculum activities included in the programme. In addition, care needs to be taken that the phrase 'fundamental movement skills' is not seen as some kind of pedagogical approach. Many 'off the shelf' physical education or school sport packages were designed to ensure that children had the opportunity to develop certain skills, but these should not necessarily be seen as synonymous with teaching them as a block of activity. The DfE has never imposed a particular way of teaching the curriculum on the teaching profession. Scheduling a six-week multi-skills programme to 'cover' fundamental movement skills as listed in the national curriculum programme of study is not, however, an approach that is expected. Opportunity to practise and develop these skills needs to be integrated, coherent and continuous.

For the purposes of this publication, we are illustrating the 22 fundamental movement skills divided into three categories by the Education Department of Western Australia (2004), which have been referenced by many countries. We are not promoting this as skill content to be covered religiously, rather as illustrative material. The table has been adapted by indicating when we might expect the various fundamental movement skills to be mastered. This will depend on a number of contexts and should only be viewed as a guide. KS2 **lower** and **upper** refer to years three and four and years five and six respectively.

Body Management	Locomotor	Object Control
Balance (KS2 – lower)	Continuous leap (KS2 – upper)	Catch (KS1)
Climb (KS2 – lower)	Dodge (KS1)	Chest pass (KS2 – lower)
Forward roll (KS2 – lower)	Gallop (KS2 – upper)	Foot dribble (KS2 – upper)
Line walk (KS1)	Hop (KS1)	Hand dribble (KS2 – upper)
	Jump for distance (KS1)	Kick (KS2 – lower)
	Jump for height (KS1)	Overarm throw (KS1)
	Side gallop (KS2 – upper)	Underarm throw (KS1)
	Skip (KS2 – lower)	Punt (KS2 – upper)
	Sprint run (KS2 – lower)	Two-handed strike (KS2 – upper)

Pupils do not develop competence in the fundamental movement skills naturally as part of their normal growth and development. These skills need to be taught. They need to be learnt and practised consistently. This is because it takes between 240 and 600 minutes of teaching and practice time to learn and become proficient in one fundamental movement skill.

The major implication for teaching in this situation is that of enjoyment. If pupils have really enjoyed their creative play in lessons, if they have really enjoyed the hopscotch playground game they were taught in physical education lessons, for example, then they will be more likely to play that game at playtime or lunchtime, and they will be more likely to go home and teach their parents the game they learnt, thereby increasing the time spent practising the fundamental movement skills.

The major implication for planning is that of developing a curriculum architecture that allows for a number of skills to be focused on in any one year so that continuity and coherence, and therefore the opportunity for progression, are increased. There is no requirement to programme activity-focused units of work of 6–7 hours' duration to dovetail with half-term calendars. In a given scenario, this has often led to throwing and catching skills being taught at the start and the end of the academic year with little or no planned continuity or progression for throwing and catching in-between.

In planning and teaching, the development of these skills is based on pupils' needs. The opportunity arises to develop them at KS1, for example, through creative play, to music, with or without equipment or apparatus to provide challenge, interest and enjoyment, and to practise both indoors and outdoors.

The implication for assessment therefore has to be for physical education teachers or coaches to have an expectation of what the skills should look like when they are mastered and when they should be mastered. This ensures informed decision-making about what skills and how many skills to focus on, which children to support and which children to extend. In addition, for effective assessment to be realised, the skills of observation and evaluation need to be developed as part of 'gap analysis', and the knowledge of what to say, how to question learners and how to feed back as part of effective intervention to progress the skills. If this is understood, together with the integrative nature of learning, then the practice of one skill per week as part of a unit of work would never have evolved.

The importance of movement is often overlooked because it is such a natural part of our development. The more opportunity for appropriate experiences that we can provide, the more likely it is that fundamental movement skills will be mastered, and this is also crucial for a child's physical, cognitive and affective development across all subjects. In addition, initial studies demonstrate no consistent association between prevalence of skill mastery and socio-economic status. There is a huge responsibility for schools, therefore, to ensure that socio-economic status does not become a barrier or an excuse as the foundations of fundamental movement skills are laid in early childhood and are essential to encourage a physically active lifestyle. If children feel good about what their bodies can do, they are more likely to seek out further opportunities.

The Cognitive Domain Pathway

KS1

afPE has always advocated that the learning experiences of physical education should focus on young people **'learning to move'** before **'moving to learn'**. Learning to move is about the learning of the fundamental movement skills required for participation in different types of physical activities. Moving to learn is the application of the skills learnt for participation in physical activities, but also the learning integrated with other aspects of school learning within and beyond the curriculum. The simple tactics required for attacking and defending include creating and exploiting space and denying space. These can be developed in a multitude of simple run and chase games such as tag, which can develop thinking and awareness of marking and dodging. Denying space while playing a pig-in-the-middle game can be through either defending the 'sender' or the 'receiver'. A natural progression is the need for the attackers to create space by making an angle for the pass. Developing and applying skills are integrative – they go hand in hand.

KS2

At KS2, a broader range of skills are applied, in particular thinking and application of linking and combining actions are the focus. Understanding how to improve by recognising what made performances successful, and evaluating these performances to improve further moves the individual from knowing facts or key points about performing a skill to an individual who knows how to improve. The threshold transition is from 'knower' to 'learner'. In terms of the basic principles of attacking and defending, the most widely accepted principles that form the basis for team play in all sports were developed by Allen Wade. When I started my teacher training in 1982, we were recommended to purchase a book entitled *The FA Guide to Training and Coaching* written by Allen Wade in 1967. I still have the book! Allen was The Football Association's Technical Director. He was a former Loughborough University physical education student, as were our lecturers. The following year, in 1983, he finished as Technical Director of the FA, having spent 20 years in post.

The five basic principles of attack are:	The five basic principles of defence are:
1 penetration	1 delay
2 support/depth	2 depth
3 width	3 balance
4 mobility	4 concentration
5 improvisation/creativity.	5 composure/discipline/patience.

In order to be secondary ready, it is important that learners know and understand these basic principles that form the foundation of all game play.

KS3

Cognitively, if pupils understand the key techniques learnt then they will be better able to apply them in different sports and activities. For example, once it is comprehended that spreading fingers slightly behind and to the side of a basketball aids control in receiving a chest pass and aids control and accuracy in sending a chest pass, then it becomes easier to apply the same concept to a shoulder pass in netball, a volley pass in volleyball or a lateral pass in rugby. It also becomes easier to make connections to applying the same concept to a handstand, where a technical point is to spread fingers. We should not have to repeatedly teach the same technical points when the concept of 'greater surface area equals greater control' is understood.

Also building on the foundations of KS2 is the development of the principles of play applied in KS3 to the employment of a range of tactics and strategies. Strategies refer to attacking, defending and transitional decisions about overcoming opponents. Strategies will reflect an approach. For example, an attacking strategy might be to attack with width and depth, and using a fast break. This may be combined with a defensive strategy that defends compactly or narrowly. Tactics might include tactical formations, patterns of play, roles and responsibilities, overlapping and zone defence. Tactics are how the strategy will be carried out.

Developing skills to solve problems can be part of games tactics and strategy, but these skills can principally be developed through outdoor and adventurous activity contexts. Research since the 1990s has demonstrated that when taught problem-solving skills, pupils' antisocial behaviour improves. A simple approach I have adapted in my career and always used is the IRAK approach to problem solving – identify, rationalise, address/act, knowledge. The first stage is to identify the problem. The second is to rationalise or make sense of the problem by explaining it from a logical perspective to enable the third stage, which is to address the problem with ideas or solutions for action. This in turn leads to the development of new knowledge, which, if applied appropriately, helps to prevent the same problem happening again. If the problem is a recurring one, then the new knowledge provides a template to follow in addressing the difficulty.

Analysis is a higher order conceptual skill that is required to be taught in KS3. If pupils have learnt this concept then they will be 'next stage' ready in terms of examination study. When teaching basic movement analysis, we must be able to break down the performance into component parts. This will involve getting pupils to describe the movement of joints; the function, actions and type of contraction of the muscles producing the movement; and the plane of the movement. Pupils should know terminology for joints, muscles and types of contraction. Analysis will also apply to tactics and strategies in games and of course compositional principles if following gymnastics or dance. It is inextricably linked to improving all aspects of performance, including in outdoor and adventurous activities.

Analysis informing the previous discursive points for the cognitive domain in KS3 provides the conceptual framework for understanding effective performance.

KS4

In KS4, pupils are expected to develop their cognitive skills, but in particular their analytical skills in moving from breaking performance information into parts in order to explore relationships to evaluating and improving or being able to justify a course of action that they have decided on. In other words, they will prioritise what they have decided to improve and be able to articulate a reason for this.

The Affective Domain Pathway

Learning the key skills, essential knowledge and concepts of the psychomotor and cognitive domains will be affected by a pupil's social and emotional intelligence. This is viewed as so important that social and emotional aspects of learning (SEAL) are taught in primary schools. In addition, children are more likely to feel confident about themselves if they are competent movers and performers. The affective domain therefore plays a huge integrative part in teaching and of course assessment.

KS1

Pupils should work well individually, and this involves them being an active participant, attentive and motivated, and possessing a positive attitude. Working with others involves listening, initiating, contributing, joining, taking turns, responding and justifying.

KS2

Pupils should continue to enjoy communicating, collaborating and competing with each other. The emphasis is on enjoyment, but importantly, pupils should be developing certain values. This is likely to be simple acceptance of values such as actively participating, positive attitudes and the importance of exercise in developing flexibility, strength, technique, control and balance, rather than the more complex state of commitment we expect to see demonstrated at KS3 and progressing on into KS4.

KS3

By the end of KS3, participation in exercise, sports and activities outside school is expected. Pupils will be organising, rearranging and assessing their values, and will begin to create unique value systems that, once constructed, become characteristic of their behaviours. At the adolescence stage, there is a constant value struggle between the notion of freedom and responsible and respectable behaviours. Adherence to rules and etiquette in competitive games and other physical activities helps synthesise values, especially when building trust and developing an allegiance or a 'faithfulness' to the long-term health benefits of physical activity. Problem-solving skills become useful in conflict resolution.

KS4

By the end of KS4, individuals should have a coherent value system that organises their behaviours. The behaviour that we expect to see at this stage is pervasive, consistent, predictable and, most importantly, characteristic of the learner. In national curriculum physical education terms, pupils will develop personal fitness, engage in an active, healthy lifestyle and take part regularly in competitive sports and activities outside school.

Writing Intended Learning and Success Criteria Aligned to the Curriculum

The task of writing learning intentions was made considerably easier by the work of the famous American educationist Benjamin Bloom and his way of organising thinking into a six-layer taxonomy, from the most basic to the more complex levels of thinking. The categories of this classification were:

- knowledge
- comprehension
- application
- analysis
- synthesis
- evaluation.

In the 1990s, Anderson – a former student of Bloom – revisited the taxonomy. As a result, a number of changes were made, although two changes clearly stand out:

- the transition from each layer being labelled as a noun to each layer listed in verb form
- the promotion of 'synthesis' to the top layer in the form of the verb 'create'.

Bloom et al's (1956) research had led to further developments of a taxonomy for educational objectives, which helped teachers use stage-appropriate assessment language in the formulation of learning intentions and success criteria for units of work or individual lessons. With reference to Bloom's taxonomy, each learning domain has been summarised in the following table:

Psychomotor	Cognitive	Affective
Layer verb (in bold) and key behaviours and words that can help focus our planning of learning intentions, learning activities and appropriate assessment methodology (see Section 5)		
Naturalise High level performance becomes likely, and skills are performed naturally *design, specify, manage, invent, produce*	**Create** Generate new ideas, products or ways of viewing things *develop, plan, build, create, design, organise, revise, formulate, invent, propose, establish, assemble, construct, integrate, rearrange, modify*	**Characterise** Individuals join community clubs and participate regularly; they become active members *act, display, compete, influence, practise*

Articulate Pupils' refined actions are performed as a series with flow, in varying combinations in varying contexts for performance *construct, solve, combine, coordinate, integrate, adapt, develop, formulate, modify, master*	**Evaluate** Pupils justify a decision or course of action *check, review, justify, assess, present a case for, defend, report on, investigate, direct, critique, judge, hypothesise, appraise, argue, project manage*	**Organise** Specialised equipment/clothing for activities is purchased, and pupils include participation in activities or clubs in their weekly schedule; they develop and modify their values *build, develop, defend, modify, relate, prioritise, reconcile, contrast, arrange, compare*
Develop precision Pupils will refine movement so that errors are rare – they develop fine motor skills, in particular sport-specific technique *demonstrate, complete, show, perfect, calibrate, control*	**Analyse** Pupils break information into parts to explore understandings and relationships *break down, interrogate, compare, quantify, measure, examine, deconstruct, experiment, relate, extrapolate, value*	**Value** Pupils attend optional clubs, participate in opportunities offered and develop values that they constantly question *argue, challenge, debate, refute, confront, compete, justify, persuade, criticise*
Manipulate Pupils perform actions following instructions and practice, often developing actions using their own ideas *recreate, build, perform, execute, implement*	**Apply** Pupils use information in another familiar situation *use, discover, execute, carry out, solve, implement, construct, conduct, perform, react, respond*	**Respond** Pupils volunteer to do things, to help, to contribute individually or in a team *react, clarify, contribute, question, present, become excited, enjoy, collaborate (compete), perform*
Imitate Pupils observe, copy and pattern movement after the teacher, a video or watching another pupil *copy, follow, replicate, repeat*	**Understand** Pupils explain ideas or concepts *explain, reiterate, reword, paraphrase, classify, critique, summarise, illustrate, review, report, discuss, interpret, give example*	**Receive** Pupils listen attentively to the teacher introducing rules of a game, the introduction of a skill or movement pattern, for example *listen, focus, attend, participate, cooperate, discuss, acknowledge, follow, concentrate, feel*
	Remember Pupils recall information *arrange, describe, list, memorise, recognise, relate, reproduce, name, select, state, find*	

This work provides an ideal bridge between the floor standard headline objectives of the national curriculum that we have provided, the challenging yet inclusive expectations mapped to childhood growth and development, and the planning of appropriate unit or learning intentions, learning activities and assessment methodology.

Reflection

Expertise in different activities requires well-organised knowledge of key skills, concepts, evaluation and analysis sequences, general problem-solving skills and the scaffolding of behaviours that lead to healthy active lifestyles. Teachers need pedagogical content knowledge (PCK) – knowledge about how to teach physical education – rather than only knowledge about a particular subject matter or sport in order to achieve the aims of physical education.

- ✔ **How do you currently develop knowledge of physical education in the three learning domains?**
- ✔ **How do you ensure an integrated approach so that the pathways are not viewed in isolation?**
- ✔ **How is our curriculum architecture coherent and continuous, and designed around what we know about 'messy' learning?**

References

Anderson, L.W., Krathwohl, D.R., Airasian, P.W. (eds), Cruikshank, K.A., Mayer, R.E., Pintrich, P.R., Raths, J. and Wittrock, M.C. (2001) *A Taxonomy for Learning, Teaching, and Assessing: A Revision of Bloom's Taxonomy of Educational Objectives*. New York: Longman. ISBN: 978-0-801319-03-7.

ARG and BERA (2013) 'Response to consultation on primary assessment and accountability', www.bera.ac.uk/wp-content/uploads/2014/02/ARG-BERA-response-to-DFE-011013-2.pdf

Bateson, G. (1972) *Steps to an Ecology of Mind*. San Francisco: Chandler.

Bloom, B.S., Engelhart, M.D., Furst, E.J., Hill, W.H. and Krathwohl, D.R. (1956) *Taxonomy of Educational Objectives: The Classification of Educational Goals: Handbook I: Cognitive Domain*. New York: David McKay Company.

Cousin, G. (2006) 'An introduction to threshold concepts', *Planet*, 17: 4–5.

Cousin, G. (2008) 'Threshold concepts: Old wine in new bottles or a new form of transactional curriculum inquiry', in Land, R., Meyer, J.H.F. and Smith, J. (eds) *Threshold Concepts within the Disciplines*. Rotterdam: Sense Publishers. ISBN: 978-9-087902-67-4. pp. 261–272.

Cousin, G. (2009) *Researching Learning in Higher Education: An Introduction to Contemporary Methods and Approaches*. Abingdon: Routledge. ISBN: 978-0-415991-65-0.

Cousin, G. (2010) 'Neither teacher-centred nor student-centred: Threshold concepts and research partnerships', *Journal of Learning Development in Higher Education*, 2.

DfE (2011) *The Framework for the National Curriculum. A Report by the Expert Panel for the National Curriculum Review*. London: DfE.

DfE (2013) *Physical Education Programmes of Study: Key Stages 1 and 2, Key Stages 3 and 4: National Curriculum in England.* London: DfE.

Education Department of Western Australia (2004) *Fundamental Movement Skills Teacher Resource.* Perth: Education Department.

Meyer, J.H.F. and Land, R. (2003) 'Threshold concepts and troublesome knowledge: Linkages to ways of thinking and practising', in Rust, C. (ed) *Improving Student Learning – Theory and Practice Ten Years On.* Oxford: Oxford Centre for Staff and Learning Development (OCSLD). ISBN: 978-1-873576-69-4. pp. 412–424.

Land, R., Meyer, J.H.F. and Baillie, C. (2010) 'Editors' preface: Threshold concepts and transformational learning', in Land, R., Meyer, J.H.F. and Baillie, C. (eds) *Threshold Concepts and Transformational Learning.* Rotterdam: Sense Publishers. ISBN: 978-9-460912-05-4. pp. ix–xlii.

O'Sullivan, E. (2002) 'The project and vision of transformative learning', in O'Sullivan, E., Morrell, A. and O'Connor, M. (eds) *Expanding the Boundaries of Transformative Learning: Essays on Theory and Praxis.* New York: Palgrave Macmillan. ISBN: 978-0-312295-08-0. pp. 1–12.

QCA (2007) *The National Curriculum.* London: QCA.

Sterling, S. (2010) 'Transformative learning and sustainability: Sketching the conceptual ground', *Learning and Teaching in Higher Education*, 5: 17–33.

Wade, A. (1967) *The FA Guide to Training and Coaching.* London: Heinemann.

Section 5: Connecting Learning and Assessment

Assessment, Progress and Inclusive Physical Education

While working on the curriculum in Kosovo, as part of a European Union donor project, I was party to government documentation that highlighted assessment as **the most important part of their curriculum reform**. In the past decade, assessment has been receiving the full attention of researchers and education systems. This attention has presented assessment as integral to planning, teaching and learning, and has helped teachers to ensure that their communication is appropriate and all learners are making expected progress. The primary purpose of assessment has become 'to improve learning for all pupils'.

With the advent of levels, this 'primary purpose' has unfortunately almost been eclipsed by the **profession's own** primary purpose that evolved, which appeared to be an obsession to convert every bit of progress a learner made into a number or a grade. An approach to assessment practice that has at its core a focus on improved learning for all pupils **has to** involve a transformation in the way we think about assessment and the way we carry out our assessment practice.

Assessment in this new era focuses schools to change in terms of ensuring curriculum provision and teaching pedagogy meet the learning needs of all pupils. This is different to a mindset that has perceived pupils as the root cause of a lack of progress and that pupils must be complicit in their learning because 'this is what we offer, and this is how we teach it'.

Assessment for change and improvement requires us to focus our actions on the deficiencies of our provision, rather than highlighting the deficiencies of the learner. The latter was the strange trend that evolved with the (mis)use of levels. Differential performance was labelled, the deficiencies of pupils were emphasised, yet little was done about it. More time and energy went into collating and processing numbers from data sheets based on a judgement of performance in isolated activities than went into ascertaining why pupils underperformed compared to national expectations and then using this information effectively to change provision and practice for all pupils' improvement. At a time when the research into best practice assessment called for a re-emphasis on the learning function of assessment and a de-emphasis on the grading function of assessment, the profession was heading in the opposite direction.

The removal of levels, and the expectation that schools will introduce their own approaches to formative assessment, to support pupil attainment and progression, has provided us with an opportunity to truly make assessment work. Schools are still working to a common standard, a common expectation, which is the attainment target written as an integral part of the national curriculum programme of study. Quite simply, the 2014 version is not structured in the form of level descriptors as previously.

To ensure that assessment works, our assessment framework should be built into the school curriculum so that schools can check what pupils have learnt and whether they are on track to meet expectations at the end of the KS. What does this mean? Clearly, although assessment has always been considered to be integral to good teaching, much of the recent research refers to the need for more deliberate actions in designing the strategies, tools and practices to support assessment as part of good teaching (ARG and TLRP, 2009). Substantial research exists on the characteristics of good practice for assessing student learning. This research has been used in outlining afPE's position on assessment in this section and begins with the three key principles below.

afPE's Approach to Assessment

The following three core principles outline afPE's approach to assessment. This should form the basis of our assessment practice:

1 The primary purpose of assessment in physical education is to improve pupil progress and attainment against the standards: assessment FOR learning.

In realising the primary purpose of assessment, teachers must understand the maturational stages of childhood growth and development, the floor standards that are being used to benchmark attainment, the way pupils learn, their individual needs and individual starting points or baselines. Only then can we truly design curriculum effectively and improve our teaching appropriately.

Assessment that is used to improve pupil progress and attainment against the standards is based on the learning we most value for pupils in our subject discipline. The DfE (2013) has provided this starting point with the essential learning or floor standards listed in the programme of study and the provision of clear purposes and aims, culminating with the aim for pupils to lead healthy active lifestyles.

Assessment for learning is a key driver in informing this evolving practice, and we should continuously use assessment information to improve ways of doing things for learners. Assessment is most effective when it reflects the fact that learning is a transformative, troublesome, liminal, bounded, discursive, integrative and messy process that is multidimensional and revealed in pupil performance over time. Assessment methodology, including how frequently we assess, what assessment information we decide to record or keep, and what assessment information we decide to report, must all be appropriate to acknowledge learning as such.

The implications of this denote that our assessment practice has to entail a variety of measures and be ongoing rather than episodic in its implementation. A single assessment instrument will not reveal all that needs to be known about pupil achievement and how it can be improved. A strategic approach to appropriate assessment methodology can provide this information and enable us to constantly improve and assemble a view of achievement over time.

2 Assessment requires clear alignment with the aims of physical education: assessment OF learning.

Assessment works best when it is based on clear statements of purpose and aims for the programme, the standards pupils are expected to achieve, and the criteria against which to measure success. The DfE (2013) has provided us with these constituent components. In aligning our units of work and lesson episodes to the physical education programme of study, it is important to communicate explicit, clear and understandable criteria so pupils know exactly what is expected of them from each learning activity or assessment task they engage with. This assessment knowledge has a huge impact on learner behaviours if the criteria they are being assessed against are unambiguous. Everything we do must be connected and ultimately lead to the achievement of programme outcomes, national standards and physical education aims. This alignment allows us more readily to quantify learning or to 'measure' it.

3 Assessment should be an integral component of programme design: assessment AS learning.

The teaching and learning elements for each stage, for each year, for each unit should be designed and planned with full knowledge of the nature of assessment pupils will take and the method of assessment that teachers will employ. This is important for all pupils to demonstrate what they know, understand and can do. The learning domains are critical to consider in planning and assessing learning. An analysis of the learning domain or outcome that is required allows us to plan for appropriate learning activities and select the method of communication. For example, we might utilise visual face-to-face, visual video, auditory speaking and listening or recording, or kinaesthetic tasks in isolation or in combination depending on the learning requirements. This simple design consideration increases the opportunity for deep learning and prevents assessment being perceived as a separate entity.

Assessment Strategy

When planning an assessment strategy, afPE's guiding principles (based on research) should be referred to. If the primary purpose of assessment is to improve learner progress and attainment against physical education floor standards, then assessment for learning practice should provide the basis for our assessment strategy, as well as become the key focus for any assessment methodology we use. We are not advocating a return to previous practice, which was corrupt, invalid and unreliable, and time-consuming. The following considerations help to determine our assessment strategy and inform our selection of methods:

- Who?
- What?
- When?
- Where?
- Why?
- How?

Who?

Who are we assessing – a range of pupils (a representative sample), a particular group (more able, pupils with SEN, pupil premium) or a random sample?

What?

What are we assessing – individual outcomes from one learning domain or a combination of outcomes across two or three learning domains?

When?

When do we assess? Most of our assessment should be ongoing and does not need to be recorded. Learning activities and assessment tasks should be integrated into each lesson. The question remains, however, when and how often should we schedule other assessments? When and how often should we have inter-learning tasks (homework)? Should we set an end of year exam? Formalised assessments can be used when appropriate and don't necessarily need to be scheduled. Assessment must, however, be timely. The influence of assessment on learning and progress can be lost if the assessment information derived from the assessment method used is not fed back immediately into the learning process.

Where?

Most of the assessment tasks will occur within each and every lesson. Assessment is a form of communication, and this ongoing 'dialogue' constantly provides information to the teacher about how to appropriately intervene to act as a springboard for pupils' progress. Certain assessment methodologies, however, lend themselves to completion online from home or even in other subject lessons across the curriculum.

Why?

The majority of assessment practice will be carried out with the sole aim of improving pupil progress and attainment. Other assessment methods may be selected to check knowledge or understanding because the teacher is unsure. An online test carried out remotely can provide important information about what to plan and teach to ensure pupils deepen their understanding of key knowledge and concepts in physical education. Assessment should have a clear purpose. If our assessment practice doesn't lead to some kind of improved practice, then we should be asking ourselves 'Why are we doing it?'

How?

There are a number of assessment methods that teachers can use, and the selection of the most appropriate method is crucial to ensuring assessment is fit for purpose. In deciding the methods to employ, however, we must follow this useful quality assurance check – VARSC:

- valid
- authentic
- reliable
- sufficient
- current.

Valid

The important notion here is purpose. Educational assessment, indeed any assessment, should always have a clear purpose. Validity is therefore the single most important aspect of worthwhile assessment. Does the assessment have a clear purpose? Does the method selected measure what it was designed to measure? If we ask pupils to complete an **analysis** worksheet, then the task language must move beyond 'list', 'identify' or 'describe' for example; otherwise, the assessment information gleaned is invalid. Is the assessment contaminated by other characteristics? An assessment that measures the application of basic attacking principles in a game is not valid, for example, if it requires a seven-year-old pupil to demonstrate the principles in the full-sided version of the adult game on a full-sized playing area. Fitness will impact on the result due to the large area being covered and the distance over which passes are played. Other factors come into play so the assessment isn't necessarily valid.

Authentic

The tasks set should be real-world tasks we want pupils to perform. Pupils' ability to apply standard driven tasks (tasks derived from the national curriculum and what we value in physical education) to real-world scenarios are assessed. Scenarios or core tasks are examples of authentic assessment. A non-authentic example would be where a teacher administers a test or an assessment lesson consisting of a battery of physical tests. In this context, the assessment is separate from teaching and learning. This is quite traditional and, unfortunately, quite common. In the authentic assessment model, the same authentic task used to measure a pupil's ability to apply the knowledge or skills of dance composition, for example, is used as a vehicle for pupil learning. So pupils might be asked to use a repeating celebratory motif in their dance composition to express the emotions that Everton players might have felt when they beat Manchester United for the second time in the 2013–2014 season to complete their first 'double' since 1969. When presented with a real-world problem to solve, pupils are **learning in the process of developing a solution**, teachers are facilitating the process, and the pupils' solutions to the problem become an assessment of how well the pupils can meaningfully apply the concepts. In authentic assessment, the teaching, learning and assessment are integrated.

Reliable

Is the method used consistent over time? Does the repeated use of an assessment method or assessment tool lead to consistent results? Is an approach that uses observation as its sole method for determining progress in the three learning domains reliable, given teacher subjectivity? Are the probing questions that the teacher asks to elicit conceptual knowledge the same for each group? Do all pupils have the opportunity to respond to the questions or engage in the task? How is this managed so that it is equitable and inclusive? Is a judgement based on a one-off performance more reliable than a judgement based on performance over time? How reliable are results based on a performance test when one group performs the assessment after lunch in wet, muddy conditions while another group undertakes the test the following morning in warm, dry conditions?

Sufficient

Is the full range of performance identified in the standards covered? The use of levels tended to be **in**sufficient in this respect. Physical skill performance tended to be the dominant assessment, and 'knowledge and understanding of fitness and health' or 'making informed decisions about healthy active lifestyles' were either overlooked or given a lesser weighting when factored into a summative judgement. Does the evidence show competence over a period of time and in a range of contexts? Even Ofsted has incorporated this 'sufficiency' criterion into their inspection process by factoring 'progress over time' into their judgements. The range of contexts for the programme of study has been highlighted by listing them apart from the headline objectives for each of the learning domains tabled in Section 4, and this helps us to ensure physical education learning experiences are broad and balanced.

Perhaps one of the worst practices that evolved in the last 14 years with levels, and one that contrasts totally with the 'sufficient' quality assurance aspect, was the emergence of the 'assessment lesson'. Typically, the last lesson of each unit (usually each half-term) was set aside for assessment. The worst example I remember was a teacher I observed using a clipboard with a spreadsheet attached comprising the year seven group's list of names in the left column, and in the top row, a list of skills to be assessed, which together formed a matrix. During the lesson, the assessment matrix was populated with level numbers and sub-level letters. A final column was left blank on the right hand side to calculate an overall level for football. The skills listed were passing, shooting, dribbling, heading, crossing and tackling. The game played was 12 v 12 because of numbers in the group. This meant 144 decisions to make (six skill judgements for 24 pupils), in what turned out to be just less than a 40-minute time period (60-minute lesson, less changing time and organisation). In other words, a decision every approximately 16–17 seconds. I despaired, not least of the fact that some children never headed the ball or made a tackle, but also that all of the skills listed were 'on the ball skills' when the vast majority of the game is played 'off the ball'. Prozone statistics, for example, highlight that in a full 90-minute game of football, players are on the ball for only 2½ minutes on average. In this example, assessment is clearly not sufficient, neither is it valid or reliable.

Current

Is the assessment information being used current? In other words, are we basing judgements on current or very recent performances contrasted with the use of assessment information from seven months previously? The common approach to the use of levels did this. If a child had been ill or injured during a unit of work, the level they had been given often counted towards an end of year average. Is the assessment timely? Is the assessment of current performance, or does it include content that was planned but wasn't covered or content that was missed by pupils through absence? Was the assessment administered, for example, as annual or end of unit traditional practice, despite the majority of the content not being covered due to the wettest winter since records began?

Assessment Methodology

This section lists the most common assessment methods from our work with schools and maps them to the 2014 curriculum requirements.

Holistic Assessment

Holistic assessment is used where learning or performance objectives are inter-related and complex, and the extent of learning or performance is measured against established standards. In physical education terms, it should incorporate objectives or intentions derived from the three domains of learning. The implications for planning and teaching are that the learning activities incorporate opportunities for pupils to demonstrate knowledge of concepts, physical skills, **and** attitudes and behaviours. Where learning or performance objectives are complex, the judgement of the teacher is a holistic one about the quality of performance, and such judgements are arrived at by recognising the performance of the integrated action, not of the performance of each part.

This can be illustrated using my two youngest children, who often carry out their own British Bake Off on a Friday after school. They each use the same ingredients, but my daughter understands the process of mixing the ingredients so that they are aerated. Her lemon drizzle sponge rises and has a better texture than her brother's. In the same way, an individual's dance performance may look better than another pupil's because they understand the importance of motif and eye focus linked to body shape in order to convey emotion. In making a judgement about what was lacking in the performance, the process and individual components will still need to be analysed so the end product or performance can be improved. Assessment isn't used to judge each individual component of the performance. The performance is judged, and assessment is used to diagnose what and how to improve. In the 1990s, research into holistic learning and assessment developed the notion of rich tasks, which was used in Australia and parts of North America. Wales adopted the idea of rich tasks. In England, we called them core tasks. The fact that this approach was used with the previous national curriculum doesn't mean that it is no longer appropriate. We must ensure, however, that any holistic assessment or core tasks planned align to the new floor standards in each KS.

Practice Activities/Tasks

While we have used the term 'holistic assessment' to refer to core tasks, which by implication have to be utilised over time for sufficient information to be gleaned, practice tasks might be an assessment method focusing on one skill, tactic or principle in isolation. The purpose of this assessment would of course be to improve the individual skill, tactical application or compositional principle. This doesn't equate to planning the teaching of the skill in an isolated drill – it can still be assessed as part of a small-sided or modified game.

Blended Assessment

While holistic assessment is a method that allows combined learning to be assessed, and a practice task focuses on one aspect to be assessed, blended assessment is such that various methods might be used for a group of pupils to allow all learners to demonstrate what they know, understand or can do, in their own way. A teaching games for understanding approach or a sport education approach, combined with the use of ICT, for example, allows multiple methods of assessment to be used.

Inter-learning Tasks

We have replaced the term 'homework' with 'inter-learning tasks'. The word 'work' conveys the notion of some kind of chore to be performed. Many pupils, my children included, associate it with something to be carried out under duress, usually in fear of a punishment should they not complete it. The word 'home' suggests that it is something completed at home. 'Inter-learning' is something that the pupil does away from the formal setting of a lesson. The task should connect the formal learning in lessons by deepening learning, extending a concept or practising a skill. In a strategic sense, inter-learning tasks could be a requirement to attend a club to develop certain learning, such as a physical skill or technique; to read an online or hard copy newspaper sports report to gain insight into how journalists use the words 'tactics' and 'strategy' to convey meaning; simple questions to complete on a virtual learning environment (VLE) page or email to check knowledge; or more open questions to check understanding. There is no need to use teacher marking and scores for these tasks to contribute to a summative numerical grade. The purpose of this type of task would be to provide assessment information about how to extend or support the learner in terms of future content in lessons and how best to teach the content or provide a context.

Journals

Journals can be used in a number of different ways. They can provide a log of achievement, a diary of participation or a record of interviews, or allow pupils to make statements of progress. This type of record could just as easily be incorporated into a portfolio.

Interviews

When I was a tutor at university, it would be common practice for us to regularly carry out tutorials for students. This type of support often gave me useful information as to where a student's thinking was conceptually, and this knowledge often contributed to subsequent lectures. Pupil 'interviews' in a school context can be a useful method of assessment in terms of knowledge of the learner, their likes and dislikes, their knowledge and understanding, and their aspirations. At KS3, I have seen this carried out strategically in 'formal' five-minute interviews at lunchtimes, sometimes as group interviews and sometimes targeted at pupils who the teacher doesn't get to know as well as others during lesson time or in after-school clubs. At KS4, I have even seen this scenario used as an actual interview as though the pupil was being interviewed for a sport-related position. This method allows pupils to prepare explanations of concepts, which helps with their understanding and behaviours. Asking 'Why is it important to be physically active?' or 'What are the main inhibitors to engaging in a healthy active lifestyle?', for example, is also conducive to reinforcing key messages.

Learner Statements

Learner statements are a useful way of getting pupils to identify how they have progressed and met key assessment criteria. This can be carried out as an inter-learning task – in this case, inter-unit, inter-term or inter-year. It would be inappropriate to request such a statement each lesson. The statement would of course relate to the headline objectives or intentions in the learning domains for national curriculum that were detailed in Section 4. This method of assessment can also be used as part of a learning portfolio, made easier when integrated with online learning platforms.

Handouts/Worksheets

As with all methods of assessment, the purpose of the assessment task should be clear, especially when using a worksheet, for example. This method allows opportunity for teachers to identify if pupils can work independently of the teacher. It also allows pupil observations, comments and feedback to be recorded. This provides information to the teacher as to whether the learner is identifying, describing, able to improve others, analysing or evaluating. As outlined in Section 4, it is imperative that these verbs are understood and used appropriately to enable not only appropriately challenging tasks and teacher intervention, but also pupil to pupil intervention.

Observation

Teachers observe learners performing planned tasks. It is key that teachers are skilled at observing children moving, and analysing movement. Otherwise, it becomes impossible to intervene effectively to make improvements. There are many teachers who are unskilled in this area, and I know where I would spend professional learning monies if I were still working in a school context. The alternative is teachers who plan a unit of work in advance that details lessons on a weekly basis and then teach them in a spoon-fed or 'Postman Pat' delivery style. Assessment in the form of observation to inform teaching and learning is absent in this example due to a focus on content and coverage.

Listening

In the same way that observation is important for intervening to improve movement skills, or game tactics, listening as a method of assessment is important to gauge learners' thinking from the language employed and make interventions to improve comprehension.

Scenarios

Scenarios are used as an effective assessment methodology as they allow pupils to demonstrate how they can apply what they have learnt in contexts that might never occur ordinarily during a lesson. Scenarios set for game play are quite common, but scenarios in other contexts are less so. For example, groups of pupils, who are one fewer in number than the opposition, are challenged to keep a clean sheet for five minutes – the scenario being that a player has been sent off. Other scenarios that challenge a team to beat three rounders in the next five minutes or to defend a small half rounder lead contribute, for example, to pupils thinking about tactical play in scenarios or contexts that are important for the teacher to devise. In athletics, individuals can be challenged to run a tight bend by narrowing the arc. Without this scenario, they will never experience the forces a top athlete experiences if drawn on an inside lane, and will never understand the need to adapt body position or the technical adaptation of the arm action while sprinting around an athletic track bend.

Group/Individual/Sample/Random

Problem-solving tasks, as in the context of outdoor and adventurous activities, are socially interactive and a great way to assess attitudes, behaviours, individual responses to stress and so on. Care needs to be taken when organising and managing these tasks as one or two people can often dominate so roles and team make-up should be rotated/changed. In terms of sampling, if a teacher selects a representative sample of six pupils from their group (two pupils who need extending, two 'middling' and two requiring additional attention/support in the context of the group) and rotates the sample each lesson, then each pupil would receive a focused assessment (eg observation) every two and a half weeks, given a class of 30 and a timetable of two one-hour lessons. In a school year, this would result in up to 16 focused observations per child. These observations, combined with other assessment information gleaned from a variety of methods, are more than sufficient to collate assessment information in order to make an informed summative (annual) judgement about whether pupils are on track to meet the floor targets.

Examinations

There is no reason why physical education written examinations aren't used in end of year exams in secondary schools as per other subjects. The examinations themselves should be an assessment of the learning covered in the three domains and therefore provide additional assessment information to that already gathered over the course of a year as to how well a pupil is progressing towards the end of KS floor standards. This information on its own should in no way be used to plot a flight path to a GCSE score given everything we now know about learning, and it should certainly not be used to share an indicative grade for an exam that is to be taken at the end of year 11. What it does do is allow learners to practise in exam conditions, and it also confirms for, or informs, the teacher, for example, whether pupils have fully understood a tactical concept or are able to illustrate the concept of analysis from their own experience. Assessment information gleaned also allows the teacher to target future provision to help the learner to either catch up (providing of course all other learners have grasped the concept), or deepen or extend the concept by applying it to another context. Supporting activities could be interviews, pairing the pupil with someone who has grasped the concept, inter-learning tasks and so on.

ICT in Assessment Of, As and For Learning

The effective use of ICT can be a foil for all of the assessment methods previously outlined. The most important aspect that informs our decision about whether to use ICT or not is if it allows us to do something that traditional methods of communication would not facilitate. ICT is an information and communications technology. It therefore provides the means to communicate more effectively with the learner. It is not only the teacher's effective use of ICT in their teaching, but also the learner's effective use of ICT in their learning that can lead to greater progress and attainment gains. Technology has moved on considerably – certainly since I used to book, collect and then wheel a TV trolley into the sports hall in order to play a video that I had spent the previous evening setting up! The beauty of modern-day technology is that it can immediately 'record' assessment information, which is easily stored and accessible. Performances that we have captured on digital video in a lesson to play back to a pupil in order to improve their performance can also be used as evidence that progress has been made or standards have been reached. The storing of this assessment information in online portfolios can promote sustainable, inclusive and time-efficient practice.

Portfolios of Evidence

My first encounter with a portfolio of evidence was in the 1990s when they were introduced into teacher training. My role was PGCE secondary physical education course leader at the University of Worcester at the time, and we were making the transition from assessment that used a matrix of competency statements to a portfolio of evidence against new Teacher Training Agency (TTA) standards. The need for change was clear.

A trainee's capability was recorded and monitored against a competency statement matrix, and by the end of a course, trainee teachers gained qualified teacher status (QTS), having marked off all the statements. The competencies might have been ticked to indicate they had all been met, but this didn't necessarily mean good teachers were the result. Competencies were activities or behaviours that teachers were expected to display, but didn't inevitably mean that any kind of standard had been reached. And so standards were born. A trainee teacher would still have to develop competencies for teaching, but it was their 'expertise' demonstrated against the standard that was judged.

Over time, the number of standards increased, and unfortunately, the task of designing courses to prove that all the standards had been met became so burdensome in terms of administration that assessment practice and monitoring actually got in the way of learning and teaching. Coding practices for each standard were adopted and then listed for each lecture, lesson, professional mentor meeting and mentor meeting, and trainee teachers were required to keep evidence for each and every one of these standards, so much so that they would be able to unfailingly recite the number and standard by rote. Unfortunately, this was a classic example of the assessment methodology moving so far from its intended purpose that it became unfit for purpose. Bloated assessment specification had led to over-assessment and too much administration.

Common sense did prevail in many institutions, and quality not quantity became the focus and a mantra that saw the purpose of portfolios as more of an **improving** document than simply a **proving** document – a document that promoted reflective thinking about practice to deepen understanding, a document that, in its formation, helped trainee teachers to identify strengths, limitations and opportunities for further development.

The teachers' standards (DfE, 2011 – for implementation from September 2012) were revised and slimmed down to reflect what was considered the essential standards a teacher should aspire to.

A teacher must:

1 *set high expectations which inspire, motivate and challenge pupils*

2 *promote good progress and outcomes by pupils*

3 *demonstrate good subject and curriculum knowledge*

4 *plan and teach well structured lessons*

5 *adapt teaching to respond to the strengths and needs of all pupils*

6 *make accurate and productive use of assessment*

7 *manage behaviour effectively to ensure a good and safe learning environment*

8 *fulfil wider professional responsibilities.*

The parallels with the changes to the national curriculum 2014 standards for all pupils in England should be evident. Administration around our assessment practice in schools had become burdensome, just as the assessment practice had become in teacher training institutions. The floor standards have focused teaching and assessment in schools on what is essential in our subject discipline.

Online/Electronic Portfolios

The advent of school VLEs has contributed to the development of online portfolios. Many schools and indeed commercial companies have developed VLE pages or school information management system compatible software respectively that provide a platform for the collation of assessment evidence. While work scrutiny, in terms of recognising progress over time, for many subjects, can be carried out using pupil workbooks, physical education is slightly different. An online portfolio is an ideal way to document assessment evidence and promote improving processes so that we do not make the same mistake as teacher training portfolio practice in the 1990s.

The use of digital cameras, digital audio sticks, mobile phones, email, online discussion forums, weblogs (blogs) and school networked systems all provide the basis for effective portfolio use. Inter-learning tasks (homework) such as group discussion, online tests and learner statements not only develop pupil learning and thinking, but also provide evidence of learning at moments in time. These snapshots build over time (eg a year or KS) and can collectively demonstrate progress over time. Digital data, such as audio, video or image that is recorded in lessons to play back to pupils in order to improve their performances, can also be saved and hyperlinked from portfolio pages or documentation. All of this documentary evidence should of course align with the key skills, essential knowledge and concepts, and vital behaviours expected in our subject. Evidence kept or recorded only needs to be sampled information taken from a representative sample of activities. It is the pupils who develop this record because they take ownership of learning. It is their images that they decide to post, it is their reflection, their statements, their inter-learning tasks that populate the portfolio. The process of collating the information becomes one of improving. Collectively, this record can be used to 'prove' progress and attainment if required.

In August 2014, my eldest son cut his head when using a zip wire we have rigged up in our garden. There was a lot of blood, and my other children were most concerned, the youngest was very upset. The first words my eldest spoke, however, when realising the amount of blood spurting from the deep cut near the crown of his head, were to his sister and brother to get his iPad mini. It turned out he wanted them to take a picture so he could post it on Instagram! I regularly check their accounts, and the collection of images my children have collated provide a useful potted account of what they perceive to be key moments in their lives.

Online portfolios are an excellent method of collating and combining assessment information using a number of methodologies (including teacher observations), which allow teachers to make informed judgements as to whether pupils are on track to meet the floor standards. More importantly, the process allows assessment methods to be used that are fit for purpose. In terms of age-appropriate software, it becomes possible to develop modified portfolios from five years of age, especially when children as young as two are capable of using a mouse or touch screen. Even if not kept in an electronic portfolio, some of the best collation of assessment evidence I have seen is in primary school classrooms with children's work on the walls. My youngest boy's cursive and big writing, his use of verbs, connectives, openers and punctuation (VCOP) was evident on the autumn wall in his year four classroom last year, and I could see a marked difference in his work on the summer wall, with his cursive writing looking neater and his more consistent and appropriate use of openers, for example. What I don't often see in primary schools, however, are images of pupils participating in physical education. When I collect my children from sleepovers at the weekend or tea with their friends during the week, I see more images of their friends participating in a variety of activities displayed on walls, on the hall console table or even in electronic slideshows than I do in schools. Such image portrayal in a school context would not only contribute to evidence of progress, but also promote a positive image of physical education to any pupil, parent or Ofsted inspector visiting the school. For me, it proclaims 'we value learners and their engagement in physical education'.

Assessment for Learning

The varying methods of assessment that we use strategically, appropriately, purposefully and in a timely manner should all be part of an AfL approach. This is the primary purpose of assessment.

Research by ARG essentially focused on the smallest interaction between teacher and pupil and between pupils themselves that teachers thought led to greater progress being made. Results from the study indicated that this approach led to improved pupil progress by up to a third. In other words, progress that would normally be observed at the end of a school academic year would be observed by Easter (on average). Projecting this finding across a number of years suggested that progress that would normally be observed at the end of three years would be observed after two years.

The approach used was termed **AfL**, and in 2002, ARG defined this as:

> *A process of seeking and interpreting evidence for use by learners and their teachers to decide where the learners are in their learning, where they need to go, and how best to get there.*

In 2007, maths and English carried out a similar study using AfL, which reported similar findings (PricewaterhouseCoopers, 2010). Local authorities disseminated the results of such studies, and in 2008, an increased expectation of two levels of progress across a KS was shared. Unfortunately, this manifested itself in practice typified by more frequent testing and more frequent data points. Schools and, in particular, senior leaders had missed the point. Greater rates of progress had resulted from AfL practice, not more measures. As Adrian Mole recorded in his diaries: 'To keep on measuring something doesn't necessarily make it grow.'

The ARG research with schools and teachers produced thousands of ideas for improving progress. These ideas were synthesised into four key actions associated with AfL:

1. eliciting information through questioning and dialogue
2. providing feedback with emphasis on how to improve
3. helping learners understand quality criteria
4. peer- and self-assessment (which incorporates 1–3).

It is not my intention to go into great detail about these actions. This has already been well documented by Frapwell (2010), and schools over the past decade will have engaged in professional development in these areas. Suffice to say, however, if the assessment methods are used integrally to teaching, then these are the key actions that inform teacher selection of appropriate methodology, provide learners with appropriate opportunity and information to make informed decisions about next steps, and ultimately lead to greater progress.

Summary

Assessment of pupils' progress towards the floor standards doesn't mean that we have to record a number by writing it on a record sheet or word processing it on a data sheet to prove that we have assessed progress or that pupils have actually made any progress at all. A record sheet with ticks or numbers strewn across it is not evidence of progress and is not accepted as such by Ofsted. Indeed, in 2007, a section headed 'Time for standards' in an Ofsted evaluative report on 'Reforming and developing the school workforce' included the subtitle 'Ticking boxes or improving learning'. It is exactly this meaningless, inappropriate tick box/numbering/labelling practice that the legislative changes have sought to remove.

Our assessment of a learner's progress towards the success criteria targeted for each lesson gives us information that we will use to plan the next lesson. At a medium-term stage, it will provide assessment information that we will use to plan the next unit of learning. At a longer-term stage, we will have annual information that can be used to plan or adjust the next year's programme. All of this will be aligned and progressive to the end of KS floor standards.

Assessment methods outlined in this section are integral to planning and teaching and not only improve learning, but also provide assessment evidence created by pupils in the process of their learning that can be documented (sampled) to 'prove' progress and attainment. An annual summative judgement is therefore qualitatively well informed, at which point the DfE requires us to report whether pupils are on track to meet the end of KS floor standards. If learners are not on track to meet the benchmark, or they are falling behind, then an evaluation will need to take place.

Reference to VARSC is important to ensure that the assessment methods we employ are fit for purpose, and our assessment decisions with regard to aligning progress against the standards are quality assured. In this regard, it is imperative to remember that the strategic design of assessment strongly affects how and what pupils learn; this may be positive (eg reinforcing intended learning) or negative (when pupils learn to pass rather than learn to learn). What is undeniable is that an AfL approach that puts the learner and their learning at the heart of everything we do **can lead to better standards**. In national curriculum 2014 speak, these standards also include a keen focus on leading healthy active lifestyles. When approached as such, the system has now become focused on the deficiencies of our provision, rather than highlighting the deficiencies of the learner.

Reflection

An assessment functions formatively to the extent that evidence about student achievement is elicited, interpreted, and used by teachers, learners, or their peers to make decisions about the next steps in instruction that are likely to be better, or better founded, than the decisions they would have made in the absence of that evidence.

Wiliam, 2011

- ✔ **What methods of assessment do you currently use?**
- ✔ **How do you strategically design your assessment approach?**
- ✔ **Is assessment viewed as integral to teaching and learning, or is it viewed as 'bolt on'?**
- ✔ **How is assessment information used to improve your teaching or curriculum provision for ALL pupils?**
- ✔ **What evidence do you have that proves progress, and is it VARSC?**

References

ARG (2002) 'Assessment for learning: 10 principles', www.qca.org.uk/libraryAssets/media/4031_afl_principles.pdf

ARG and TLRP (2009) *Assessment in Schools: Fit for Purpose?* London: TLRP. ISBN: 978-0-854738-92-2.

DfE (2011) 'Teachers' standards: Guidance for school leaders, school staff and governing bodies', www.gov.uk/government/uploads/system/uploads/attachment_data/file/301107/Teachers__Standards.pdf

DfE (2013) *Physical Education Programmes of Study: Key Stages 1 and 2, Key Stages 3 and 4: National Curriculum in England*. London: DfE.

Frapwell, A. (2010) 'Assessment for learning', in Bailey, R. (ed) *Physical Education for Learning*. London: Continuum. ISBN: 978-1-847065-02-5. pp. 104–117.

Ofsted (2007) 'Reforming and developing the school workforce'. Manchester: Ofsted.

PricewaterhouseCoopers (2010) *Evaluation of the Making Good Progress Pilot*. London: DCSF. ISBN: 978-1-847756-11-4.

Wiliam, D. (2011) *Embedded Formative Assessment*. Bloomington: Solution Tree Press. ISBN: 978-1-934009-30-7.

Section 6: Game-changing Practice

> *Change is hard because people overestimate the value of what they have – and underestimate the value of what they might gain by giving that up.*
>
> **James Belasco and Ralph Stayer**

Fourteen years ago, with the advent of an attainment target that was structured with hierarchical level descriptors, a majority of the profession began a pattern of behaviour for assessment practice that was to become largely inappropriate and ineffective. Reform of the reform led to many physical education teachers using level descriptors in a formative numeric way that was entirely inappropriate and never intended by government or government agencies. This unquestioned pattern of behaviour re labelling differential performance and managing data never made any impact on headline measures for leading healthy active lifestyles. The behaviour was repeated until it became automatic. It became **the** way of doing things. Many teachers couldn't explain the process, nor could they defend the practice embraced, a practice that had created so many anomalies.

Blame for this way of doing things was largely apportioned to senior leadership teams who allegedly 'forced' subject teachers to conform to exactly the same assessment practice for each subject. Teachers would highlight disparity and inequality in their assessment practice, but despite these huge inconsistencies, would not change anything for fear of reprisal. The current legislation (Statutory Instrument 2232, 2013) has provided us with a new attainment target, written as an integral part of the programme of study with no levels.

The most important action to take now, in moving to a new, more appropriate way of doing things, is reflection in and on practice. The purpose of reflection is to bring our reasoning processes and behaviour to the surface, make them transparent and begin to align what we know to be effective assessment practice with our behaviour. This is difficult because so much of our behaviour has been tacitly accepted without question, and the change we are required to make will challenge our values, thinking and practice enormously. It is this profound thinking about the very process of change we are engaging with that will deepen our understanding, and impact not only on our assessment practice, but our very being itself. Discussions I have had with many teachers bear testament to this. Learning and change can be difficult, but they can also be rewarding. Stick with it.

This section outlines the ideas that departments have applied in order to improve pupil learning and progress. No one department in the pilot studies has implemented a comprehensive systemic approach to assessment, rather attempts have been episodic, but they are a start. Ideas and practice have been used to illustrate the components of assessment that are important for a holistic assessment approach, including assessment that is integral to our planning. Together, they form a more robust and comprehensive approach than any one department in isolation. Look out for further case studies in future afPE *Physical Education Matters* journals and afPE newsletters. This is a journey that will endure.

A Model for Improvement – Going SOLO

One of the physical education departments has engaged in a focus on the structure of observed learning outcomes (SOLO). Bloom's taxonomy (introduced in Section 4) is based on sequential progress through different layers. Work on threshold concepts, however, has highlighted the fact that learning is not linear. While the categories of verbs provide a useful resource for writing objectives and outcomes, the SOLO approach ensures our planning, teaching and assessment are appropriately mapped to learning and progress, which we know can be messy and unpredictable.

Biggs and Collis (1982) developed a five-stage model that essentially consists of three layers of understanding – **superficial, deep** and **conceptual**. This is because the first and the last stages are not viewed as an integral part of the learning cycle. The five-stage model is outlined below.

Stage 1: Pre-structural

Pupils do not understand the knowledge they are expected to learn. They guess things and answer 'I don't know' or 'We're supposed to', for example, when responding to questions on why they should engage in healthy active lifestyles. Pupils have not entered the learning cycle, and no verbs from Bloom's taxonomy are associated with this stage.

Stage 2: Unistructural

At this stage, learning is superficial. Pupils will have learnt relevant aspects of the whole. They might be able to remember (Bloom's taxonomy) an aspect on its own, but not understand the relationship with the whole. For example, learning about a motif in dance, or a skill as part of the game, doesn't mean that learners understand it in the context of the performance or game. Pupils might be able to repeat things, but any kind of probing questioning highlights a superficial understanding of the relational content. Teaching methodologies can help make these connections. Structure and context are important when everything can appear to be chaotic to 'beginner' learners.

Stage 3: Multistructural

At the multistructural stage, learners start to connect several relevant aspects or understand the relevance of several components, but the bigger picture still eludes them. While they may be operating at higher layers of Bloom's taxonomy, the significance of focus and motif in a dance performance as a whole may still elude them. Learning at this stage can still be superficial, but it can also demonstrate a more meaningful association with the activity. An individual may be able to run forward and pass back in rugby, but in a competitive game still runs 30 metres across the pitch while gaining only one metre for the team. Questioning might reveal the individual is unable to connect the aspects of running forward in the context of the game and gaining territory, or they might be able to articulate the concept, but this may often be repeating what the teacher has already informed them without understanding, because they are unable to demonstrate it in performance. If they are able to truly explain the concept, then with the right environment – for example, fewer players on teams – they will be able to make the right decision. Learning, however, is messy so while it might appear they understand the concept in a relational way, a more complex environment may result in them reverting back to the multistructural stage.

Stage 4: Relational

The relational stage signals a more evocative association with learning. Pupils can integrate ideas into a whole, recognise relationships and connect ideas to each other. The ability to make connections makes it more likely that this new way of viewing the world and these new associated ideas can be applied to new situations. At this stage, learners are less likely to accept learning at the superficial stages, and deep, more meaningful learning results in a conceptual understanding, which begins to embrace more abstract ideas.

Stage 5: Extended Abstract

Learners can make connections not only within their subject, but between other subject disciplines and with the outside world. They make sense of new learning from their understanding of the world, but also by challenging assumptions and reordering or replacing ideas, creating new connections and new understandings. This very stage is considered transitional, for as soon as learners reach this new 'plane', they are back to attempting to learn new aspects relevant to the whole, and a new learning cycle begins.

Having briefly explained the five stages, it is hugely important to remember that learning is contextual and non-linear, and can be messy. Teachers and learners may find themselves in a different learning stage of the cycle for different activities and, for each of those stages, different layers of Bloom's taxonomy. In the pilot school, even if a pupil had reached the relational stage of learning about an activity, he or she often regressed back to a previous stage if challenged with new information, such as the offside rule or a different tactical formation in football, or a problem that is unsolvable in outdoor and adventurous activities. That shudders his or her connective foundations of relational learning, resulting in a multistructural understanding of the activity or area.

As the teacher records:

> *I learnt that there is an appropriate way to plan for progress, which at times moves 'backwards' when considered against the SOLO way of looking at learning.*
>
> *The focus is not on what is taught, but what we want the pupils to learn. We might have to go back before we move forward. The first steps are always to list the learning intentions for learners. The national curriculum provides an initial reference point for this. I mapped these to the learning domains, and the verbs really help this process. Teaching and assessment can then be designed to align to these outcomes.*
>
> *This approach has helped me to understand why levels have gone, and I now realise that much of how I used to teach didn't take learning beyond a superficial stage.*
>
> *I can report that my kids are on track to reach the floor standard even if they have gone backwards. When we used levels, we might record a level 5c to a level 4b, for example, and when it came to reporting that, it didn't make sense to us, senior leaders or parents. And the kids didn't feel good about it, often challenging us as to why they had received a lower score. Now, it does (make sense), but we don't have to highlight it!*

For me, the most significant statement the teacher made was:

> *This has changed the way we teach. We have utilised a teaching games for understanding (TGfU) and a sport education (SE) approach because we know they help learners make connections in terms of their relational or deep and conceptual learning. We have tried to use a similar approach (TGfU and SE) in terms of its holistic approach in our dance and gymnastics units.*
>
> *We have used SOLO to help us design learning outcomes, learning experiences, teaching methods and assessment tasks that ('scaffold') link (sic) our units of work, helping our kids understand PE (physical education) as a subject, rather than see PE (physical education) as isolated sports or activities. It has helped* ***me*** *understand PE (physical education) better and helped me teach it better!*
>
> *As a department, we also used SOLO to help us plan key questions related to the (SOLO) stage kids were at and the Bloom's taxonomy layer. It sounds complicated, but it was really quite simple. You can ask kids key questions in lessons, on tests for homework, in end of year exams, and we also asked them to plan questions for us. Focusing on the Bloom's taxonomy verb ensures that we develop appropriate questions so that kids have to explain stuff or analyse movement etc and are challenged to think.*

The teacher in this case used the work of Bloom and Biggs and Collis to complement each other. Visually, the model can be illustrated as a 3D pyramid with the SOLO learning cycle represented by a sphere.

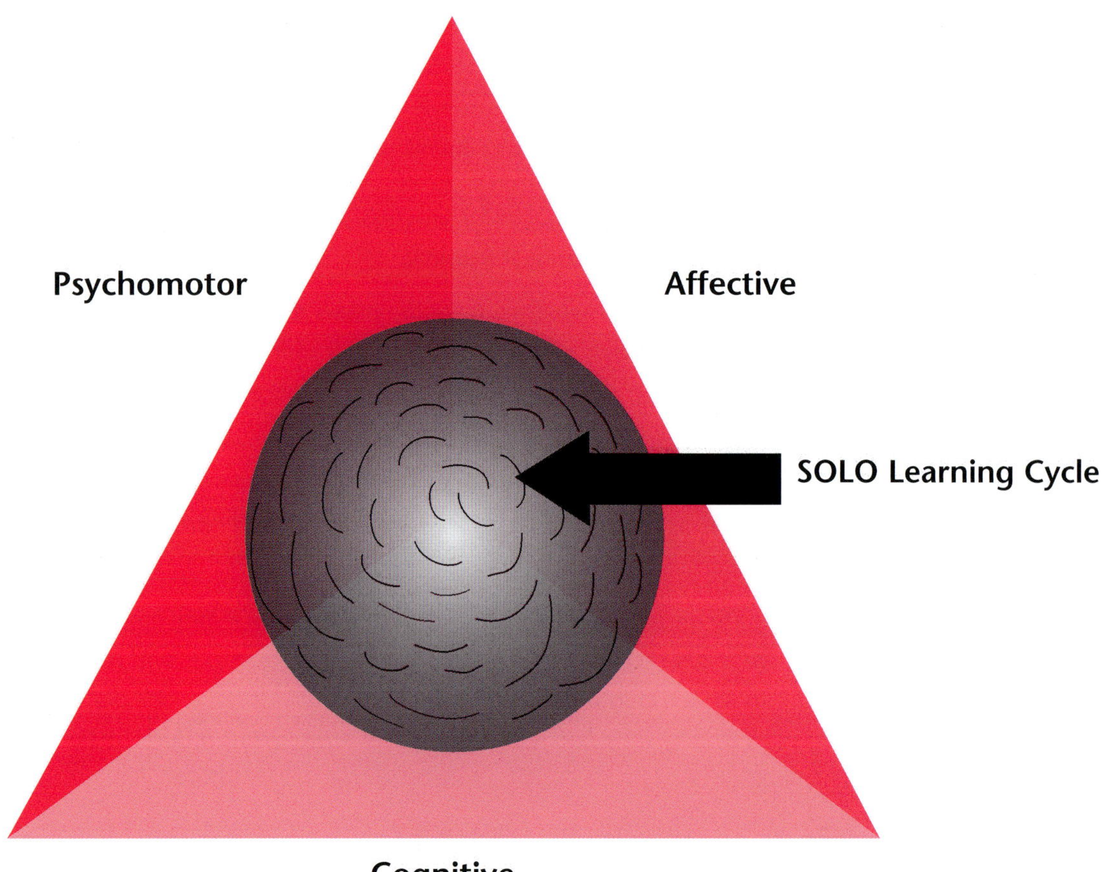

Planning a Unit of Work Embedding Assessment (Using the SOLO Approach)

At a planning meeting in Kosovo, while discussing planning resources to support teachers, on the table in front of me were more than 15 different templates for a medium-term plan. These ranged from several A4 documents of three or four pages to a nine-page epic. The nine-pager wasn't actually a medium-term plan or unit of work; rather, it was a series of seven individual lesson plans that built learning on one skill per week. Interestingly, some meeting attendees were quite precious about a particular template, usually because it was theirs, and often because of the work that had gone into the detail. By using an approach that England Rugby World Cup 2003 winning coach Clive Woodward calls 'white rooming', we developed guidance to help teachers. This way of working involves imagining a room, and everything is removed from it – the furniture, furnishings and carpets – and it is then painted white. The room can only be painted another colour or items can only be brought back into it if they are fit for purpose. In our context, we asked key questions to determine fit for purpose:

- What is a medium-term plan?
- Who is it for?
- What is its purpose?

'Form', as my now deceased father always used to inform me, 'should always follow function', and so it did.

What is a Medium-term Plan?

When analysed carefully, planning for learning involves a myriad of considerations about teaching and learning, pupils, their needs, their prior learning, equipment and facilities available, curriculum, content, context, objectives, activities and success criteria, but put quite simply it is **the process of deciding what you will teach and how you will teach it**. Short-term planning is usually accepted to be one or two lessons, and a medium-term plan is generally accepted to be one or more units of work that consist of learning planned over a number of hours or weeks. In England, this is traditionally a half or a full term consisting of 6–12 weeks.

In 1999, the QCA published a physical education scheme of work for KS1 and 2 and a scheme of work for KS3 and 4. These schemes of work, or long-term plans, consisted of a number of units of year-group-focused medium-term plans for primary, and link, development, intermediate and advanced units for secondary. Many of these units were planned for 12–18 hours. Other countries differ according to their contexts, but medium-term will generally range from 6–24 hours. Even though many definitions describe a medium-term plan as a sequence of learning planned, it is more realistic and appropriate that the plan details the learning expected, and lists possible content and contexts for this to be achieved. Formative assessment practice then informs the teacher about how to order or sequence the learning activities and experiences in order to best meet the outcomes/success criteria. A medium-term plan or unit of work **is not** a series of pre-planned lessons. Each successive medium-term unit or units planned should be constructed to align to and 'progress' learning towards the floor standards.

Who is It For?

A medium-term plan should be written for learners by the teacher. I am genuinely enthused by teachers who approach this positively and attempt to understand the process, rather than ask to be spoon-fed an approach to teaching and learning that has been written by someone else, or worse still, who purchase commercially produced plans and then make no attempt to adapt them to their learners.

The justification for not planning is almost entirely one of time. Teaching and learning will be most effective, however, when teachers themselves have given thought to the learning intentions, content and context, and resulting success criteria. To teach a unit 'off plan', a plan that someone else has developed, is akin to buying a property before it is constructed – it is difficult to understand aspects of the design or imagine what it might look like. The process of constructing the plan helps focus a teacher's thoughts and ideas for their teaching in order to effectively progress each individual pupil's learning within a group. The planning process is, therefore, by its very nature, a professional learning exercise. Consequently, a medium-term plan is a document written by a teacher for him or herself. As long as what is planned is constructively aligned and gives sufficient information for the teacher to create a picture of learning intended, then this is appropriate. There is no right or wrong way to do this. There are, however, less burdensome ways of doing it. If a unit of work has been provided by the school or department, it should be flexible enough for the teacher to think through the process, make adaptations and take ownership.

What is Its Purpose?

The purpose of 'planning' a medium-term plan comprises several aspects:

- To outline the learning intended in order to build on and/or support prior learning.
- To provide opportunity for teachers to clarify their thoughts and think deeply about teaching and learning.
- To allow time for the teacher to 'assess' any equipment, resources, financial, safety or professional learning implications of teaching the unit to reach the expected learning for all pupils.
- To plan effective assessment strategies (see Section 5).
- To monitor effective teaching in terms of pupil engagement and progress in achieving the unit outcomes.

What Should a Medium-term Plan Contain?

In short, it should contain information that allows teachers to achieve its purpose (see the previous section). In the example that follows, the bare minimum essential information for learning and teaching is listed. Schools can add sections that they deem appropriate. Risk assessment sheets should accompany medium-term plans, and any financial implications for resources, for example, can be recorded elsewhere.

Pupil Learning and Assessment at the Heart of the Process

[Verb] [Context] [Content] [Assessment Strategy] [Success Criteria]

1 Identify the learning objective or learning intention and select the appropriate verb.

Assessment information re pupil prior learning informs this step.

[Verb] [Context] [Content] [Assessment Strategy] [Success Criteria]

2 Select the context for learning.

What context? What stage of learning? What prior learning – competitive games, dance, outdoor and adventurous activity, other; individual, pairs, groups, challenge; facility, on site, off site?

[Verb] [Context] [Content] [Assessment Strategy] [Success Criteria]

3 Select the content.

Content selected must be linked to the three learning domains **and** to the verb selected. If physical skills in small-sided games in football define the content and context, for example, and assessment of prior learning indicates that year eight learners are ready to **refine** skills, then the content and teaching of the content will be focused on making small adjustments and improving technique.

[Verb] [Context] [Content] [Assessment Strategy] [Success Criteria]

4 Develop an effective assessment strategy.

This will involve selecting appropriate assessment methods. Peer observation, learner statements and videoing performance are methods integral to learning activities and learning experiences that help improve learning. Assessment information recorded in this way can also be kept as sampled assessment evidence.

[Verb] [Context] [Content] [Assessment Strategy] [Success Criteria]

5 Identify success criteria.

If pupils have achieved the intended learning, what does this achievement look like? Using the example in point three above, if pupils have refined their techniques, what will this look like? Movement used in the performance of the skill, phrase or sequence should flow. It looks better because of the technical adaptations. In a dance or gymnastic phrase or sequence, for example, the clarity of body shape looks better, and transitional movement flows because of minor technical adjustments to body lines – head, wrist and finger position, and ankle and toe position. If they are at the relational stage of learning, these adjustments should be implemented by learners quite rapidly.

Constructive Alignment

The five-point process outlined reflects an approach called 'constructive alignment', a term conceived by Biggs (1999), which has been an influential concept in planning, teaching and assessing. It is best summarised by Biggs (2002) himself:

> *The 'constructive' aspect refers to what the learner does, which is to construct meaning through relevant learning activities. The 'alignment' aspect refers to what the teacher does, which is to set up a learning environment that supports the learning activities appropriate to achieving the desired learning outcomes. The key is that the components in the teaching system, especially the teaching methods used and the assessment tasks, are aligned to the learning activities assumed in the intended outcomes. The learner is 'trapped', and cannot escape without learning what is intended.*

Planning Case Studies

The following two examples demonstrate the planning process, which integrates and aligns assessment opportunity, strategy and success criteria. The first example is a medium-term plan, and the second example illustrates what the process might look like as part of an annual programme.

Planning Using SOLO as Part of Constructive Alignment

The exemplar two-page medium-term plan template below illustrates two contexts for constructive alignment – competitive games (football) and dance.

<table>
<tr><th>KS3</th><th>Y8</th><th colspan="2">Refining, Analysing and Participating</th><th>Number of Hours</th></tr>
<tr><td colspan="2">Teacher Expectations
The teacher will, for example:</td><td colspan="3">Pupil Expectations
All pupils will:</td></tr>
<tr><td colspan="2">1 teach through games-based activity/'Erlebnis' and 'Erkennis' in dance
2 use authentic, holistic and inter-sessional learning assessment methods
3 promote inclusive physical activity and commitment (value).
These are expectations for the teacher and their teaching. What aspect of their teaching are they looking to improve so that improved outcomes for pupils are the result?
Examples include promoting school or departmental values, expectations linked to the teachers' standards, a departmental teaching approach, a departmental trialling of assessment methodology, or a focus on the implementation of particular departmental policy.</td><td colspan="3">1 develop expert technique to improve performance
2 analyse and improve performances compared to previous ones
3 participate in exercise, sports and activities (out of school).
Headline expectations linked to KS-appropriate national curriculum floor standards are listed here. In this example, one focus has been taken from each learning domain. It is expected that expert technique will be demonstrated in this activity (eg football or dance) because the primary schools have provided opportunity for all pupils to follow these activities each year both within and beyond the school day. Analysis is a target for the end of the KS so an activity is selected where pupils are already technically competent in order to begin breaking down movement to improve their overall performance. Finally, it is expected that all pupils attend an extra-curricular club in their chosen activity throughout the term.</td></tr>
<tr><th colspan="2">Professional Development Support Required</th><th>Pupils to Extend</th><th>Pupils to Support</th><th>Other</th></tr>
<tr><td colspan="2">1 In-house professional mentoring re TGfU approach
2 Department meeting extending and developing understanding of the various methods of assessment
These are examples of how identified professional learning support can be implemented in order to support the learning needs of pupils. They can be ongoing and might include courses, qualifications or mentoring and coaching.</td><td>Names of pupils and possibly the learning domain focus can be listed here.
Ross Barkley (PAC)
Jayne Stones (AC)
P = psychomotor
A = affective
C = cognitive</td><td>Leon Osman (A)
Romelia Lukaku (C)</td><td>Bryan Oviedu (has been injured and missed six weeks of PESS, P)
Tina Howard (autistic, A)</td></tr>
</table>

	Learning Intention (Select verb)	Learning Activities/Learning Experiences Context and content (select assessment methodology)	Success Criteria Pupils will be able to:
Doing	**Refine** technique to improve performance	**Football:** Individual performance and small-sided games (more complex and demanding); beating an opponent; practice, pairs and group work; introduce more technique (eg step-over, step-turn, scissors, double scissors, Ronaldo chop/scoop turn, Cruyff turn, McGeady spin); passing with different parts of the foot; receiving with cushioned control using head, chest, thigh and foot; strategy linked to analysis; peer and self-assessment; feedback with an emphasis on how to improve	make small technical adjustments (fine motor skills) to ensure the skill is performed more effectively; identify and explain the adjustments; 'upgrade' their performance; be consistent and precise, with quite rapid adjustments
		Dance: Dance performance including sporting motifs in pairs, eye focus in stillness and movement, expression, posture, body alignment, stretch, steps, step combinations, leaps; link to fitness (eg use of plyometric training to help improve technical performance); peer and self-assessment; feedback with an emphasis on how to improve	make small technical adjustments (lines, hands, alignment) to ensure the motif, the skill, the expression is communicated and performed more effectively; identify and explain the adjustments; be consistent and precise, with quite rapid adjustments
Thinking	**Analyse** and improve performances compared to previous ones (multistructural/relational)	**Football:** Observe partner's performance; use ICT to video and watch performances; improve technique through small-sided games and practices to help relational/big picture understanding; teams can reciprocate the effectiveness of the opposition's attacking and defending tactics after games; play a tournament over a number of weeks with league and knockout stages with a plate competition so everyone is always competing; inter-sessional learning; learner statement; highlight the roles that the skill set pupils are engaging with is developing (eg tactician, coach)	identify the muscles, levers and joints involved; comment on balance and coordination and what inhibited or allowed flowing movement; analyse the effectiveness of tactics in relation to the technique and decision-making
		Dance: Observe video of last year's year seven and set benchmark for performance; develop ideas of how to improve technique, phrases and composition as an individual, pair and group; video performance regularly, focusing on identified technique and phrasing to improve; highlight the roles that the skill set pupils are engaging with is developing (eg choreographer, coach)	identify the muscles, levers and joints involved; comment on balance and coordination and what inhibited or allowed flowing movement; analyse the effectiveness of composition in relation to technique, expression and motif
Feeling	**Participate** in exercise, sports and activities (out of school)	**Football:** Offer opportunity to attend before-/after-school or lunchtime clubs, including fitness for sport; invite local club representative to talk to pupils about opportunities available in their local club; promote fun side of activity, but make it challenging; constantly recognise success; promote sporting etiquette before, during and after games; promote health and fitness benefits	commit to attending either a school or community club regularly (once or twice per week)
		Dance: Offer opportunity to attend after-school clubs; invite local club representatives to talk to pupils about opportunities available in their local clubs; promote fun side of activity, but make it challenging; constantly recognise success; promote health and fitness benefits	commit to attending either a school or community club regularly (once or twice per week).

Using Assessment Information to Track, Monitor and Improve Progress Towards the Floor Standards: Assessment OF, AS and FOR Learning

Aim

A primary school wanted to raised standards and improve outcomes for all children in physical education. They used assessment information to:

- make informed decisions about planning for their teaching and pupil learning between lessons and units to improve progress
- develop authentic contexts and construct aligned assessment opportunities for learning (SOLO)
- promote an even-handed approach to learning in the three domains (cognitive, affective, psychomotor).

1 A Year 3 class teacher outlines her curriculum plan for the year. Using SOLO and Bloom's taxonomy, she develops learning intentions aligned to the KS2 floor standards that she believes the pupils should develop **in** the three learning domains. She uses the programme of study requirements to guide her choice for the context **through** which to meet the learning intentions. She selects six activities: modified competitive games (handball, rounders); dance; outdoor and adventurous activity challenges (low risk problem-solving activities); gymnastics; and running, jumping and throwing challenges of an athletic nature. She then plans the content.

2 In formulating a curriculum plan, the teacher in the case study elected to:

forecast for this group the standards that, as a result of her teaching, she expected the children to have achieved by the end of the year

identify key examples/milestones of performance she believed were achievable by the end of:

a **December** – to be able to recognise their own success and comprehend some basic attacking and defending principles

b **March** – to compare performances with previous ones and demonstrate improvement; and be able to link skills to make actions and sequences of movement.

She also:

explained to the pupils why she believed they could achieve these standards in the coming year and outlined the reasons behind her decisions

shared further opportunities available for the pupils who could see what the year had in store for them.

3 Having laid her plans, the teacher began teaching the first modified competitive games unit – handball. In each lesson, the teacher sought to **share learning intentions** and **clear success criteria** with the pupils. She was improving her own professional skills against the **teachers' standards** in her use of formative assessment specifically – feedback and key questions to promote dialogue to secure pupils' progress. Pupils were also involved in **self- and peer assessment** and played a key part in the lesson plenaries leading to **informed decisions about learning for the next lesson**. At the end of the modified handball unit, she involved pupils in **reviewing and targeting learning** for the next dance unit. She assessed the pupils to have achieved most of the **success criteria** from the handball unit. She shaded these **green** on her medium-term unit plan. There were three outcomes shaded in amber and one in red, however, that she felt the pupils needed to revisit. She adapted the learning intentions, learning activities and success criteria for the next dance unit to ensure coherence and continuity.

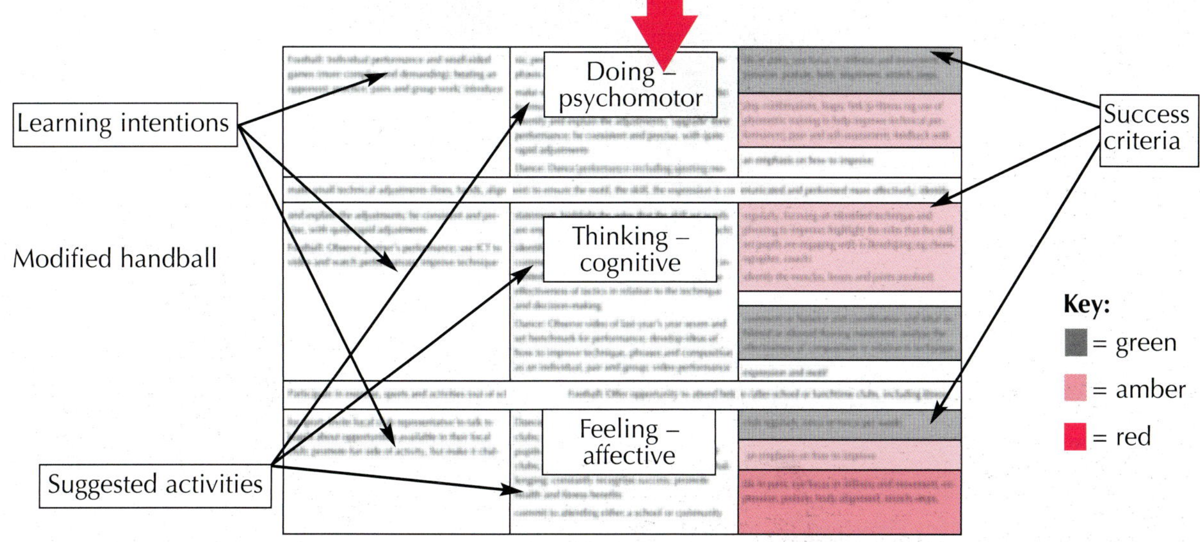

Dance

Outdoor and adventurous activity challenges

Gymnastic activities

Running, jumping and throwing challenges

Modified rounders

4 The teacher then continued to teach the remaining units, focusing on appropriate intervention as a result of strategic **ongoing observation and questioning**. This ensured all pupils accessed learning and helped progress to floor standards. She used the **milestone targets** she had set for December and March to step back and check overall progress. Assessment information, in the form of big writing about physical education (written in English lessons), videos and images of performance, and teacher notes stored in an electronic portfolio, helped to inform a judgement as to whether pupils were on track to meet floor standard expectations.

Immediately, it is possible to see the **even-handed approach she has used to the teaching and learning of the three learning domains in national curriculum physical education, and this is a very good habit.** She has adapted her teaching to promote continuity of the three learning domains across units. Where she noticed a pattern emerging with other teachers in the school, also shading too much amber for the affective domain, she ascertained the reason and targeted PE and Sport Premium funding to bring in a qualified practitioner who provided ideas for learning integration.

5 Reflection

How do you currently embed assessment for learning practices into your long-, medium- and short-term planning?

How do you currently monitor:

- an even-handed approach to the three learning domains
- the effectiveness of your teaching
- learner progress
- the need for CPD
- the impact of CPD?

How do you currently adapt your planning and teaching in the three learning domains as a result of your assessment practice and:

- incorporate into future units
- extend units
- other?

Notes

- The record is a class record.
- It is used to monitor the progress of pupils towards the end of year expectations, which in turn should be progressive to the end of KS floor standards.
- The judgement **of** pupils' learning being 'on track' or 'requiring additional support' (including the most able) doesn't lead to the recording of a number. Rather, it leads to adaptation of the learning planned – in other words, the learning intention, the learning activities and learning experiences, and the success criteria are changed/tweaked.
- The planning record created therefore becomes evidence that schools are using assessment information to identify pupils who are falling behind in their learning or who need additional support to reach their full potential, including the most able.
- Information about pupils requiring this additional support will be listed on the next unit of work front sheet. In a secondary school where teachers may not teach the same group consecutively, this necessary sharing of information can be carried out in regular moderation meetings. This practice is essential so that each teacher can be informed of the learning needs of pupils in their various groups and can plan appropriately to meet these learning needs.
- The process of planning the unit of work documents, together with teacher annotations and adaptations and a judgement on whether outcomes have been achieved (red, amber and green), can contribute useful information about whether the curriculum and our teaching of it is appropriate. If an outcome is shaded red and no pupil has achieved it, is it because of the wettest spring season on record, which meant we didn't teach it and children did not have opportunity to learn? Is it because we didn't have the knowledge or confidence to teach it? Or is it because we taught it, but pupils didn't learn it? In an amber scenario, did some pupils not progress as expected because stage-related content was too difficult? (Certain children, due to their birth date, might be 12 months behind in their growth and development compared to other children in the same year.) Or have they only just returned from illness or injury? Whatever the reason, the onus is on the teacher to change the curriculum context or content (change the activity or differentiate the task), or change the way the content is taught so that all learners make progress.
- The recording of a number or grade for pupils in any activity when much of the unit was written off due to poor weather is a nonsense. In the same way, the use of 'I can' statements, which for pupils who 'can't' is a process that highlights deficiency in performance and is not conducive to developing a connection or a love of learning in physical education, is also a nonsense.
- The act of monitoring pupils' progress toward end of unit success criteria and annual expectations using the planning record does not require additional teacher assessment records with 'I can' statements or tick box sheets of any kind. This practice is simply a duplication of the decision-making process already carried out in arriving at the shading of the unit success criteria. Assessment is integral to this improving process. A tick sheet creates more administration and is a separate activity. For secondary, however, where pupils will often be in different groups for physical education, an overview or mapping sheet that allows the subject leader to easily identify which pupils require additional support for whatever reason (weather, injury, absence, fear, special need, more able) provides a useful mechanism for monitoring whether teachers are adapting their planning and teaching to ensure pupils narrow the notional gap between current performance and floor standards, or at the very least do not fall further behind.

- The planning record is not 'assessment evidence'. Assessment evidence is 'documentary' evidence, which if required can form part of a work scrutiny for physical education (see assessment methodology, in particular electronic portfolios, Section 5). Some of the departments in the pilot studies have carried out work scrutiny as part of their moderation process. Assessment becomes embedded in a process that demonstrates rigour and an integral part of deepening individual teacher understanding of assessment **of**, **as** and **for** learning.

Learning and Progress

Due to the nature of learning and what we know about 'progress' to floor standards, learning in terms of the planning of constructive alignment could well be depicted as per the following diagram, where planned learning in the units of work may consolidate or strengthen the relational aspects linked to previous learning, 'take a step backward' when contrasting contexts and new challenges are introduced, or may advance rapidly.

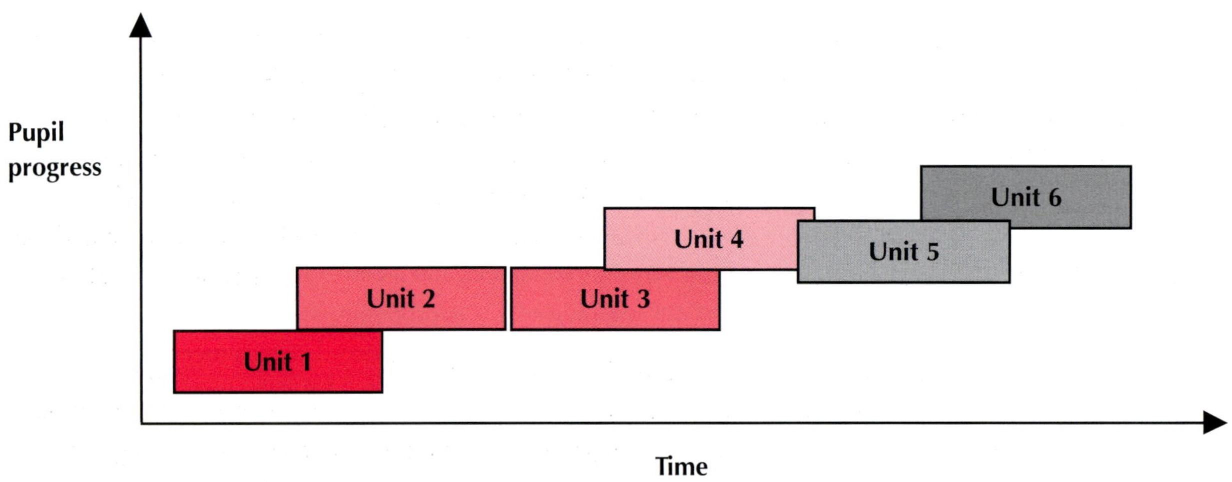

Diagram to illustrate possible 'progress' through successive units of work

A Seasonal and Cultural Approach to Integrated Delivery

One teacher used an extended 'sport education' approach to the delivery of the programme. There are no activity areas and no range of content listed in the national curriculum for 2014. Departmental discussions about opportunities created by the requirements of the physical education programme of study led to an idea that extended the approach the school used to the teaching of competitive games (rugby). Previously, they used an SE approach. The trial, taking advantage of the flexibility created by the framework of the DfE (2013) programme of study for physical education, is summarised as follows for their year nine pilot group:

Phase 1: Three blocked weeks (six hours) of fitness training focusing on contrasting skill-related and health-related fitness.

Phase 2: Three blocked weeks (six hours) of 'pre-season training' focused on the development of technique and unit skills, with input from the teacher about advanced attacking and defending strategies. This phase also included time in the lesson where pupils developed their own haka dance style, based on the stimulus of videos from the 1973 New Zealand haka performed to the Barbarians at Cardiff Arms Park and a performance of the haka at the Millennium Stadium performed to the Welsh team in 2008. Discussion led to pupil suggestions about the frequency of practice and how the New Zealand All Blacks might have incorporated the performance of the haka into their overall training schedule. In a wet weather lesson, the pupils were able to practise the haka indoors.

Phase 3: Three blocked weeks (six hours) of 'pre-season friendly' games, which also included further refinement of their technique, tactics and the haka performance. Pupils were working in four groups of seven (28 pupils in the class), which equated to one pre-season game per week. Pupils refereed their own games. Please note this was one 'playing referee' from each side, not a pupil excluded from refining their skills or being physically active competing in the games, for example. Inter-learning tasks set included requiring pupils to reflect on their own and the opposition's strengths and weaknesses in order to determine tactics for the competitive phase.

Phase 4: Three weeks of competition and three weeks of outdoor and adventurous activities (six hours total). A competitive game was played each week, which started with each team's performance of the haka. Pupils fed back to each other on the performance. Outdoor and adventurous activities (low-risk problem-solving activities) were scheduled to further develop a sense of belonging, a sense of team cooperation and problem-solving skills, which were also applied to their competitive team games. This arrangement also created flexibility if the schedule was affected due to inclement weather so that the competitive game could be played, and prevented too many competitive games being played each week – especially if pupils played for the school and/or an outside club.

Phase 5: Three weeks of fitness and three weeks of outdoor and adventurous activities (orienteering) (six hours total). The department attempted to mirror a season by engaging in fitness-type activities to develop strength, stamina and speed after the Christmas break.

Phase 6: Three weeks (six hours total) of further competition and technical/tactical learning.

Notes

1 While the school moved to a traditional approach for the remainder of the year, blocking badminton, gymnastics, athletics and cricket, staff are already devising ideas for an integrated approach that spans the whole year.

2 Rather than plan six-week consecutive blocks of fitness, rugby, dance and outdoor and adventurous activities, the approach integrated these activities and ensured the programme was engaging for the pupils. Boys' dance became part of an authentic approach to their programme, which mirrored a seasonal approach that a top player might engage in.

3 The department found it difficult to plan for this approach, but if we analyse the combined unit of work example earlier in this section, it becomes achievable. The planning focus is on appropriate learning that is developed through a context and content. This context was one that pupils in this school found exciting and engaging.

Backward Planning

Since The Mexico City 1968 Olympic Games, when Richard Fosbury first used a new technique in competition, the world high jump record has improved dramatically. Previously, the 'western roll' and 'straddle' techniques had led to improvement in the world record over time. The advent of a new technique, however, which involved the athlete going over the bar backwards, made previous improvements appear incremental and insignificant when compared to the steep slope transformational improvement achieved using the 'Fosbury flop'. In the same way, the advent of backward planning as a curriculum design tool has had a similar effect on standards in teaching and learning. Frapwell (2013) has developed a simple seven-step process based on backward planning research that creates the opportunity for higher standards, maps to the national curriculum and supports constructive alignment.

Step 1

The first step is to focus on a key objective taken from the DfE (2013) programme of study. For this example, we have taken it from the 'doing' physical being at KS3 **(NB: curriculum targets will obviously be developed from all three learning domains)**:

Develop expert technique to improve performance.

The **contexts** to allow opportunity for this development are listed in the KS3 three-column table in Section 4 (page 56). There are three years to develop this (usually years seven, eight and nine).

Step 2

As a department, decide which activities best meet the needs of your learners. Many schools have developed a year seven programme whose purpose is to lay the foundations for pupil choice of a selected pathway for years eight and nine (and subsequently years 10 and 11, which will dovetail to qualifications, eg GCSE physical education). In other words, pupils should know what they like and what type of activities they are successful at, and use this information to choose a pathway in year eight.

We are laying the foundations at this stage for a springboard to greater progress and engagement in later school years.

Step 3

An **annual target** for year seven might be, for example:

By the end of year seven, we expect all learners to demonstrate:

- **developing technique** in each component of their programme
- **expert technique** in at least one team or individual activity
- **improved performance** in all components.

When combined with the 'feeling' physical being, we **might**, for example, target 100% of learners attending at least one extra-curricular activity during the course of the year. Opportunity needs to be explored in this context. We need to change our thinking from providing greater opportunity for the more able to providing greater opportunity for all. A school might, for example, target a minimum number of activities to be followed for extra-curricular, but shouldn't necessarily expect a greater frequency of attendance from someone who is recognised as gifted in physical education and/or talented in a sport. Someone with special needs might require greater opportunity to fulfil their potential than a more able pupil. This change in our thinking and approach is required if we are to meet not only the floor standard but also the aims of physical education.

Step 4

We should align our assessment so that **learning intentions** for **each unit** and **each lesson** must be shared and use the same criterion-referenced language: **expert, technique and an appropriate verb**. These are not the only criterion-referenced language we might use as the NCPE programme of study is only a minimum entitlement. Our teaching must provide plentiful opportunities to develop these aspects.

Step 5

AfL strategies and appropriate assessment methodologies should be developed, implemented and consistently used to promote learning, success and progress (see Section 5).

Step 6

Periodically, teachers (and pupils) should assess whether all learners are on track to meet their end of year targets (and therefore the end of KS floor standard).

Many of the process targets developed will be integrated with AfL strategies, but should also target the soft skills to enable the learner to develop as a learner and engage with the content and achieve criteria more effectively – for example, skills such as:

- leadership skills (captaincy, individual decision-making)
- team-working skills (relationships, collaboration, cooperation, communication)
- roles and responsibilities (effective participant/effective competitor, reciprocity)
- values (determination, commitment, respect).

Periodic or **milestone** targets will be progressive to the end of year targets.

Step 7

Review and revise. After each episode, whether it a lesson, unit, milestone or end of year, targets can be reviewed and revised.

School Moderation Case Study

A school that had employed an 'assessing pupils' progress' (APP) process for making judgements against the previous attainment target used the same moderation process towards standardisation, using the new programme of study attainment target or floor standard.

The purpose of the moderation process was to:

- quality assure their assessment judgements
- build confidence and trust in their own and others' assessment judgements
- check progress
- provide a benchmark using sampled pupils, to agree if they were on track or otherwise to meet the floor standards
- develop ideas for and share best practice
- provide opportunity for professional learning
- build a picture of progress over time.

The moderation process the school employed included the following:

- A staff 'buddying' system – staff were placed in pairs or small groups called learning pods. Teachers planned individually and/or collaboratively within these groups and had 'go-to' buddies during the teaching of the units.
- Units of work were planned with **assessment as learning** activities integrated (constructive alignment).
- Collating **assessment evidence** from everyday teaching and learning that staff judged to be clear evidence of pupils who were on track – this was completed for two assessment moderation meetings during the year (December and March).
- Meeting discussion, deliberation and consensus of the collection of evidence that demonstrated a pupil was 'on track'.
- Keeping a portfolio of evidence – the collection of evidence was kept in an electronic portfolio (VLE) and also hard copy format that provided a benchmark for staff making a judgement as to whether pupils were on track. In other words, a standardised **assessment of learning** judgement about a pupil's progress and attainment against a floor standard benchmark.
- Using assessment information to improve subsequent planning, teaching, integrated assessment and extra-curricular opportunities for all learners.

Staff reported the following:

- The moderation process was something that became embedded in their practice, a way of doing things, rather than 'just turning up to a meeting'. It became a professional development activity. They 'learnt lots' from the process, especially the use of appropriate verbs in constructive alignment to ensure inclusive, challenging activities to progress all pupils.

- They gained deeper insight into the national curriculum and raised their expectations, and this also helped foster a more progressive and inclusive approach.
- Although staff had previously followed an APP approach, it was experienced as an administrative chore. It was felt that their decisions had become too focused on skilled performance in an activity, summative, rather than formative, and focused on key skills, essential knowledge and concepts, and vital behaviours

Reporting to Parents

We do not have examples of reporting to parents, given the combined timescales of the legislation and the writing of this book. Many schools, however, are adopting their previous practice of reporting an indicative grade and whether pupils are on track to meet their GCSE target grades. The 9–1 numbering scale is being/has been used to replace grades. Some schools have adapted this to use the 9–1 scaling to indicate a GCSE score each year in order to indicate progress.

What should become immediately apparent is that this practice mirrors previous levelling practice and recreates a system that was corrupt and led to grade inflation. At the time of writing, we also do not know the grade descriptions or indeed if any will even be published. The practice therefore of labelling a child with a score of three in year seven or five in year nine becomes just that – a labelling practice that actually means nothing.

Rather, we should develop a system that is fit for purpose – a system that accepts and trusts qualitative assessment methodologies alongside the use of tests (quantitative), aligns reporting with the floor standards expected for each KS, aligns reporting with the purpose and aims of physical education and the aims of the school, personalises reporting of the learning and progress achieved, and reports reliable information to parents about how their child and the school is doing (DfE, 2014) in their core physical education. Too often, I view reports that depersonalise the learner and their learning, using a number or grade serving only to highlight deficiencies in progress to a numerical target. This, believe it or not, contrary to some practice, **is not** the raison d'être of education.

What Might a Report that is Fit for Purpose Look Like?

> *Elliott is on track to meet the standard expected by the end of the key stage. He is able to break down movement and analyse technique to improve others' performance beyond expectations. His technical skill improvement was less than expected due to his broken back, but this is understandable. Elliott is committed to improve and has joined a lunchtime circuit training club we established, to improve his core stability, and he displays good lifestyle habits, regularly attending school clubs. He has a great sense of humour.*
>
> *Targets: Consider joining the local rugby club. Join the school's online healthy active lifestyle blog.*

Notes

- The above exemplar report and associated targets are 101 words.
- The report succinctly gives an account in relation to headline national curriculum targets in the three learning domains.

- It highlights beyond-expected progress.
- It highlights less-than-expected progress in a positive way and explains the reason for this.
- The targets are process targets – in other words, essential actions that the school or pupil can do in order to stay on track or catch up/close or narrow the gap.
- An effective quality assured process will ensure that the information contained in the report is aligned, reliable and robust.
- Some schools have used the early years stage categories to report to parents – those of 'emergent', 'expected' or 'exceeding' in relation to the end of KS floor standards expected. The reporting of a single judgement, however, can obscure or distort key elements of the subject if teachers do not also unpack the standards and take explicit account of the different but integral progressive pathways (head-heart-hands). There is a danger that reporting progress only in terms of a single judgement obscures accurate and perceptive understanding of the pupil's actual strengths and weaknesses, and performance in the different pathways (head-heart-hands) should be built in to the report.

Reporting to Senior Leadership

a If we understand how assessment is integral to the curriculum at the intended, enacted and achieved stages (see Section 3) and our curriculum planning is robust, then senior leadership should be confident that the subject leader has a clear understanding of their subject, including the ability to recognise, assess and describe progress in the different pathways (head-heart-hands) of physical education.

b If we use appropriate hierarchical vocabulary that helps to illustrate progress against the standards and ensure pupils understand what they have achieved, what they did to achieve it and what they have to do to improve, then senior leaders should be confident that assessment criteria are being applied.

c If the principles of assessment (Section 5) are embedded in practice and used to improve learning, then senior leaders should also be secure that assessment for learning practice underpins and informs everything we do.

d If we take account of appropriate timescales, assessment methods and VARSC; recognise what constitutes evidence; and use this assessment information as part of a departmental moderation strategy that informs teacher CPD and standardises not only an appropriate start point (baselining) and appropriate learning tasks (challenge) but also judgement against the required standard, then senior leaders should trust teachers' professional judgement when they articulate progress in a report to parents.

e If assessment information that informs teacher professional judgement also forms evidence of self-evaluation in reporting to senior leadership department standards, pupil progress and the strengths and areas to improve; and subject specific targets are identified on the basis of this, then senior leaders should trust this information.

f If, as a result of our appropriate planning, teaching, ongoing assessment, moderating, monitoring and self-evaluation, we now quantify as a percentage (eg 85%) the number of pupils who are on target to meet the end of KS floor standards and report this information internally and annually to senior leaders, then this quantitative measure should be trusted.

Conclusion

The intentions outlined in Section 1 were to support teachers in developing:

- a more reliable and valid approach to assessment without the use of levels
- a robust system where the changes, especially for assessment, are understood, quality assured and fit for purpose
- a system where a broad and balanced curriculum and AfL strategies that promote inclusive practice and drive higher standards are understood.

In this book, we have argued for the need to rebalance the seemingly competing demands of effective AfL to improve learning and progress and higher standards for all pupils, with the limited approach requiring too frequent use of data to monitor and record progress and standards. We have raised concerns that the system has in the past reformed the reform, and some schools are currently following this same path in reinventing levels in various guises. We have highlighted overzealous data monitoring regimes that have become over-burdensome and inhibited the development of effective AfL throughout the system. We have explored essential relationships in terms of curriculum, assessment and pedagogy, and outlined key statutory changes in relation to the language of physical education and the language of learning, progress and higher standards so that assessment criteria are transparent. In doing so, we have shared background theory behind the rationale for change, especially that of threshold concepts and transformational and messy learning, and sought to develop an assessment system that is fit for purpose and inclusive in meeting the aims of physical education. This requires an understanding of the three key assessment principles afPE has provided, and targeted assessment methods used as part of a robust strategy (VARSC). This diligent approach moves assessment from a separate data-driven activity to assessment as integral and essential to planning, teaching and improving learning for all, including professional learning for teachers. Finally, examples have been shared as to how teachers and departments have developed purposeful assessment ideas in practice.

Thank you for reading.
We wish you well in your endeavours.
Make a difference.

Once upon a time, there was a wise man who used to go to the ocean to do his writing. He had a habit of walking on the beach before he began his work.

One day, as he was walking along the shore, he looked down the beach and saw a human figure moving like a dancer. He smiled to himself at the thought of someone who would dance to the day, and so, he walked faster to catch up.

As he got closer, he noticed that the figure was that of a young man, and that what he was doing was not dancing at all. The young man was reaching down to the shore, picking up small objects, and throwing them into the ocean.

He came closer still and called out 'Good morning! May I ask what it is that you are doing?'

The young man paused, looked up, and replied 'Throwing starfish into the ocean.'

'I must ask, then, why are you throwing starfish into the ocean?' asked the somewhat startled wise man.

To this, the young man replied, 'The sun is up and the tide is going out. If I don't throw them in, they'll die.'

Upon hearing this, the wise man commented, 'But, young man, do you not realize that there are miles and miles of beach and there are starfish all along every mile? You can't possibly make a difference!'

At this, the young man bent down, picked up yet another starfish, and threw it into the ocean. As it met the water, he said,

'It made a difference for that one.'

Loren Eiseley

Reflection

Summary *(noun), a brief statement or account of the main points of something.*

The list below represents the summary responses to teachers' frequently asked questions.

- ✔ **The current system of levels has been removed and will not be replaced – for all subjects.**
- ✔ **Ofsted will not be looking for two levels of progress between KS1 and 2 or three levels of progress between KS2 and 4. Why? Because levels have gone.**
- ✔ **The rationale for the shorter programmes of study is to foster an ambition for all children to excel no matter what their background – to set pupils up to succeed.**
- ✔ **Shorter programmes of study allow for the maximum level of innovation at school level in the development of content in the subject areas and should support deep learning at each KS.**
- ✔ **The subject disciplines are described in such a way as to attempt to make clear both what should be taught and what pupils should know and be able to do as a result.**
- ✔ **New aims and a clear purpose for physical education emphasise competence, competition, being physically active and leading healthy active lifestyles.**
- ✔ **Have high expectations. High expectations shape outcomes. 'Whether you think you can or whether you think you can't, you're probably right.'**
- ✔ **The programme of study outlines the key skills, essential knowledge and concepts, and vital behaviours expected of someone who is physically educated.**
- ✔ **Understand and apply floor standards in the light of threshold concepts and learning that is messy.**
- ✔ **Design curriculum that meets all learners' needs.**
- ✔ **Teach well, progressing learning in each of the domains.**

- ✔ Ensure assessment is fit for purpose – be clear about the purpose and aims of physical education, and ensure assessment is matched to these.
- ✔ Develop assessment policies that acknowledge assessment cannot be separated from the processes of planning, teaching and learning.
- ✔ Re-emphasise the learning function of assessment, de-emphasise the grading function – develop AfL practice, embed it in your practice. It is this 'for learning' practice that leads to greater progress being made within lessons (four key teacher actions) and between units, modifying units of work and reviewing teaching.
- ✔ Concentrate on making sure that all pupils reach the expected standard, rather than on labelling differential performance.
- ✔ Ensure constructive alignment in planning learning and teaching, assessment strategy and reporting.
- ✔ Involve pupils in the process – understand assessment criteria, and explain these clearly to learners so they can also be clear and engage.
- ✔ Use quantitative measures sparingly (eg test scores) and a range of qualitative evidence (assessment information) to provide a clear and reliable picture of progress and attainment.
- ✔ Build moderation procedures into the subject meeting calendar at least twice a year.
- ✔ Trust professional judgement that is the result of rigorous, robust and fair processes that aren't influenced by external pressures resulting in grade creep.

References

Biggs, J. (1999) *Teaching for Quality Learning at University*. Buckingham: SRHE and Open University Press. ISBN: 978-0-335211-68-5.

Biggs, J. (2002) 'Aligning teaching and assessment to curriculum objectives', Learning and Teaching Support Network.

Biggs, J. and Collis, K. (1982) *Evaluating the Quality of Learning: The SOLO Taxonomy*. New York: Academic Press. ISBN: 978-0-120975-52-5.

DfE (2013) *Physical Education Programmes of Study: Key Stages 1 and 2, Key Stages 3 and 4: National Curriculum in England.* London: DfE.

DfE (2014) 'Assessment Principles', www.gov.uk/government/uploads/system/uploads/attachment_data/file/304602/Assessment_Principles.pdf

Frapwell, A. (2013) 'National curriculum 2014 and assessing without levels', Wychbold: afTLC Ltd.

Statutory Instruments (2013) *No. 2232 Education, England: The Education (National Curriculum) (Attainment Targets and Programmes of Study)(England) Order 2013*. Norwich: The Stationery Office. ISBN: 978-0-111103-66-1.

A complete resource pack for primary music

Carol Donaldson Carmel McCourt

Acknowledgements

Thanks to Felix Donaldson, Isla Donaldson, Leah Molyneux and Saskia Speed for performing the rap on 'Neesa'

United Kingdom: Folens Publishers, Apex Business Centre, Boscombe Road, Dunstable, LU5 4RL. Email: folens@folens.com

Ireland: Folens Publishers, Greenhills Road, Tallaght, Dublin 24. Email: info@folens.ie

Poland: JUKA, ul. Renesansowa 38, Warsaw 01-905

Editor: Sara Peacock
Layout artist: Ken Vail Graphic Design, Cambridge
Illustrations: Celia Hart
Cover design: Ken Vail Graphic Design, Cambridge

First published 2006 by Folens Limited.

British Library Cataloguing in Publication Data. A catalogue record for this publication is available from the British Library.

ISBN 1-84303-858-7

Contents

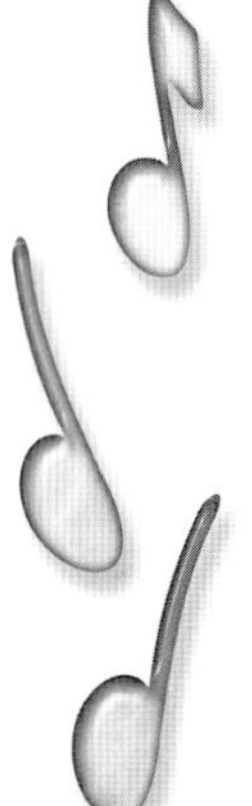

Music Works
Creative Approach to Music in Education

Dear Teacher,

We hope you find this music resource pack helpful and easy to use. The main idea behind this pack is for your lesson-planning to be done for you to enable you to relax. No special musical ability or aptitude is required!

What does *Music Works* do?

Music Works provides three sections for every age group. Within each pack are different themes, for example, for Years 1 and 2, Healthy food, World music and Mammals and me.

Each individual pack contains six 40-minute lesson plans (along with a CD), all working towards the end performance of a specially composed and themed song. The emphasis is on learning through singing, but percussion and rap is also used and, along the way, many music curriculum requirements for Key Stages 1 and 2 will be met.

You are led through each step simply, using the CD tracks to guide you through the song, vocal exercises, rhythm and pulse exercises (all of which are very easy to follow).

Each pack may also be used cross-curriculum with English.

What's different about *Music Works*? The 'WOW' Factor!

This pack has an original contemporary 'pop' song, written especially for *Music Works*. This means the children are more likely to want to engage with it as they will like the sound of it!

Each song has space for a rap in it. Part of this is already written and part of it needs to be written by the class. This seems to work especially well with some of the boys – they identify with rap more easily than some other forms of music and think it's 'cool' to join in with! It encourages them to express themselves and give ideas.

The children also feel the song becomes theirs and is part of their genre – not the teacher's.

How to get the best out of *Music Works*

Read through the lesson plan and get comfortable with starting and stopping your CD player so you don't spend time during the lesson trying to figure out how it works. All machines are slightly different and can thwart the best of us! Make sure you have a good CD player that has sufficient volume.

The feeling that the children 'own' the song rather than the teacher is key to the success and enjoyment of *Music Works* and should be encouraged. (For example, I might say, 'Well, you could do that rap movement with your hands', which I imitate badly and say, 'Oh I can't do it, I'm too old, you show me.' I let them laugh at my pitiful attempts to try and move and rap and they will try to show me and the other children how to do it.)

Children with differing abilities

Children who may not engage in other subjects well can be very musical and the difference between learners is far less obvious.

Ensure that less able children make a big contribution to the rap section. A sense of ownership starts to develop and the resultant building in their confidence is very rewarding.

Note from the authors:
We hope these lessons will be useful to you as a teacher and make learning about music fun for the children. Don't hesitate to let us know how things work or don't work for you so we can update our design and provide you with further resources for the future.

Lesson 1 The song: 'The Carrot Song'

Music objective

Introducing 'The Carrot Song'.

Learning activity

- Doing a vocal warm-up (QCA units 1:1, 1:4 and 1:5).
- Learning basic techniques for building confidence in using the singing voice (QCA unit 1:1).
- Following and learning a new song in two parts (QCA units 1:1, 1:4 and 1:5).

QCA learning objectives

Unit 1 Ongoing skills

'This unit highlights the musical skills that require regular practice and ongoing development throughout the key stage.'
'Singing songs with control and using the voice expressively.'
Children should learn:

- Section 1 – to use different voices and find their singing voice.
- Section 4 – to control pulse and rhythm.
- Section 5 – to control pitch.

Scottish attainment targets

Using materials, techniques, skills and media (voice)

- Level B – Control rhythm, speed and leaps in melody.
- Level C – Sing confidently in unison with some awareness of dynamics, phrasing and expression.

Evaluating and appreciating

- Levels B/C – Recognise the sounds of instruments and groupings; demonstrate aural retention through playing phrases from familiar tunes by ear; give opinions of own music making; and discuss the characteristics of music with a clearly identifiable mood.

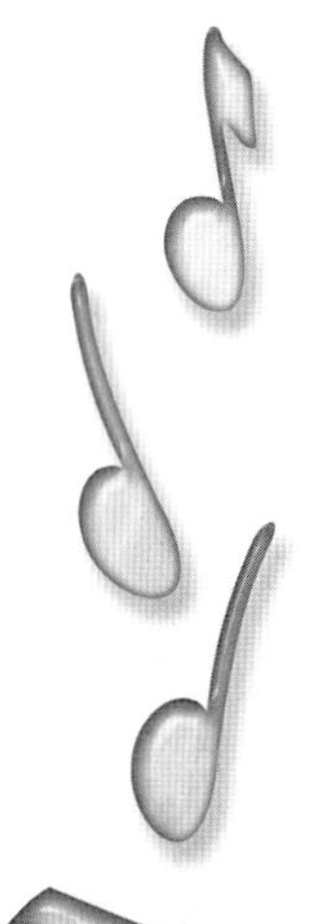

The song: 'The Carrot Song'

1 Tell the children to listen really carefully to the song you are about to play for them because you will be asking them questions about it. Play TRACK 1 on the CD – 'The Carrot Song'.

2 Discuss the song with the children. See if they have understood what the song is about – the journey of the carrot from being planted as a seed to being served on our dinner plates. Discuss the different ways of eating carrots as mentioned in the song (raw, cooked, chopped, grated, and so on). Explain that the carrots will be covered with earth and will need to be washed and scraped. Discuss why carrots and other vegetables are good for you (bring in the concept of vitamins as mentioned in the song).

3 Vocal warm-up – we sing using our whole body, not just the vocal chords! We therefore need to make sure we are relaxed and open physically in order to release the voice. Take ten minutes to do the warm-up.

- Ask the children to stand in a circle and make sure they are standing in 'neutral' – with un-folded arms and legs shoulder-width apart. Ask them to imagine that their head is attached to a piece of string from above, which is pulling their head and shoulders up straight.
- Take deep breaths in and do loud exaggerated yawns going from a high to a low noise. Ask the children if they can feel the note go from high to low in their body as well. Encourage them to see how high or how low they can go.
- Get the children to shout 'Hey!' as loud as they can after the count of three (just a short sound, not a long one!) then get them to shout 'Ho!' even louder after three (no screeching!). Try all the vowels (Hee, Hoo, Hah, Hi, and so on). Point out how loud the children are. Often children can bellow really loudly across the playground, but have voices like mice when it comes to singing. They have now found their loud voices and can and should sing loudly from now on. (Note: It's always more difficult to get children to sing louder than softer. Once you've got them to sing loud it is far easier to bring their volume down than the other way around.)
- Listen and follow TRACK 6 on the CD. The CD guides you through some exercises, in the form of 'call and answer': something is sung on the CD, then there is a gap for you to copy this and sing it back. These exercises will help children to learn about pitch. Stress the 'b' of 'banana' to help sound out the notes.

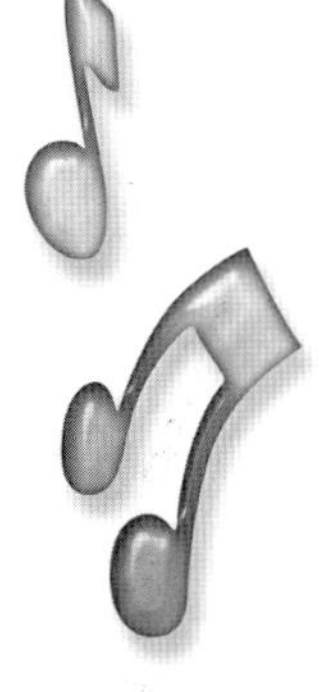

The song: 'The Carrot Song'

4 Listen to TRACK 1 on the CD again and this time listen out for just the choruses. The tune is the same for each chorus, but the words are slightly different each time: 'Watch those carrots grow' on the first chorus, 'Gonna dig my carrots up' on the second, 'Gonna eat my carrots up' on the third and 'Watch my muscles grow' on the fourth chorus. Note that the tune goes from high to low on the choruses. Use your hand to follow the shape of the melody from high to low.

5 Spend some time going over just the words of each chorus:

- Have the children practise just saying the words of the chorus. Listen to TRACK 4 to hear the pulse of the song; you can speak it over this.
- Point out the gap at the end of each line.
- Point out how in each chorus there are three lines with the same words and rhythm (for example 'Watch those carrots grow') and that the fourth line is different: it lasts longer and the tune goes down even lower ('Down, down, deep in the ground').

6 Now sing along to just the choruses on TRACK 1. Point out to the children how you have to start the phrase slightly earlier on the two middle choruses starting with 'Gonna'. Practise just singing along with the choruses a few times round until the children are familiar with it. Again, indicate the fall in pitch with your hands.

7 Listen to TRACK 1 on the CD again. Pay attention to the verses this time. Point out how the tune goes from lower to higher in pitch for the verses. Use your hand to indicate the rising pitch.

8 Split the class into three groups and give them a verse each to learn. Now get each group to sing along to their verse on TRACK 1, but leave out the choruses this time. Have the children use their hands to indicate the climb up in pitch on each verse. Sing along to TRACK 1 again, with everyone singing together on the choruses and each group singing their verse.

9 This song may take some time for the children to remember it all! Take time to practise singing the song a few times through with TRACK 1.

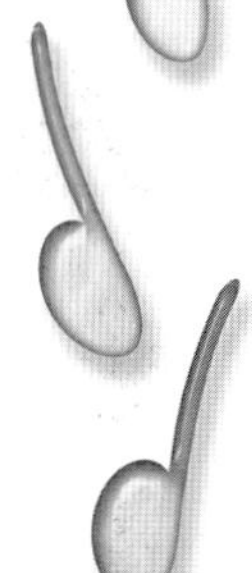

Chill out time!

Ask them to listen to the sounds around them in silence. After one minute ask them to put up their hands and say what they've heard.

Adding percussion

Note – You will be using the percussion trolley for this lesson.

Music objective

Recapping the song and learning percussion parts.

Learning activity

- Doing a warm-up (QCA unit 1:1, 1:4 and 1:5).
- Building confidence in using the singing voice and singing in parts (QCA unit 1:1).
- Learning simple percussion parts (QCA units 4:1–3: and 4:7).

QCA learning objectives

Unit 1 Ongoing skills

'This unit highlights the musical skills that require regular practice and ongoing development throughout the key stage.'
'Singing songs with control and using the voice expressively.'
Children should learn:

- Section 1 – to use different voices and find their singing voice.
- Section 4 – to control pulse and rhythm.
- Section 5 – to control pitch.

Unit 4 Feel the pulse – Exploring pulse and rhythm

'This unit develops children's ability to recognise the difference between pulse and rhythm and to perform with a sense of pulse.'
'What is pulse?'

- Section 1 – Children should learn what is meant by pulse or steady beat.

'Exploration'
Children should learn:

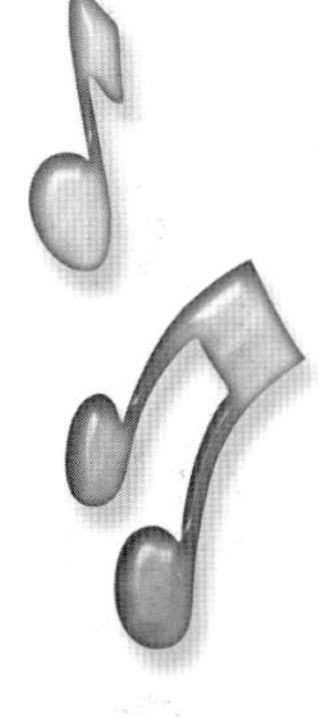

- Section 2 – how to control a pulse.
- Section 3 – what is meant by rhythm.

'Bringing it all together: Can we use pulse and rhythm to make accompaniments?'

- Section 7 – Children should learn how to use pulse and rhythm to create an accompaniment for a chant or song.

Scottish attainment targets

Using materials, techniques, skills and media (instruments)

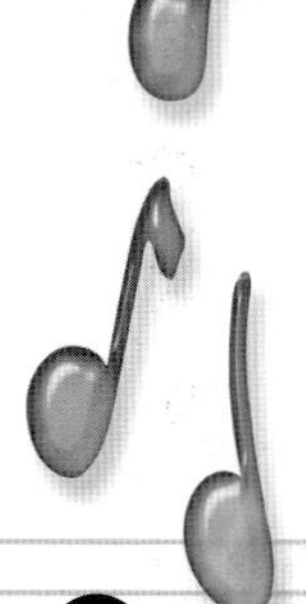

- Level B – Play simple rhythmic parts showing some control over speed and volume.
- Level C – Display two-handed co-ordination in playing straightforward melodies and rhythms.

Lesson 2 Adding percussion

1 Play TRACK 1 on the CD ('The Carrot Song') to remind the children of the song.

2 Ask children to put hands up if they remember what the song is about. Can they remember about the pitch climbing up in the verses and climbing down in the choruses?

3 Do a short vocal warm-up as described in Lesson 1 and by listening to TRACK 7 on the CD, where there are gaps for the children to repeat what is being sung.

4 Split the class into their three groups and practise the words of the song.

5 Now practise singing the song all together over TRACK 1.

6 Listen to TRACK 4 on the CD, which is the pulse of the song. Get the children to clap with the pulse and sing through a chorus of the song over the top.

7 Now get the children to sing the words of the song over the pulse again (use TRACK 4). This time, get them to clap the rhythm of the words rather than the pulse as they sing (that is, a clap for each syllable: 'Watch those car-rots grow'). Once the rhythm is established, stop the singing and have the children just clap the rhythm over the pulse. Point out how the pulse stays the same, but the rhythm changes.

8 Listen to TRACK 5 on the CD. This is a simple percussion part to accompany the song. Have the class clap along to this rhythm.

9 Now split the class into three (it will be easier to stick to the same three groups as established in the previous lesson). Have Group A clap the pulse whilst Group B claps the new rhythm and Group C claps the rhythm of the chorus words. This can get complicated, so start with Group A and then add Group B. Once these rhythms are firmly established, add Group C with the rhythm of the words for the chorus. This may be very hard! Tell the children that it is OK if they make mistakes – it will get easier.

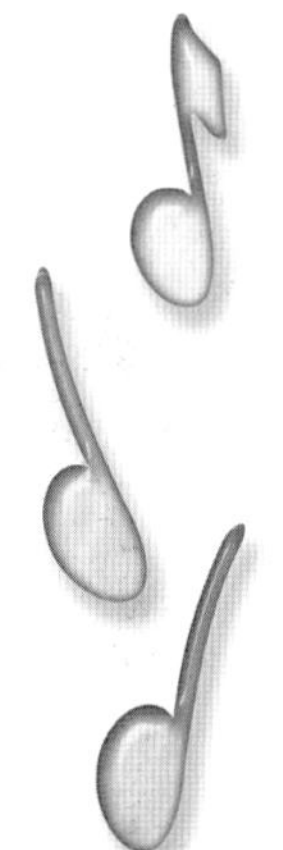

Adding percussion

10 Keep the class in these three groups and give out percussion from the trolley. You could try giving all the shakers to the pulse group, all the woodblocks to the rhythm group and tambourines to the 'words' rhythm group, but any mixed percussion will work. Start Group A off with the pulse and, once established, add Group B with the rhythm, then Group C with the 'words rhythm'.

11 Now practise the song over TRACK 1 whilst playing both the rhythms and the pulse on percussion on the chorus sections only. This may be easier said than done! The children will probably find it too difficult to remember the words as well; so just let them concentrate on playing the percussion this time through. (Note: It may help to stand the three groups quite far apart so they don't get too easily drawn in by each others' cross-rhythms. It would definitely help the 'words rhythm' group to sing the words of the chorus while they play.)

12 When you feel the children are ready, have them sing and play along to TRACK 2 (the backing track).

Chill out time!

Have the children sit down at their desks. Each child should lay their head on their arms with eyes closed, breathing slowly through their nose. Ask them to imagine the journey of the carrot from planting it as a tiny seed in the soil, with the sun beating down and the rain falling on the green shoots that can be seen starting to poke out through the soil. Describe the bit we can't see – the bit that's growing in secret under the ground – its orange body starting off thin, pale and scrawny and gradually fattening up into a big, juicy, bright orange carrot. Ask the children to imagine the carrot being dug up and washed and think about what their adult at home would do with it next. Grate it? Boil it? Make carrot soup? Have it raw? Have it chopped up? Feed it to their rabbit? Throw it away? Ask them to put up their hands to share what they think.

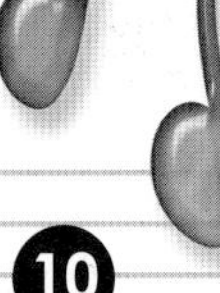

Lesson 3 The rap

Note: You will need the instrument trolley for this lesson.

Music objective

Writing their own rap for the song.

Learning activity

- Creating their own rap over a pulse (QCA units 4:1–4 and 4:7).
- Recapping the song (QCA units 1:1, 1:4 and 1:5).

QCA learning objectives

Unit 1 Ongoing skills

'This unit highlights the musical skills that require regular practice and ongoing development throughout the key stage.'
'Singing songs with control and using the voice expressively.'
Children should learn:

- Section 1 – to use different voices and find their singing voice.
- Section 4 – to control pulse and rhythm.
- Section 5 – to control pitch.

Unit 4 Feel the pulse – Exploring pulse and rhythm

'This unit develops children's ability to recognise the difference between pulse and rhythm and to perform with a sense of pulse.'
'What is pulse?'

- Section 1 – Children should learn what is meant by pulse or steady beat.

'Exploration'
Children should learn:

- Section 2 – how to control a pulse.
- Section 3 – what is meant by rhythm.
- Section 4 – how to combine pulse and rhythm.

'Bringing it all together: Can we use pulse and rhythm to make accompaniments?'

- Section 7 – Children should learn how to use pulse and rhythm to create an accompaniment for a chant or song.

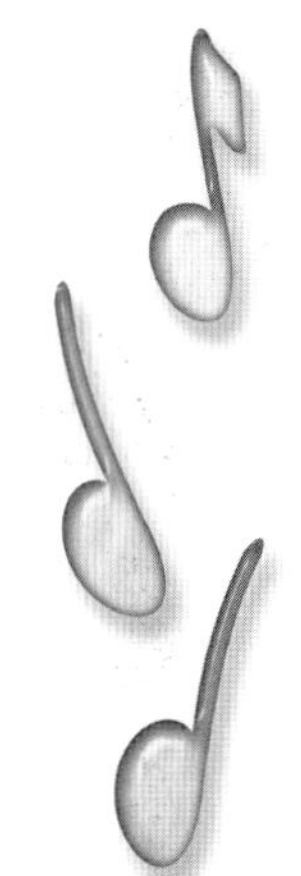

Scottish attainment targets

Using materials, techniques, skills and media (voice)

- Levels C/D – Sing confidently in unison producing a good clear vocal tone with awareness of dynamics, phrasing and expression.

Expressing feelings, ideas, thought and solutions

- Level C – Create sound pictures which convey mood and atmosphere, displaying imagination.
- Level D – Invent music [rap] which incorporates simple melodic and rhythmic features and shows imagination and the ability to select appropriate sound sources.

Healthy food

Lesson 3 The rap

1 Play TRACK 1 on the CD ('The Carrot Song') to remind the children of the song.

2 Do a short vocal warm-up as described in Lesson 1 and by listening and singing along to TRACK 6 on the CD.

3 Split the class into the same three groups as the previous lesson and sing the song, without the percussion. Have the groups sing a verse each, with everybody joining in on the chorus.

4 Listen to TRACK 3 on the CD to hear the rap bridge: 'scoop, scoop, scooby doo, scooby doo wah'. Next the children are going to write their rap, which fits in the middle section of the song after the chorus: 'Gonna dig my carrots up, Gonna dig my carrots up, Gonna dig my carrots up, Dig my carrots up from the ground'. There's a gap the length of a verse for the children's rap. There are a few different ways you can approach the rap so choose whatever you feel suits your children the best: to start with, get the children to come up with names of all the vegetables they can think of and write these down on the whiteboard.

a) You could divide the vegetables into three categories:

- Root vegetables, which grow in the ground (potatoes, parsnips, turnips, etc.)
- Leaves (lettuce, cabbage, etc.)
- Flowers/florets (broccoli, cauliflower, etc.) and vegetable 'fruits' (cucumber, peas, pumpkin, courgette, squash, etc.)

b) You could get the children to suggest different ways to eat the vegetables: for example, pumpkin pie, cauliflower cheese, mashed potatoes, mushy peas and tomato sauce.

c) You could get the children to describe their favourite foods, then divide the foods into 'healthy', 'unhealthy' and 'not-too-bad's.

Whichever option you choose, you will end up with a list of vegetables, food or meals. Write all these down on the whiteboard. These can be just words, phrases or short sentences.

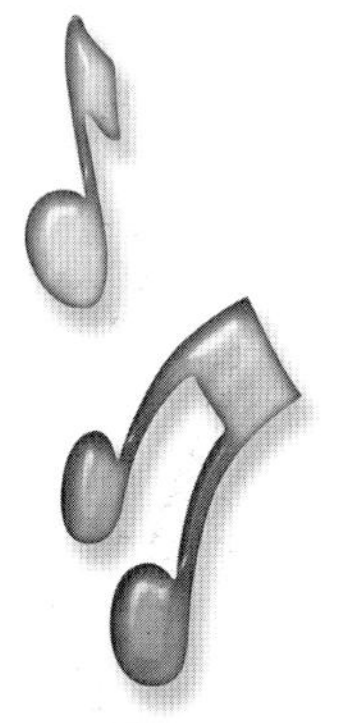

Lesson 3 The rap

5 Pick out as a team what you definitely want to include and circle or star these on the board. Try to craft this, with the children's help, into a rap. Speak the words over TRACK 4, the pulse, or get the children to clap the pulse and see what works over it. Arrange them in a fitting order.

6 Practise your rap. (Clapping along with the pulse will help you to rap in time.)

7 Now practise the whole song through from start to finish, using TRACK 2 (the backing track).

Chill out time!

Have the children sit down at their desks. Each child should lay their head on their arms with eyes closed, breathing slowly through their nose. Ask them to go through the whole song and rap in their heads, without saying anything, and see if they can hear the pulse and the rhythm as well. This is using their 'thinking voice' – i.e., they are hearing the song in their heads without singing it, like reading a book without speaking the words. This is a good way to help them to remember the song.

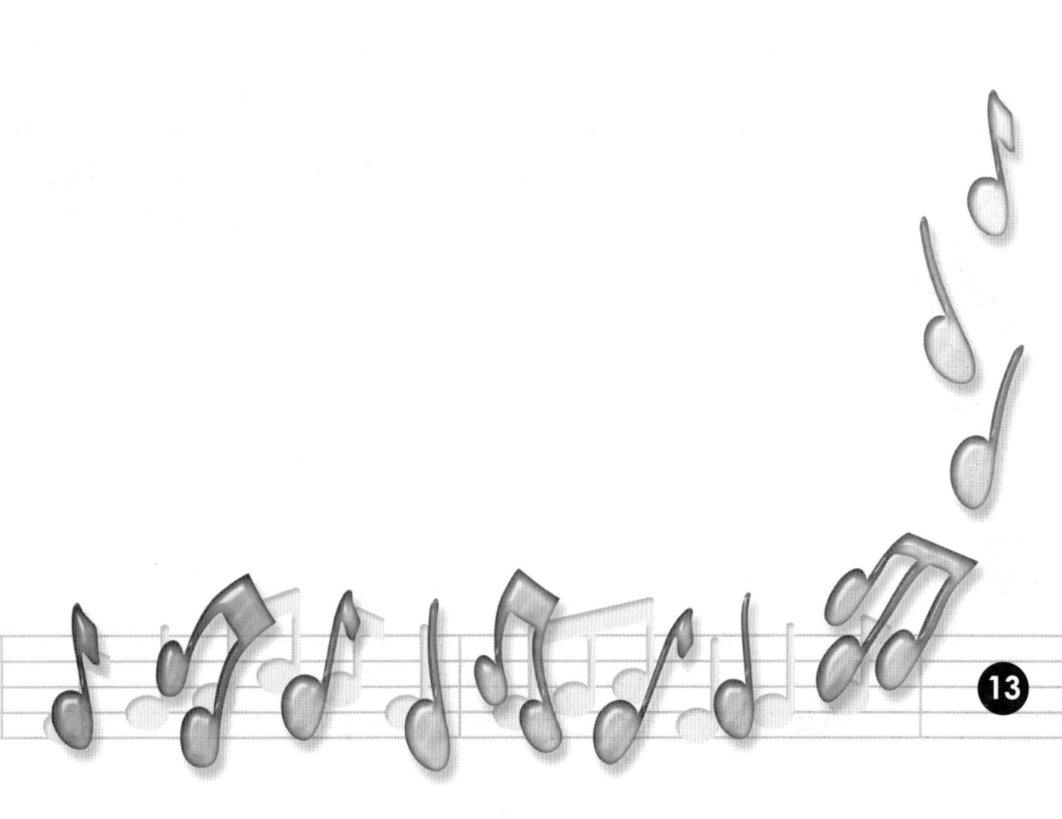

Moods and feelings

Note – You will be using the instrument trolley for this lesson.

Music objective

Identifying different sorts of weather with different pieces of music; improvising musical moods; recapping the song.

Learning activity

- Listening to three contrasting pieces of music and identifying which moods they portray(QCA unit 3:3).
- Composing music with the aim of portraying different sorts of weather (QCA units 2:3 and 2:6).

QCA learning objectives

Unit 2 Sounds interesting – Exploring sounds

'This unit develops children's ability to identify different sounds and to change and use sounds expressively in response to a stimulus.'
'How can we make and use sounds expressively?'
Children should learn:

- Section 3 – to focus their listening.
- Section 6 – to explore expressive use of sounds.

Unit 3 The long and the short of it – Exploring duration

'This unit develops children's ability to discriminate between longer and shorter sounds, and to use them to create interesting sequences of sound.'
'How can we use instruments to make long and short sounds?'

- Section 3 – Children should learn that music is made up of long and short sounds.

Scottish attainment targets

Using materials, techniques, skills and media (voice/ investigating: exploring sound)

- Level C – Experiment with different combinations and qualities of sound to represent contrasting moods and effects.
- Level D – Experiment and explore melodic, harmonic and rhythmic patterns.
- Level D – Sing together confidently in harmony and unison demonstrating awareness of dynamics, phrasing and expression.

Evaluating and appreciating

- Level D – Discuss the effect of the use of particular instruments on the mood and character of music; give and accept constructive criticisms of performing and inventing.

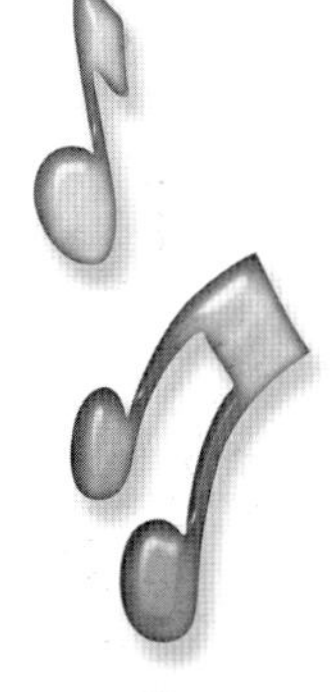
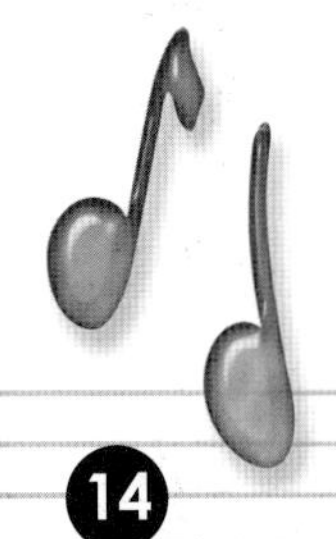
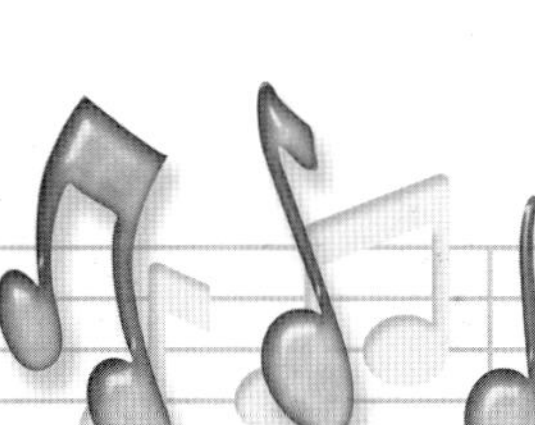

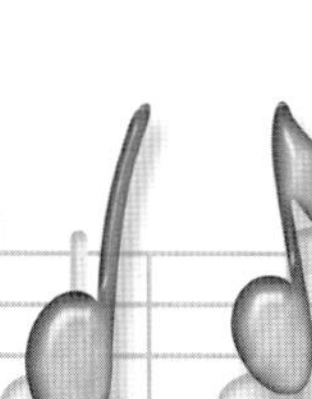

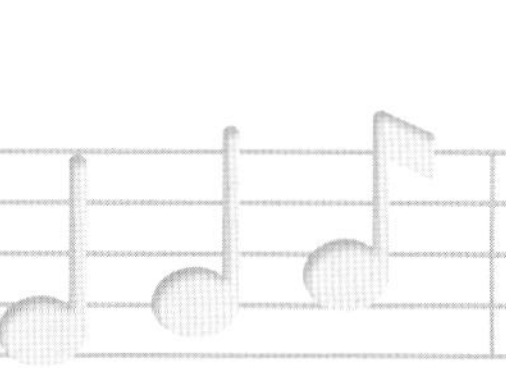

Healthy food

Lesson 4 Moods and feelings

1 To begin with, demonstrate to the children the various sorts of sounds that can be made with instruments on the percussion trolley. Show how some instruments make a short sound (for example, the woodblock), some make a long sound (for example, the chime bar – play one note and let it ring), and some instruments can make a long or a short sound (for example, the maracas – give them a quick flick and then a sustained shake to show the difference). Hand out the percussion and get the children to demonstrate short or long sounds.

2 To demonstrate the variety of speed, play a drum with even beats spaced out slowly (for example one beat per second) to demonstrate slowness. Then use the same drum to play, for example, three beats per second to demonstrate quickness. Get the children to do the same thing.

3 Next work on changes in volume. Ask the children to play all their instruments loudly, then softly. Use a signal to indicate you want them to go louder or softer. See if they can follow your signals.

4 Tell the children to put their instruments down, as they will be listening to three different pieces of music. One is describing rain, one wind, and the other thunder and lightning. Challenge them to see if they can tell which is which. Now listen to TRACKS 8, 9 and 10.

5 Ask the children why the pieces of music sound different: what instruments made it sound rainy/windy/thundery? Was the music played slowly or quickly? Did it use long or short notes? What instruments were used? Split the class into three groups and assign one of the weather conditions described earlier to each group.

6 Get each group to create a short piece of music describing their weather using their voices, and tuned and un-tuned instruments. These should last for only a minute. For example:

- Rain: Children could: say 'Pitter patter'; use rain sticks; use fingertips on a tambourine. Children could tap their palms of their left hand with the middle fingers on their right. (If this is done by lots of children randomly at different times without a pulse, it sounds very much like rain!). All should be played softly and slowly without a change in speed or volume.
- Wind: Children could play tambourines and shakers starting moderately, then gradually building in both speed and volume reaching a sustained climax. They could use their voices too, making whooshy wind noises.

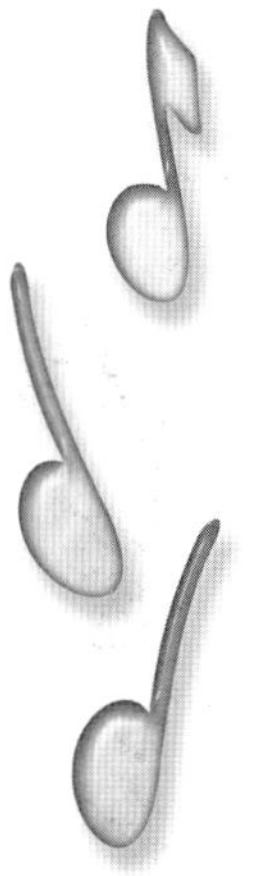

Moods and feelings

- Thunder and lightning: use a cardboard sheet (wobbling the sheet will make a thunder sound). The children could also make sudden loud noises such as a series of bangs from a loud drum with a stick, a loud clash of cymbals, and so on.

The children should perform these to the rest of the class in turns.

7 Create a composition together of a storm. They should stay in their three separate groups for this. Explain how a storm starts gently with rain and then builds through a crescendo (gets louder), sustains, then gradually dies down, leaving just the gentle rain, then silence again.

- Demonstrate what signals you will give to indicate an increase in the volume and then the decrease as the storm dies down (palms up for an increase, down for a decrease). Then show what signal you will use for an increase in frequency/speed of sound (perhaps making fast circular motions with a hand to speed up, and slow downwards motions for slowing down).
- Start gently with the rain group and then add the wind. Have the wind and rain groups increase in volume and frequency, then bring in the thunder and lightning group. After a short while, have the volume and frequency gradually decrease, with the groups dropping out in reverse order, leaving just the gentle rain decreasing to silence at the end.
- Comment and praise appropriately, sharing what you felt worked and why – give the children the opportunity to do the same.

8 After you've put the percussion away, listen to TRACK 6 on the CD for a gentle vocal warm-up, making sure you exaggerate the words.

9 Listen to TRACK 1 on the CD to remind you of the song. Practise the words of your rap too. Now split into the three verse groups and sing and rap along to TRACKS 1 and 2. Just use hands to clap the percussion parts on the choruses.

Chill out time!

Have the children sit down at their desks. Each child should lay their head on their arms with eyes closed, breathing slowly through their nose. Ask them to think of themselves sat outside in their garden or a nearby park, and to think of all the different sorts of weather that happen there and how it would feel, sound and look to them (e.g. the smell of wet leaves after rain, the scrunch of walking on the snow, the dazzling sunshine warming them). At the end, ask them to put up their hands to share what they think.

Lesson 5 Singing techniques

Music objective

Improving vocal quality; learning the rap section of the song.

Learning activity

- Full vocal warm-up (QCA unit 1:1)

QCA learning objectives

Unit 1 Ongoing skills

'This unit highlights the musical skills that require regular practice and ongoing development throughout the key stage.'
'Singing songs with control and using the voice expressively.'

- Section 1 – Children should learn to use different voices and find their singing voice.

Scottish attainment targets

Using materials, techniques, skills and media (voice)

- Levels C/D – Sing confidently in unison producing a good clear vocal tone with awareness of dynamics, phrasing and expression.
- Levels D/E – Sing together confidently, in unison and straightforward harmony, producing good vocal tone.

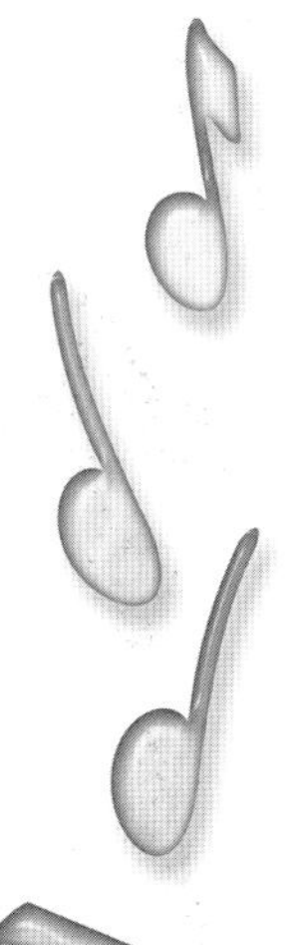

Singing techniques

1 Begin the lesson with a vocal warm-up. Have the children form a large circle.

- Ask the children to make sure they are standing in 'neutral' – with unfolded arms and legs shoulder-width apart. Ask them to imagine that their head is attached to a piece of string from above, which is pulling their head and shoulders up straight.
- Take deep breaths in and do loud exaggerated yawns going from a high to a low noise. Ask the children if they can feel the note go from high to low in their body as well. Encourage them to see how high or low they can go.
- Ask them to bend their arms at the elbows then to join their hands to form a circle with their arms. They should stretch their arms out, then up, relaxing the chest area. Next encourage them to imitate the Tarzan call, beating on their chest as they do it.

2 Play the vocal warm-up on TRACK 7, which begins with a vowel exercise emphasising 'Oh', 'Ah' and 'Eee' and continues with a tongue-twister. Follow the exercises, listening to the voice and singing with the children in the gap that is left for them. Exaggerate the consonants in the song. With the whole group, sing the tongue-twister slowly at first, then getting faster and trying to sing it as fast as the voice on the CD. Show the children how to use the consonants to express the notes.

Lesson 5 Singing techniques

3 Play TRACK 1 and sing through the song.

4 Then play TRACK 3, sing along to the bridge then run through the rap part.

Chill out time!

Have the children sit down at their desks. Each child should lay their head on their arms with eyes closed, breathing slowly through their nose. Ask the children to think back and see if they can remember what they had for lunch. Next, ask them to think about their favourite food. Then ask them to imagine they are going to have a special party and to think about what *healthy* party food they could serve. Finally, have the children sit up, open their eyes, and share their ideas around the class.

The performance

Note – You will be using the percussion trolley for this lesson.

Music objective

Developing the ability to take part in a class performance with confidence, expression and control.

Learning activity

- ◆ Performing together (QCA units 1:1, 1:7 and 2:1).
- ◆ Playing percussion parts (QCA unit 4:1 and 4:7).
- ◆ Doing a vocal warm-up (QCA unit 1:1).

QCA learning objectives

Unit 1 Ongoing skills

'This unit highlights the musical skills that require regular practice and ongoing development throughout the key stage.'
'Singing songs with control and using the voice expressively.'

- ◆ Section 1 – Children should learn to use different voices and find their singing voice.

'Listening, memory and movement'

- ◆ Section 7 – Children should learn to listen carefully and develop their aural memory.

Unit 2 Sounds interesting – Exploring sounds

'What sounds can we hear?'

- ◆ Section 1 – Children should learn to recognise different sound sources.

Unit 4 Feel the pulse – Exploring pulse and rhythm

'This unit develops children's ability to recognise the difference between pulse and rhythm and to perform with a sense of pulse.'
'What is pulse?'

- ◆ Section 1 – Children should learn what is meant by pulse or steady beat.

'Bringing it all together: Can we use pulse and rhythm to make accompaniments?'

- ◆ Section 7 – Children should learn how to use pulse and rhythm to create an accompaniment for a chant or song.

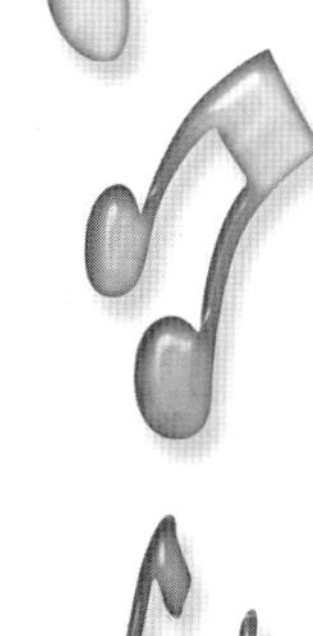

Scottish attainment targets

Using materials, techniques, skills and media (voice/instruments)

- ◆ Levels C–E – Work co-operatively and with confidence to show a respect for others when presenting and communicating with others through the music medium.

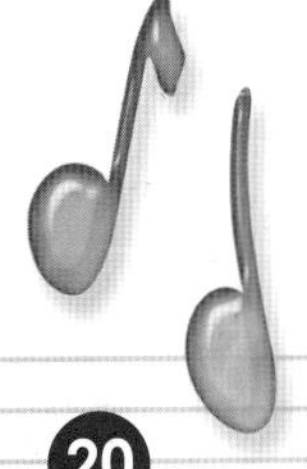

Lesson 6 The performance

1 This performance can be limited to the classroom. It can be later performed at a school assembly or included in a school play. You will need to use TRACK 2 (the backing track) for the performance.

2 Take the children through a vocal warm-up, as in Lesson 1.

- Ask the children to stand in a circle and make sure they are standing in 'neutral' – with un-folded arms and legs shoulder-width apart. Ask them to imagine that their head is attached to a piece of string from above, which is pulling their head and shoulders up straight.
- Take deep breaths in and do loud exaggerated yawns going from a high to a low noise. Ask the children if they can feel the note go from high to low in their body as well. Encourage them to see how high or how low they can go.
- Get the children to shout 'Hey!' as loud as they can after the count of three (just a short sound, not a long one!) then get them to shout 'Ho!' even louder after three (no screeching!). Try all the vowels (Hee, Hoo, Hah, Hi, and so on). Point out how loud the children are. Often children can bellow really loudly across the playground, but have voices like mice when it comes to singing. They have now found their loud voices and can and should sing loudly from now on. (Note: It's always more difficult to get children to sing louder than softer. Once you've got them to sing loud it is far easier to bring their volume down than the other way around.)
- Listen and follow TRACK 6 on the CD. The CD guides you through some exercises, in the form of 'call and answer': something is sung on the CD, then there is a gap for you to copy this and sing it back. These exercises will help children to learn about pitch. Stress the 'b' of 'banana' to help sound out the notes.

3 Practise the rap part first, using TRACK 4 on the CD.

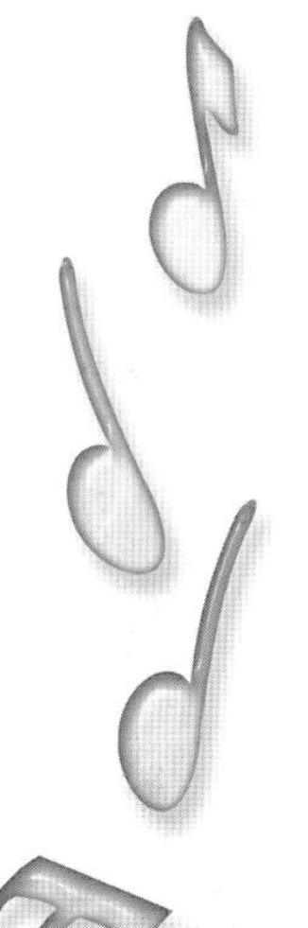

The performance

4 Get all percussion instruments ready and run through the percussion parts, playing TRACK 5 if necessary.

5 Arrange the children into their performing positions and using TRACK 2, rehearse the song.

6 Remind the children about the performance decisions you have made. For example, you could try allowing the last chorus to get louder and louder, ending with a long held note on 'toes'. Or perhaps you have some movements to go along with the song.

7 Children often do their best rendition the first time through, so if you are going to get the children to perform in front of others, try not to let them sing it all the way through, just refresh sections beforehand.

For fun, let half the class perform to the other half and then swap over, or boys to girls then girls to boys. The half listening are allowed to pull faces and try to 'put off' the performers but they must not make a sound. This leads to stifled laughter and a great deal of fun. Explain to the children the reason for this is so they may get use to performing in front of people without being 'put off'. It can lead to a strengthening in concentration.

8 Finally, have the children all stand up and perform the song together.

Chill out time!

Play some soft music in the background and have the children lie relaxed on the floor, stretched out with their eyes closed. Ask them to think about relaxing up from the ankles, legs, body, arms, neck to the head. After a period of relaxation and reflection, ask the children to sit up and volunteer to share with the rest of the class what part of the music lessons they liked the best and which they disliked.

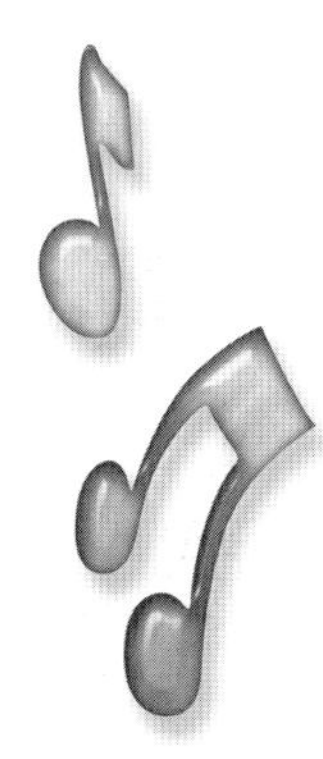

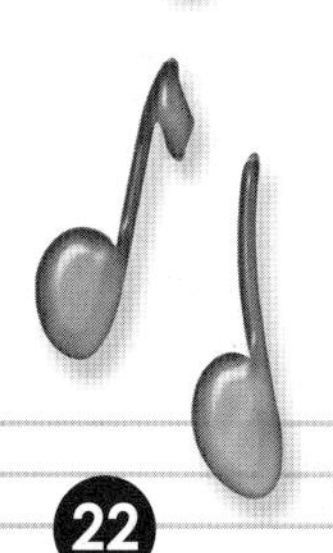

The Carrot Song

GOOD LUCK WITH YOUR PERFORMANCE!
(Note: This performance can take place in the classroom, in front of the whole school at assembly, or as part of a school play. Wherever you perform it, make sure you all have fun doing it!)

Verse 1
Plant that seed in the ground
Sunshine and water help it to grow
Then the green shoots start to show.

Chorus 1
Watch those carrots grow
Watch those carrots grow
Watch those carrots grow
Down, down, deep in the ground.

Verse 2
Put them in a soup or put them in a stew
Cooked or raw – it's up to you
Scrape them, grate them, chop them up.

Chorus 2
Gonna dig my carrots up
Gonna dig my carrots up
Gonna dig my carrots up
Dig my carrots up from the ground.

Rap bridge
Scoop, scoop, scooby doo, scooby doo wah
Scoop, scoop, scooby doo, scooby doo wah
Scoop, scoop, scooby doo, scooby doo wah
Scoop, scoop, scooby doo, scooby doo wah

Your rap

Chorus 3
Gonna eat my carrots up
Gonna eat my carrots up
Gonna eat my carrots up
Yum, yum they taste really scrum!

Verse 3
Vitamins A, C and E
I know they are good for me
Make me strong and help me to grow.

Chorus 4
Watch my muscles grow
Watch my muscles grow
Watch my muscles grow
Grow, grow from my head to my toes.

Lesson 1 The song: 'Neesa'

Music objective

Introducing the song, a two-part Native American round, and learning to sing it.

Learning activity

- Doing a vocal warm-up (QCA units 1:1, 1:4 and 1:5).
- Learning basic techniques for building confidence in using the singing voice (QCA unit 1:1).
- Following and learning a new song in two parts (QCA units 1:1, 1:4 and 1:5).

QCA learning objectives

Unit 1 Ongoing skills

'This unit highlights the musical skills that require regular practice and ongoing development throughout the key stage.'
'Singing songs with control and using the voice expressively.'
Children should learn:

- Section 1 – to use different voices and find their singing voice.
- Section 4 – to control pulse and rhythm.
- Section 5 – to control pitch.

Scottish attainment targets

Using materials, techniques, skills and media (voice)

- Levels C/D – Sing confidently in unison and harmony with some awareness of dynamics, phrasing and expression.
- Level E – Sing in unison and harmony with an appropriate vocal technique and a sense of interpretation.

Lesson 1 The song: 'Neesa'

1 Vocal warm-up – we sing using our whole body, not just the vocal chords! We therefore need to make sure we are relaxed and open physically in order to release the voice. Take ten minutes to do the warm-up.

- Ask the children to stand in a circle and make sure they are standing in 'neutral' – with un-folded arms and legs shoulder-width apart. Ask them to imagine that their head is attached to a piece of string from above, which is pulling their head and shoulders up straight.
- Take deep breaths in and do loud exaggerated yawns going from a high to a low noise. Ask the children if they can feel the note go from high to low in their body as well. Encourage them to see how high or how low they can go.
- Have the children pretend they are chewing an extremely large toffee, making exaggerated chewing shapes with the mouth (this releases the jaw). Then ask them to open the mouth as wide as possible. Explain that when we sing, we need to let the sound out and so need to exaggerate our words, opening our mouths wider than in speech.

2 Listen and follow TRACK 19 on the CD. The CD guides the pupils through some exercises in call-and-answer form. Something is sung on the CD, then there is a gap for you and the children to copy this and sing it back. When the singer on the CD asks 'Can you sing up high?' the children should sing back 'I can sing up high' to the same tune. When she sings softly, or low and loud, the children should respond with their answer in the same way it is sung to them.

3 Tell the children to listen really carefully to the next song because you will be asking them questions about it. Play TRACK 11 on the CD – 'Neesa'.

4 Discuss the song. Ask the children to guess what language the song might be in and where the song might be from. Is the song old or new? Is the song gentle or lively? Does it make you feel calm or excited?

5 Explain that the song is from the Native American (Indian) tradition, from the Seneca tribe. It is very old and has been sung for many hundreds of years. Have a brief discussion with the children about who the Native Americans are and their place in history.

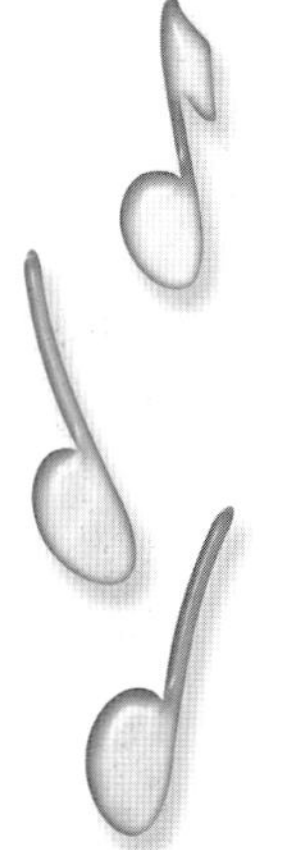

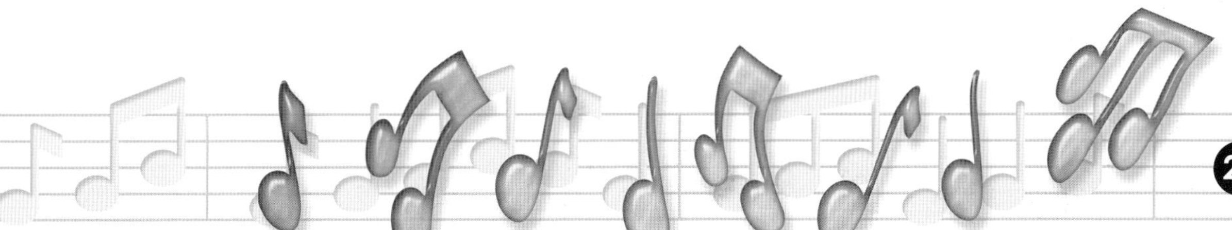

Lesson 1 The song: 'Neesa'

6 It is a good idea to give an explanation of the words at this point. Explain that the word 'Neesa' means 'The first full moon in winter'. Practise with the whole class saying the word together. The word 'Gai-wey-oh' loosely means 'It is a beautiful part of nature/creation'. Discuss this with the class. Practise saying the word together.

7 Listen to TRACK 11 on the CD again. Practise the words 'Neesa, Neesa, Neesa, Neesa, Neesa, Neesa, Neesa, Neesa, Neesa, Gaiweo, Gaiweo'. How many times is 'Neesa' sung? What about 'Gaiweo'? Tell the children to remember to hold the long 'o' at the end of 'Gaiweo'.

8 Now sing along to TRACK 11.

9 Listen to TRACK 12 on the CD. This is the same song but sung in a two-part round. Explain to the children that they start the song at different times. This creates some nice harmonies, but is quite difficult to do. Explain how it can put you off singing your part if someone else is singing something different, so it is necessary to concentrate really hard.

10 Sing along to TRACK 12 with the children singing along from the start. Did they manage to follow the first voice and not the second?

11 Now sing along to TRACK 12 again, this time with the children singing along from the second start point in the repeated refrain (after three 'Neesa's).

12 Split the class into two equal groups. Try the round without the help of the CD. Explain that the second group should start after the first group have sung 'Neesa' three times and that they have to try very hard not to sing along with what the first group are doing!

13 Try swapping the groups round so that the group who went second has a chance to start this time.

Chill out time!

Have the children sit down at their desks. Each child should lay their head on their arms with eyes closed, breathing slowly through their nose. Ask them to listen to the sounds around them in silence. After one minute, ask them to put up their hands and say what they've heard.

Lesson 2 Adding percussion

Note – You will be using the percussion trolley for this lesson.

Music objective

Recapping the song and learning percussion parts.

Learning activity

- Doing a warm-up (QCA units 1:1 and 1:4).
- Learning simple percussion parts (QCA units 4:1 and 4:7).

QCA learning objectives

Unit 1 Ongoing skills

'This unit highlights the musical skills that require regular practice and ongoing development throughout the key stage.'

'Singing songs with control and using the voice expressively.'

Children should learn:

- Section 1 – to use different voices and find their singing voice.
- Section 4 – to control pulse and rhythm.

Unit 4 Feel the pulse – Exploring pulse and rhythm

'This unit develops children's ability to recognise the difference between pulse and rhythm and to perform with a sense of pulse.'

'What is pulse?'

- Section 1 – Children should learn what is meant by pulse or steady beat.

'Bringing it all together: Can we use pulse and rhythm to make accompaniments?'

- Section 7 – Children should learn how to use pulse and rhythm to create an accompaniment for a chant or song.

Scottish attainment targets

Using materials, techniques, skills and media (instruments)

- Level B – Play simple rhythmic parts showing some control over speed and volume with the ability to be led.
- Level C – Display two-handed co-ordination in playing straightforward melodies and rhythms.
- Level D – Play confidently sustaining more challenging melodies and rhythms.
- Level E – Demonstrate increased musicianship and technical abilities whilst playing a widening range of instruments, such as keyboard, xylophone and so on.

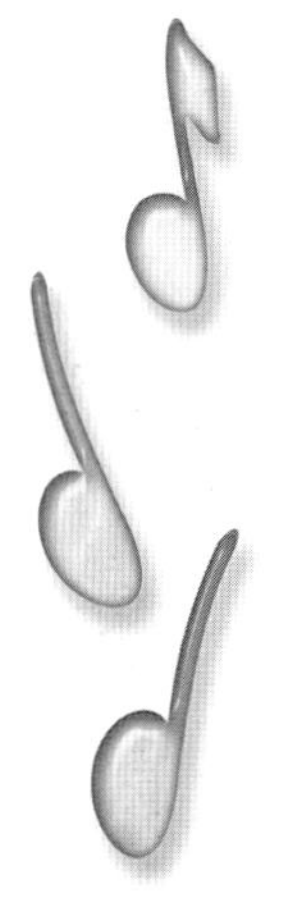

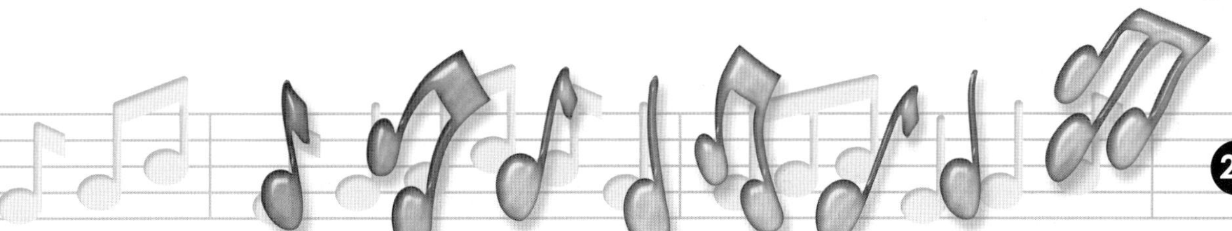

World music – Neesa

Lesson 2 Adding percussion

1 Play TRACKS 11 and 12 on the CD to remind the children of the song and the way the round works.

2 Ask if the children can remember what the song is about and where it is from.

3 Do a short vocal warm-up as described in Lesson 1 and by listening to TRACK 19 on the CD.

4 Practise the words: 'Neesa, Neesa, Neesa, Neesa, Neesa, Neesa, Neesa, Neesa, Neesa, Gaiweo, Gaiweo'. How many times is 'Neesa' sung? What about 'Gaiweo'? Remind the children to hold the long 'o' at the end of 'Gaiweo'.

5 Sing the song all together in one part.

6 Now try splitting the class into two and starting at different times, doing the song as a round. Swap the groups over.

7 Listen to TRACK 16 on the CD, which is the pulse of the song. Have the children clap the pulse and sing the song in unison. Point out how the pulse stays the same throughout the song. You can count '1, 2, 3, 4. 1, 2, 3, 4...' along with the pulse and put emphasis on the 1 as you clap. This first beat of the bar should always be louder than the others. Try (without using TRACK 16) to speed up the pulse a bit and get the children to sing over that. Get faster and faster over a few times and show how the speed of the pulse means that the speed of the song increases too.

8 Now, get the children to sing the words of the song over the pulse again (use TRACK 16). This time, ask them to clap the rhythm of the words as they do so instead of the pulse. Once the rhythm is established, stop the singing and have the children just clap the rhythm over the pulse. Can they hear how the pulse stays the same, but the rhythm changes?

9 Listen to TRACK 17 on the CD. This is a simple percussion part to accompany the song. Get the class to clap along to this rhythm.

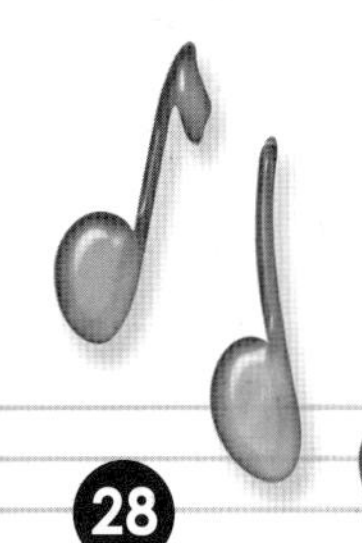
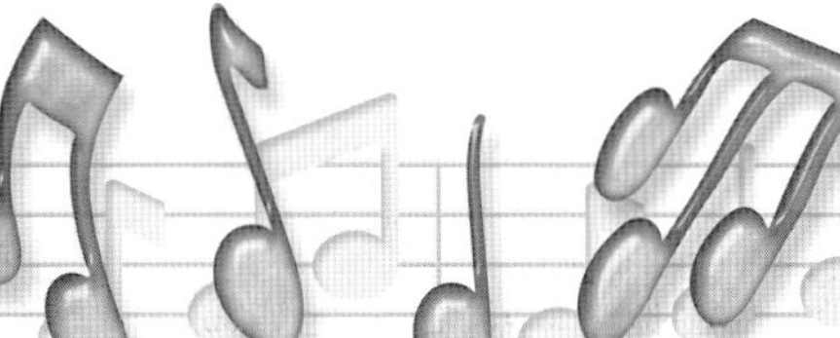

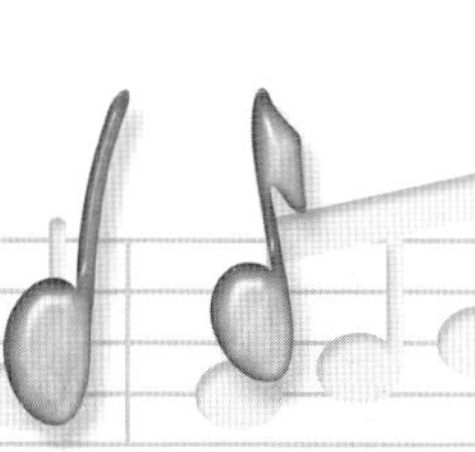
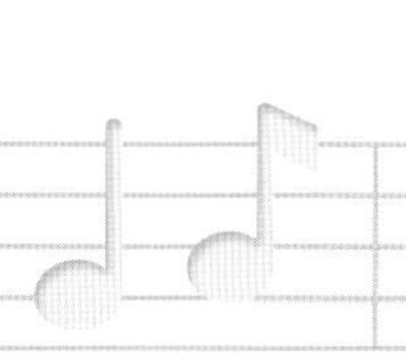

Lesson 2 Adding percussion

10 Split the class into two. One group should clap the pulse whilst the other claps the rhythm. Once you have successfully done this, swap the groups round.

11 Keep the class in two groups (A and B). Group A should play the pulse and Group B should play the rhythm. These groups are also for the two parts of the round.

12 Give out percussion from the trolley. (You could try giving all the woodblocks to the pulse group and all the shakers and tambourines to the rhythm group, but any mixed percussion will work.) Start Group A off with the pulse and, once established, add Group B with the rhythm. Now practise singing through 'Neesa' in unison whilst playing both the rhythm and the pulse on percussion.

13 Sing and play along with TRACK 12 on the CD, singing the round, then adding the percussion break.

Chill out time!

Have the children sit down at their desks. Each child should lay their head on their arms with eyes closed, breathing slowly through their nose. Ask them to go through the song in their heads without saying anything. Remind them the song is about the beauty of the full moon in winter. Ask them to imagine a full moon hanging in the sky at night. After a minute or so, ask them to sit up and initiate a discussion about the moon: is the moon always round? What other shapes can the moon be? Do they know why? Ask them to put up their hands with their replies. Do give them an appropriate brief explanation of the 28-day cycle of the moon from new (invisible to crescent shape) to half-moon to full moon and back again.

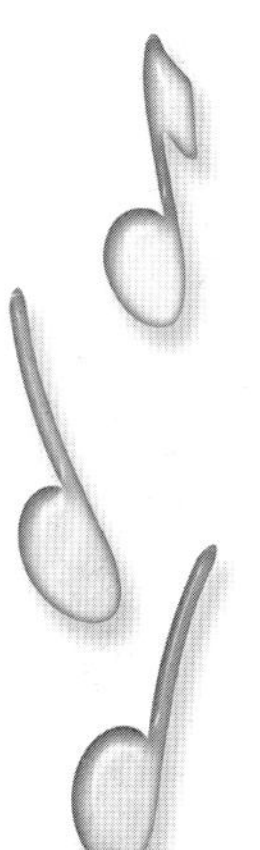

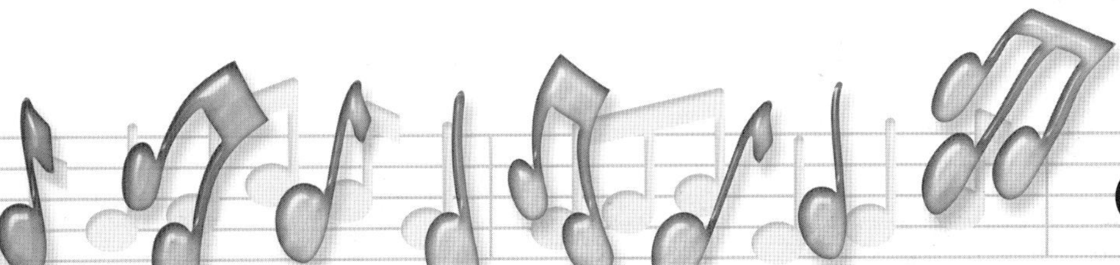

Lesson 3 Moods and feelings

Note – You will be using the instrument trolley for this lesson.

Music objective

Identifying different moods with different pieces of music; improvising musical moods; recapping the song.

Learning activity

- Experimenting with the sounds of percussion instruments (QCA unit 3:2).
- Remembering the song (QCA Unit 1:1).

QCA learning objectives

Unit 1 Ongoing skills

'This unit highlights the musical skills that require regular practice and ongoing development throughout the key stage.'

'Singing songs with control and using the voice expressively.'

- Section 1 – Children should learn to use different voices and find their singing voice.

Unit 3 The long and the short of it – Exploring duration

'This unit develops children's ability to discriminate between longer and shorter sounds, and to use them to create interesting sequences of sound.'

'How can we use instruments to make long and short sounds?'

- Section 2 – Children should learn how to make sounds of different duration on pitched and unpitched percussion instruments.

Scottish attainment targets

Using materials, techniques, skills and media (voice)

- Levels C/D – Sing confidently in unison producing a good clear vocal tone and with some awareness of dynamics, phrasing and expression.
- Levels D/E – Sing with a good sense of interpretation, sustaining enjoyment of singing during the transitionary period when the voice changes in range.

Expressing feelings, ideas, thought and solutions

- Level C – Create sound pictures which convey mood and atmosphere, displaying imagination.
- Level D – Invent music which incorporates simple melodic and rhythmic features and shows imagination and the ability to select appropriate sound sources.

Evaluating and appreciating

- Level D – Discuss the effect of the use of particular instruments on the mood and character of music.
- Level E – Recognise simple concepts such as repetition, sequence and pattern.

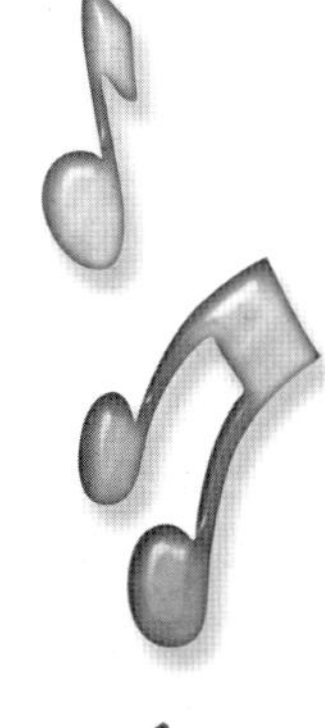
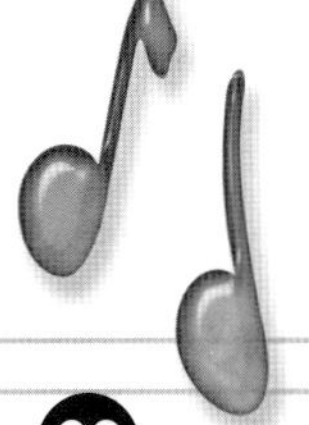
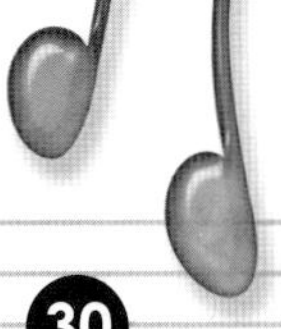

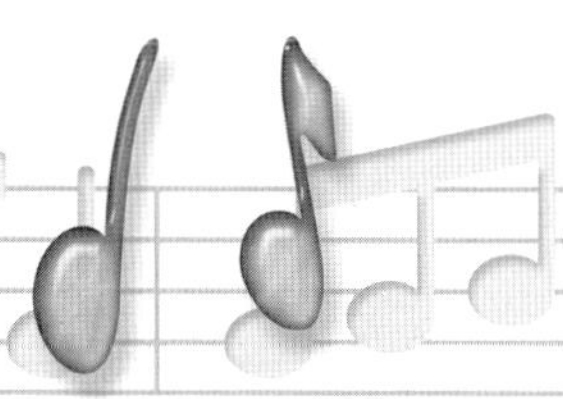

Lesson 3 Moods and feelings

1 To begin with, demonstrate to the children the various sorts of sounds that can be made with instruments on the percussion trolley. Show how some instruments make a short sound (for example, the woodblock), some make a long sound (for example, the chime bar – play one note and let it ring, and some instruments can make a long or a short sound (for example the maracas – give them a quick flick and then a sustained shake to show the difference).

2 Hand out the percussion and get the children to demonstrate short or long sounds.

3 To demonstrate the variety of speed, play a drum with even beats spaced out slowly (for example, one beat per second) to demonstrate slowness. Then use the same drum to play, for example, three beats per second to demonstrate quickness. Get the children to do the same thing.

4 Next work on changes in volume. Ask the children to play all their instruments loudly, then softly. Use a signal to indicate you want them to go louder or softer – for example, raising palms to indicate louder and bringing hands down for softer. See if they can follow your signals.

5 Tell the children they will be listening to two different pieces of music – one of the full moon on a still night and the other of a storm at night in a forest – and that they will have to try to tell which is which. Now listen to TRACKS 13 and 14.

6 Ask the children the following questions: Why did the pieces of music sound different? What instruments made it sound calm? Was it played slowly or quickly? Were long or short notes used? What instruments made it sound stormy? Was it played quickly or slowly?

7 Listen to TRACK 15. This is the sound of animals of the night, such as owls and foxes, coming out. Do they sound big, bold and brave, or timid and small? Perhaps a mixture of both? How could you tell which were the little, scared animals?

8 Split the class into three groups and assign one of the moods/scenes described earlier to each group.

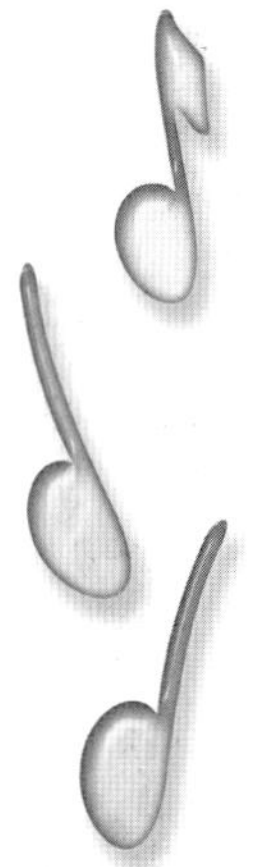

Lesson 3 Moods and feelings

9 Pick instruments from the trolley and ask each group to create a short piece of music describing their mood using tuned and un-tuned instruments. These should last for only a minute. For example:

- Moon on a calm night – chime bars played very slowly; gentle rustling of the leaves indicated by a shaker. All played softly and slowly without a change in speed or volume.
- Storm at night in a forest – tambourines, shakers and cymbals, starting moderately, then gradually building in both speed and volume reaching a sustained climax. The children could also use their voices, for example, making whooshy wind noises.
- Animals of the night coming out – tentative and slow woodblocks gently tapping, shakers gently shaking, building in volume and speed a bit, then coming down, then up again, eventually attaining a sustained volume and speed. The children could also use their voices: for example, imitating owls hooting.

The children should perform these to the rest of the class in turns. Comment and praise appropriately, sharing what you felt worked and why. Give the children the opportunity to do the same.

10 Now listen to TRACK 19 on the CD for a gentle vocal warm-up.

11 Sing along to TRACK 12 to remind the children of the song.

12 Split the children into two groups and sing the song as a round.

Chill out time!

Have the children sit down at their desks. Each child should lay their head on their arms with eyes closed, breathing slowly through their nose. Ask them to imagine they are out at night in the woods sitting quietly; it's winter and they can see the full moon hanging in the sky. Suggest that they think about what animals might be around in the woods at night, what noises they might hear, and what else they could hear. After one minute, ask them to put up their hands and say what they've imagined. (Make a note of what they say, as you will need it for the next lesson.)

Lesson 4 The rap

Note – You will be using the instrument trolley for this lesson.

Music objective

Learning the rap section and writing their own rap for the rap section.

Learning activity

- Creating their own rap and soundscape over a pulse (QCA unit 4:1).
- Recapping the song (QCA units 1:1 and 1:4).

QCA learning objectives

Unit 1 Ongoing skills

'This unit highlights the musical skills that require regular practice and ongoing development throughout the key stage.'
'Singing songs with control and using the voice expressively.'
Children should learn:

- Section 1 – to use different voices and find their singing voice.
- Section 4 – to control pulse and rhythm.

Unit 4 Feel the pulse – Exploring pulse and rhythm

'This unit develops children's ability to recognise the difference between pulse and rhythm and to perform with a sense of pulse.'
'What is pulse?'

- Section 1 – Children should learn what is meant by pulse or steady beat.

Scottish attainment targets

Using materials, techniques, skills and media (investigating: exploring sound)

- Level D – Experiment and explore melodic, harmonic and rhythmic patterns with a view to using combinations of sound in inventions.

Using materials, techniques, skills and media (voice)

- Levels D/E – Sing with a good sense of interpretation, sustaining enjoyment of singing during the transitionary period when the voice changes in range.

Expressing feelings, ideas, thought and solutions (creating and designing)

- Levels D/E – Invent music which incorporates simple melodic, harmonic and rhythmic features, and shows imagination and some awareness of structure and contrasts; lead others in playing inventions.

Evaluating and appreciating

- Level D – Discuss the effect of particular instruments on the mood and character of music.
- Level E – Recognise simple concepts such as repetition, sequence and pattern.

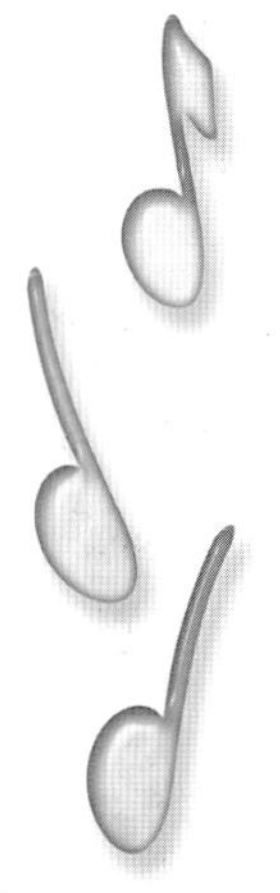

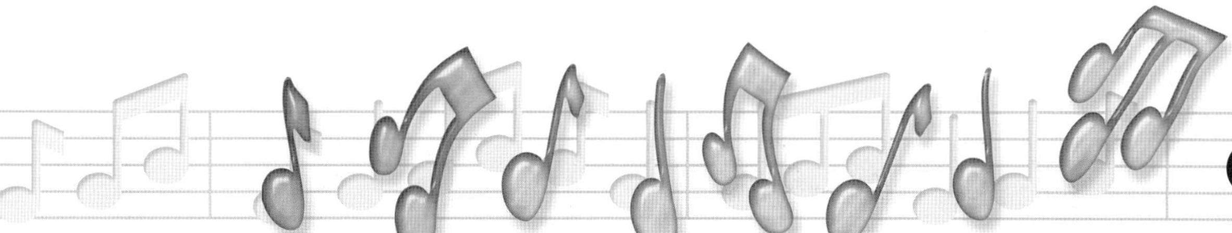

Lesson 4 The rap

1 Play TRACKS 11 and 12 on the CD – 'Neesa' – to remind the children of the song and the way the round works.

2 Do a short vocal warm-up as described in Lesson 1 and by listening to TRACK 19 on the CD.

3 Sing the song all together in unison.

4 Now try splitting the class into two and starting at different times, singing the song as a round.

5 Listen to TRACK 18 – the rap.

6 Ask the children to learn the words of the rap a line at a time by call and answer: for example, you say the first line and the children repeat until they remember it. Then do the same with the second line. Do the two lines together and get them to repeat it.

7 Ask the children to rap along with TRACK 18.

8 Discussion time. Use the ideas children came up with from the previous lesson's chill-out session. To remind them, get them to imagine again that they are out at night in the woods sitting quietly. It's winter and they can see the full moon hanging in the sky. Ask them prompting questions: What animals might be around in the woods at night? So what noises might they hear? Would they hear anything else? What might they see? Are there any other words to describe the moon? Write all their ideas down on the whiteboard. These can be just words, phrases or short sentences.

9 Pick out as a team what you definitely want to include in your rap and circle or star these on the board.

10 Clap the pulse of the song. Use the pulse to try to fit in some of the phrases you have chosen on the theme. Try clapping the rhythm of your words over the pulse. You may have to adapt them – lengthen them, shorten them and so on – to fit. Arrange them in a suitable order. (Note – the rap doesn't have to rhyme. It could be a series of descriptive words, a short list of animals and so on.)

Lesson 4 The rap

11 Listen to TRACK 12, which includes a gap for the rap. After they hear the last line of the existing rap ('Full circle made of gold'), the children should come in with their new rap, keeping to the pulse. The gap is the same length as the existing rap – four lines long. (Note: this is only for purposes of the backing track to learn the song. Once they are confident that they know it, they won't need the backing track. This means the rap can be as long or as short as you like.)

12 Practise the rap. (Ask the children to clap along with the pulse to help them to rap in time.)

13 Now guide the children in adding some descriptive sounds to their rap. Ask them to think about what percussion would help describe their words, reminding them they could also use their voices (for example, making whooshy wind noise or imitating owls hooting). Get the children to come up with ideas, reminding them of what they did in the previous lesson. Choose a few children to add some descriptive sounds to the rap and practise putting this in.

14 Have the class practise the whole song through from start to finish – they can use TRACK 12 to help them if they need it. (Note: If their rap is longer than the rap gap, they won't be able to use the backing track.)

Chill out time!

Have the children sit down at their desks. Each child should lay their head on their arms with eyes closed, breathing slowly through their nose. Ask them to go through the whole song and rap in their heads, without saying anything. Can they imagine the two parts of the round? Can they hear the pulse and the rhythm as well? This is using their 'thinking voice'. They are hearing the song in their heads without singing it, like reading a book without speaking the words. This is a good way to help them to remember the song.

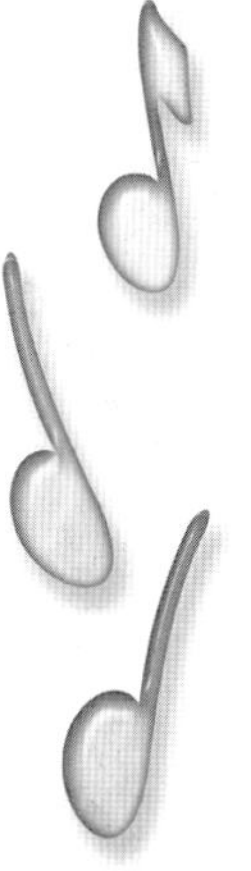

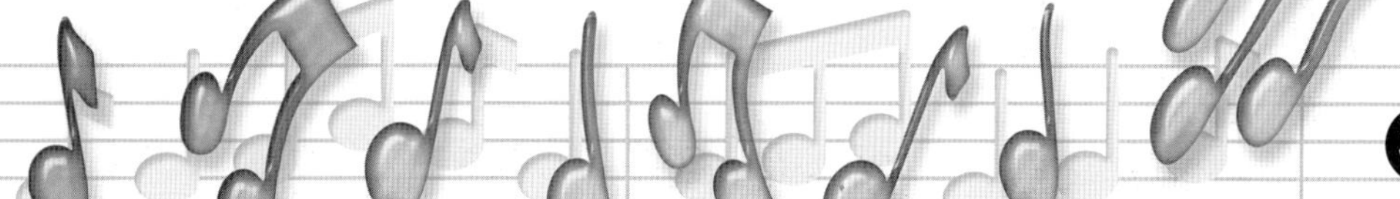

World music – Neesa

Lesson 5 Pitch and movement

Note – You will be using the percussion trolley for this lesson.

Music objective

To develop a greater vocal control and greater range; learning about pitch; movement and music.

Learning activity

- Singing games involving pitching higher and lower, and moving to the pitch (QCA units 5:1–3).
- Recapping the song (QCA units 1:1, 1:4 and 4:1).

QCA learning objectives

Unit 1 Ongoing skills

'This unit highlights the musical skills that require regular practice and ongoing development throughout the key stage.'
'Singing songs with control and using the voice expressively.'
Children should learn:

- Section 1 – to use different voices and find their singing voice.
- Section 4 – to control pulse and rhythm.

Unit 4 Feel the pulse – Exploring pulse and rhythm

'This unit develops children's ability to recognise the difference between pulse and rhythm and to perform with a sense of pulse.'
'What is pulse?'

- Section 1 – Children should learn what is meant by pulse or steady beat.

Unit 5 Taking off – Exploring pitch

'This unit develops children's ability to discriminate between higher and lower sounds and to create simple melodic patterns.'
'What is pitch?'

- Section 1 – Children should learn what is meant by pitch.

'How can we make sounds higher/lower?'
Children should learn:

- Section 2 – how to control the pitch of the voice.
- Section 3 – to respond to changes in pitch.

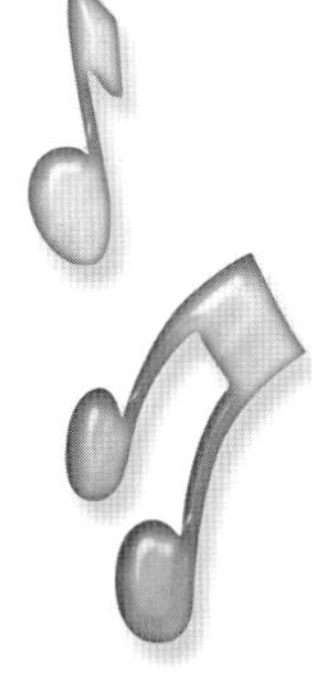

Scottish attainment targets

Using materials, techniques, skills and media (voice)

- Levels D/E – Sing together confidently in harmony and unison, with a sense of interpretation.
- Using materials, techniques, skills and media (investigating: exploring sound)
- Levels D/E – Explore melodic, harmonic and rhythmic patterns and contrasts, electronic and acoustic effects and simple harmony.

Lesson 5 Pitch and movement

1 Guide the children through a warm-up, as in Lesson 1.

2 Listen to TRACK 20 on the CD and have the children copy the sounds being made – there is a gap for them to do this. Encourage them to listen to the pitch of the owl sound as it goes higher. As they repeat the sound, ask them to lift their arms up by their sides to follow the pitch of the sound – the higher the sound, the higher their arms should go.

3 Listen to TRACK 21 on the CD and once again have the children copy the sounds being made. Encourage them this time to listen to the pitch of the cat sound as it goes lower. As they repeat this sound, tell them to lift their arms out to the front and down like a cat clawing. Follow the pitch of the sound – the lower the sound, the lower their arms should go.

4 Listen to TRACK 22 on the CD and, again, ask the children to copy the sounds being made. Listen with them to the pitch of the hen sound: it's very rhythmic, with the same tone four times, and then goes up in pitch at the end. As they repeat the sound, they should nod their head in time with the rhythm and lift it up at the end.

5 Divide the class into three groups: O, C and H. Assign a different animal (owl, cat or hen) to each group, then call out the names of the groups in turn. When you call out 'Cat!', for example, the cat group should all respond with one 'miaaaw' as they did earlier, doing the movement as well – each group should respond with their own sound and movement.

6 Repeat with each group several times, then ask them all in turn. Try to make things trickier by asking the same group twice, varying the speed of your commands and so on.

7 You can now call out 'higher' or 'lower' several times with each particular group, pushing them to their vocal limits. Do they go faster when they go higher or slower as they go lower? (They may do.) Point this out and say that's not what you asked for!

8 Next try calling out two groups at once, then all three groups (what a cacophony!). Try 'higher' and 'lower' with everyone in.

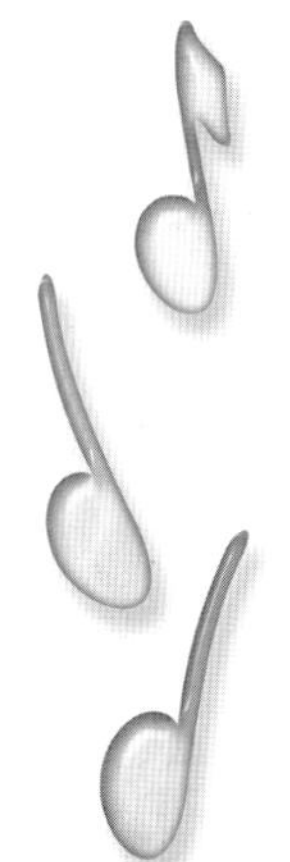

Lesson 5 Pitch and movement

9 Sing slowly through the melody of 'Neesa' in unison. As you do, get the children to move their hands up and down to follow the pitch of the melody: the higher the note, the higher the hand goes. If two consecutive notes are the same, the hand should stay at the same level (for example, 'Gaiweo' is all on the same note). Tell the children not to be too fussy about it; just to get the general shape of the tune.

10 Song practice. Prepare the class to run through the entire song, including the rap and the percussion break. Get all the percussion ready and hand it out to the children. Divide the class into two groups, then recap the rhythm, the pulse and the rap section.

11 Sing, rap and play along to TRACK 12 on the CD. How did they do? Comment on their progress.

12 If the children are ready, try the song without TRACK 12 to help them (the start note is C).

Chill out time!

Have the children sit down at their desks. Each child should lay their head on their arms with eyes closed, breathing slowly through their nose. Ask them to think about a song or tune of their choice – it might be a nursery rhyme, a pop song or a TV theme tune. Give them a minute to choose one in silence. Then get them to hum the tune very quietly to themselves. Can they hear where the melody goes up and down? After a couple of minutes, choose one or two children to hum through their tune whilst doing hand movements up and down to indicate the pitch.

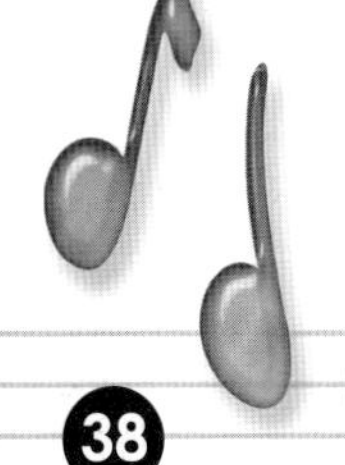

Lesson 6 The final rehearsal and performance

Note – You will be using the percussion trolley for this lesson.

Music objective

Practising performance skills and final polishing of the song.

Learning activity

- Full vocal warm-up (QCA unit 1:1).
- Practising the song (QCA units 1:1, 1:4, 1:5 and 4:1).
- Performing the song to each other (QCA units 1:3 and 1:6).
- Giving constructive feedback to each other (QCA unit 1:3).

QCA learning objectives

Unit 1 Ongoing skills

'This unit highlights the musical skills that require regular practice and ongoing development throughout the key stage.'
'Singing songs with control and using the voice expressively.'
Children should learn:

- Section 1 – to use different voices and find their singing voice.
- Section 3 – to sing with others.
- Section 4 – to control pulse and rhythm.
- Section 6 – to control the expressive elements, for example timbre, dynamics, tempo.

Unit 4 Feel the pulse – Exploring pulse and rhythm

'This unit develops children's ability to recognise the difference between pulse and rhythm and to perform with a sense of pulse.'
'What is pulse?'

- Section 1 – Children should learn what is meant by pulse or steady beat.

Scottish attainment targets

Using materials, techniques, skills and media (voice/instruments)

- Levels C–E – Work co-operatively in a group while music making or inventing, showing a respect for the opinions of others. When and where appropriate, present and perform music to the teacher, another group, the rest of the class, or a wider audience.

Evaluating and appreciating

- Levels D/E – Give and accept constructive and informed criticism of performing and inventing.

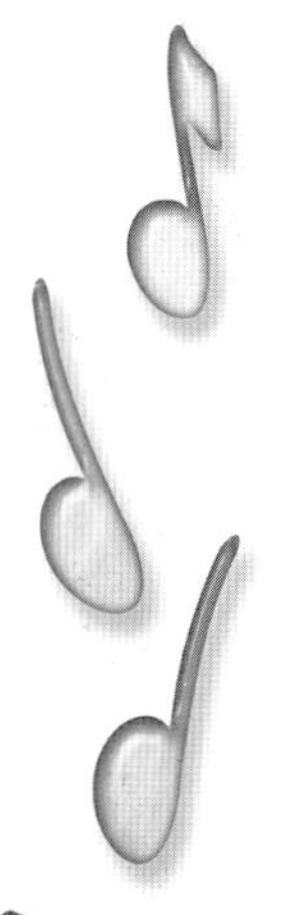

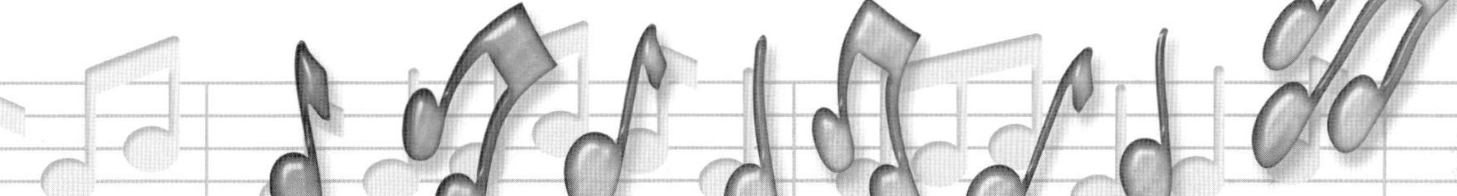

Lesson 6 The final rehearsal and performance

1 Do a vocal warm-up (as described in Lesson 1), then listen to TRACK 19 on the CD for the vocal warm-up.

2 Next, work on practising diction. Explain that we can't sing in the same way that we speak – we need to make our mouths into bigger shapes to let the sounds out and make the words clearer.

- The children should say 'pizza' slowly and in an exaggerated way, like 'Peeeeezaaaaaaaaah', making their mouths go as wide as possible on the 'eeeee' sound and as vertically big as possible on the 'aaaaah' sound. Now ask them to try saying 'Neesa' in the same way ('Neeeeeesaaaaaaah'!).
- Get the children to do an exaggerated 'Eye' sound in a similar manner, opening their mouths as wide as they can, then an 'Eh', then an 'Oh', in the same way.
- Put the three vowel sounds together – 'Eye, eh, oh' – and say them for the children to copy, call-and-answer style. Once they are doing it properly, then change it to 'Gaiweo' for them to copy back.
- Ask the children to speak through the words of the song as if they were talking through a window at somebody who couldn't hear them properly. They have to exaggerate the word shapes as if they were being lip-read. This is how they should sing the words of the song. It may feel odd, but it will sound right!

3 Talk through the order of the song with the class. Point out that it is a very complex arrangement: they sing 'Neesa' twice through, then the percussion break, rap, then their own rap, then 'Neesa' twice through to finish.

4 Hand out percussion instruments. Practise the song all the way through together without the backing track. Just concentrate on getting everything in the right order this time. (Remember the start note is C.)

5 Discuss together how the run-through went.

6 Now to bring some dynamics into the song. Try starting the first round of 'Neesa's at a 'normal' volume, with the second round a bit louder. After the rap sections, they should come in with a loud round of 'Neesa's with the final round being very soft. They may even want to add an even softer one at the end. Practise this until you and the children are happy with it. (Note: You can change these dynamics to whatever you're happy with.)

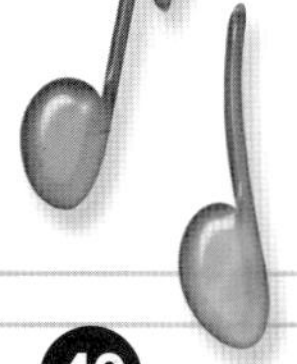

Lesson 6 The final rehearsal and performance

7 Next practise a performance. Split the class into two groups (A and B), having a mixture of call and answer people in both. Group A should now perform to Group B. Remind the children to look at the audience, stand up straight, smile and sing the words with good diction.

8 Group B should give feedback to Group A. Encourage them to think about what they have learnt and ask them to put their hands up if they have comments about the performance. Ask them to comment about specific areas, for example:

- Was the singing loud and soft in the right places?
- Did the children enunciate the words properly?
- Did the percussion bits go well?
- How could it be improved?
- What went well and sounded really good?
- Does everybody look happy when they are performing?

9 Now swap the groups over and repeat the process – have Group B perform to Group A and give feedback as before, then practise any individual bits that need addressing.

10 Lastly, have the whole class perform to the teacher, making sure that they are standing up straight, looking out to the 'audience' and singing loud (or soft) and clear. Note: Remember to praise the children on how well they've done and how much they've achieved.

Chill out time!

Have the children sit down at their desks. Each child should lay their head on their arms with eyes closed, breathing slowly through their nose. They should relax into their bodies and slow their breathing down. Get them to think back and remember the whole journey of learning the song and writing their rap. They should try to remember each lesson, what they have learned and how much of the song they've written themselves. Ask them if they feel proud of what they've done. Get them to sit and think for a minute about what they have achieved and their feelings. Finish by inviting them to put up their hands and share their responses.

Neesa (Traditional Native American Indian song)

Chorus

Neesa Neesa Neesa
Neesa Neesa Neesa
Neesa Neesa Neesa
Gaiweo Gaiweo

Neesa Neesa Neesa
Neesa Neesa Neesa
Neesa Neesa Neesa
Gaiweo Gaiweo

Neesa Neesa Neesa
Neesa Neesa Neesa
Neesa Neesa Neesa
Gaiweo Gaiweo

GOOD LUCK WITH YOUR PERFORMANCE!
(Note: This performance can take place in the classroom, in front of the whole school at assembly, or as part of a school play. Wherever you perform it, make sure you all have fun doing it!)

Rap

Full moon burning bright
Lighting up the sky at night
In the winter when it's cold
Full circle made of gold

Your rap

Chorus

Neesa Neesa Neesa
Neesa Neesa Neesa
Neesa Neesa Neesa
Gaiweo Gaiweo

Neesa Neesa Neesa
Neesa Neesa Neesa
Neesa Neesa Neesa
Gaiweo Gaiweo

Lesson 1 The song: 'Mammals and Me'

Music objective

Introducing the song and learning parts of it.

Learning activity

- Doing a vocal warm-up (QCA unit 1:1).
- Building on vocal techniques and building confidence in singing (QCA unit 1: 2).
- Following and learning the verses and choruses in the new song (QCA unit 1: 7) .
- What sounds can we hear? (QCA unit 2:1).

QCA learning objectives

Unit 1 Ongoing skills

'This unit highlights the musical skills that require regular practice and ongoing development throughout the key stage.'
'Singing songs with control and using the voice expressively.'
Children should learn:

- Section 1 – to use different voices and find their singing voice.
- Section 2 – to develop an awareness of phrase.

'Listening, memory and movement.'

- Section 7 – Children should learn to listen carefully and develop their aural memory.

Unit 2 Sounds interesting – Exploring sounds

'This unit develops children's ability to identify different sounds and to change and use sounds expressively in response to a stimulus.'
'What sounds can we hear?'

- Section 1 – Children should learn to recognise different sound sources.

Scottish attainment targets

Using materials, techniques, skills and media (voice)

- Level B – Control rhythm, speed and leaps in melody.
- Levels C/D – Sing confidently in unison and harmony demonstrating awareness of dynamics and expression.

Evaluating and appreciating

- Level C – Recognise the sounds of obvious groupings; demonstrate aural retention through playing phrases from familiar tunes by ear; and give opinions of own music making.

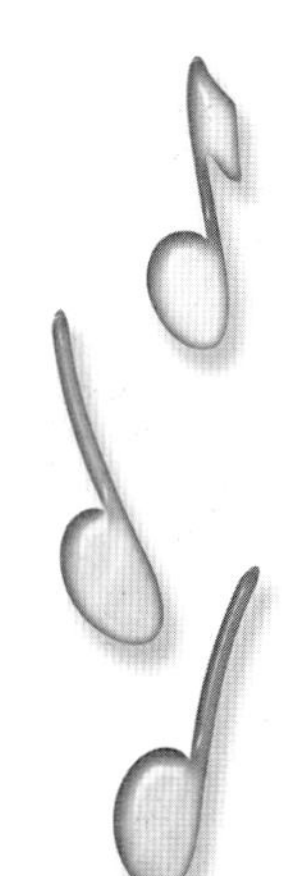

The song: 'Mammals and Me'

1 Play TRACK 23, 'Mammals and Me', on the CD.

2 Listen again and point out the arrangement: Chorus, Verse 1, Chorus, Verse 2, Chorus, Rap, Rap gap, Chorus, Verse 1 repeat. Listen for the animal noises at the end.

3 Vocal Warm-up – we sing using our whole body, not just the vocal chords! We therefore need to make sure we are relaxed and open physically in order to release the voice. Take ten minutes to do the warm-up.

- Ask the children to stand in a circle and make sure they are standing in 'neutral' – with un-folded arms and legs shoulder-width apart. Ask them to imagine that their head is attached to a piece of string from above, which is pulling their head and shoulders up straight.
- Loosen up the body in whatever way is preferred (for example, rotating the head in a circle, doing large circles clockwise and anti-clockwise with the arms from the shoulder, circles with the hips, circles with the feet and knees, then shaking the whole leg away).
- Take a deep breath into the lower abdomen to the count of three through the nose, then continue to breathe in for a further three counts, bringing the breath into the upper chest. Then breathe out slowly to a count of 20. This ensures diaphragmatic, rather than shallow, breaths. Ask the children to put one hand on their stomach and the other on their upper chest, so they can feel them both rising and falling as they breathe.)
- Repeat, now doing a 'Sss' sound on the out-breath.
- Repeat doing a hum on the out-breath.

4 Now sing along with TRACK 25 on the CD. Encourage the children to learn the chorus of 'Mammals and me'. Ask the children to sing the 'ee' sound on a smile – demonstrate to them and have them notice the change of tone with and without a smile.

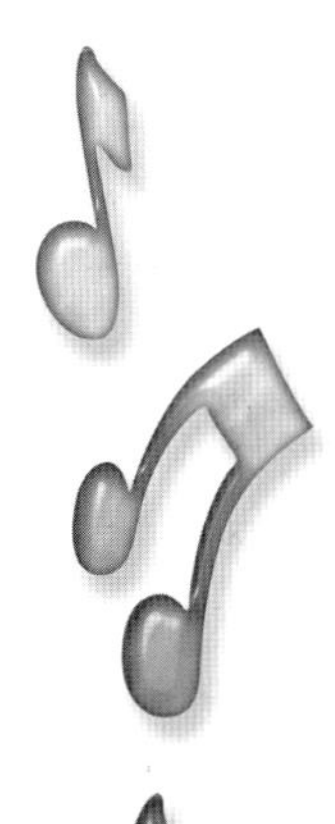
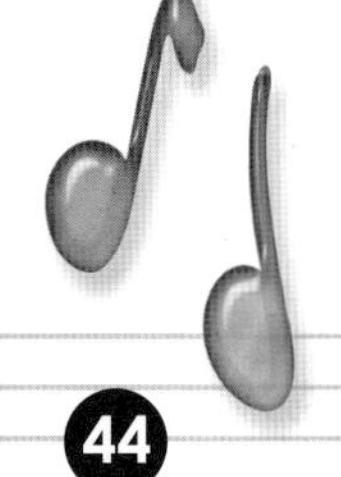

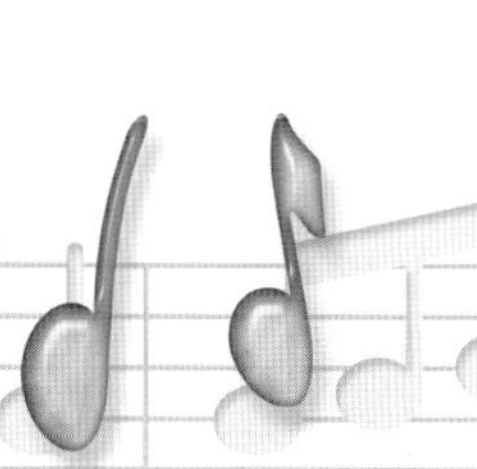

The song: 'Mammals and Me'

5 Next listen to TRACK 26 and learn verses 1 and 2.

6 Go back to TRACK 23 and sing the song again, this time adding some movements. Ask the children to copy you as you add some appropriate arm and leg movements – for example, walking on the spot for 'we live in the land', swimming arm movements for 'we live in the sea', waving hands for 'paw, fin or hand' and miming rocking a baby for 'have little babies'. Choose simple ideas that don't confuse the children – perhaps only using one or two. If there is room, let the children form a circle and hold hands then walk around slowly while singing the first half of the song.

7 Finally listen to the rap on TRACK 27 but don't worry about learning this today. The children could copy the idea of the whale by swimming with their arms, or mimic the monkey with arms dangling or a human being rubbing his chin.

Chill out time!

Have the children sit down at their desks. Each child should lay their head on their arms with eyes closed, breathing slowly through their nose. Tell them that they should sit in total silence and allow their mind to drift. Ask them to listen carefully, to think about sounds around them and to see how many different sounds they can hear.

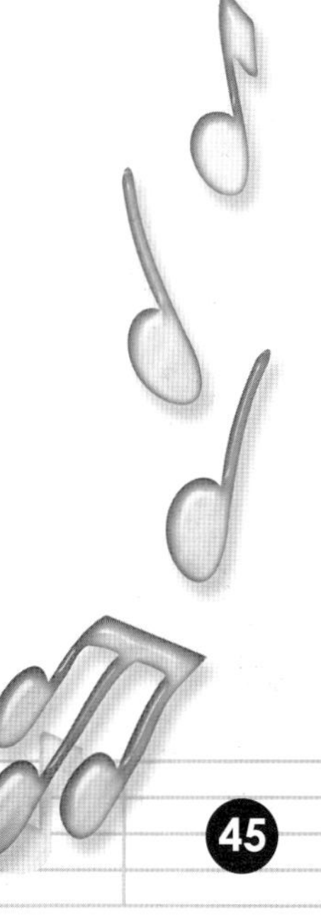

Mammals and me

Lesson 2 The rhythm

Music objective

Becoming aware of structure; confidently playing pulse and rhythm parts.

Learning activity

◆ Playing percussion (rhythm and pulse) (QCA units 4:1, 4:2 and 4:7).

◆ Remembering the chorus/verse and middle section of song (QCA unit 1:7).

◆ Recapping basic techniques for building confidence in singing (QCA unit 1:1).

QCA learning objectives

Unit 1 Ongoing skills

'This unit highlights the musical skills that require regular practice and ongoing development throughout the key stage.'

'Singing songs with control and using the voice expressively.'

◆ Section 1 – Children should learn to use different voices and find their singing voice.

'Listening, memory and movement.'

◆ Section 7 – Children should learn to listen carefully and develop their aural memory.

Unit 4 Feel the pulse – Exploring pulse and rhythm

'This unit develops children's ability to recognise the difference between pulse and rhythm and to perform with a sense of pulse.'

'What is pulse?'

◆ Section 1 – Children should learn what is meant by pulse or steady beat.

'Exploration'

◆ Section 2 – Children should learn how to control a pulse.

'Bringing it all together: Can we use pulse and rhythm to make accompaniments?'

◆ Section 7 – Children should learn how to use pulse and rhythm to create an accompaniment for a chant or song.

Scottish attainment targets

Using materials, techniques, skills and media (instruments)

◆ Levels B/C – Play simple rhythm parts showing some control over speed and volume.

◆ Level C – Display two-handed co-ordination in playing.

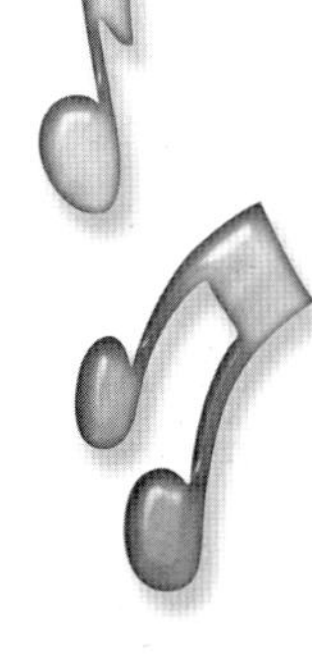

Lesson 2 The rhythm

1 Start with a vocal warm-up, as in Lesson 1:

- Ask the children to stand in a circle and make sure they are standing in 'neutral' – with un-folded arms and legs shoulder-width apart. Ask them to imagine that their head is attached to a piece of string from above, which is pulling their head and shoulders up straight.
- Loosen up the body in whatever way is preferred (for example, rotating the head in a circle, doing large circles clockwise and anti-clockwise with the arms from the shoulder, circles with the hips, circles with the feet and knees, then shaking the whole leg away).
- Take a deep breath into the lower abdomen to the count of three through the nose, then continue to breathe in for a further three counts, bringing the breath into the upper chest. Then breathe out slowly to a count of 20. This ensures diaphragmatic, rather than shallow, breaths. Ask the children to put one hand on their stomach and the other on their upper chest, so they can feel them both rising and falling as they breathe.)
- Repeat, now doing a 'Sss' sound on the out-breath.
- Repeat doing a hum on the out-breath.

2 Continue with another vocal warm-up: sirens. Ask pupils to place their hands on their heads, lightly, and imitate the sound of a fire engine or the sound of a police siren. As the sound gets higher, the mouth should get wider. They should feel the 'buzzing' sensation coming from the top of the head. Ask the children to let their 'siren' sound higher and higher.

3 Play TRACK 25 on the CD. As a class, sing along gently with the choruses.

4 Listen to TRACK 28, which plays the pulse. Clap along with the pulse and count 1, 2, 3 and 4. Point out to the children that this is a steady regular beat, giving us the tempo or speed of the music.

Mammals and me

Lesson 2

The rhythm

5 Listen to the rhythm on TRACK 29. It is different to the pulse and the beats are not evenly spaced as before. Encourage the children to hear how it fits in well with the pulse.

6 Hand out percussion instruments and ask the children to play along with TRACK 23 – those with tambourines on the pulse and those with wood blocks on the rhythm.

7 Play TRACK 29 for the children to listen to. They should play the rhythm. Do they notice how different this is to the pulse?

8 Play TRACK 23 again and tell the children to sing along with the song to refresh their memory. They shouldn't be afraid to sing gently at first with heart-felt expression. Remind the children to smile and make happy faces while they are singing.

9 Play TRACK 24 (the backing track) for the children and see if they can sing the song all by themselves. Prompt them if or when they get lost, and use a lot of arm and hand movements to signal the lyrics.

10 Have the children sing along with TRACK 23 again, but this time add the percussion at the given part of the arrangement.

Chill out time!

Have the children lie down on the floor and close their eyes, then relax in complete silence. After a minute, ask them to think about their favourite animal, what this animal eats and where it lives. Ask everyone to open their eyes and sit up, then lead the class in sharing their thoughts quietly.

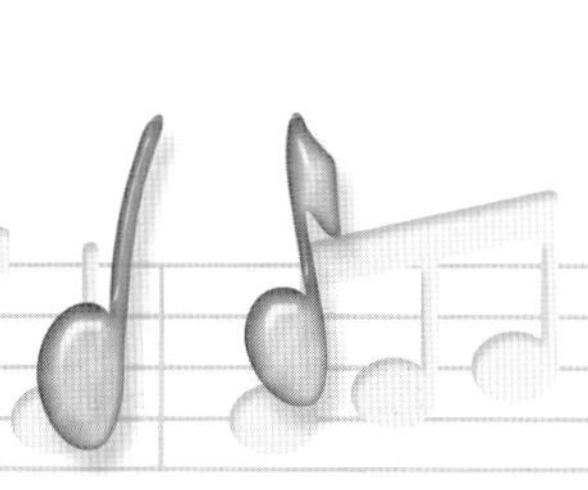
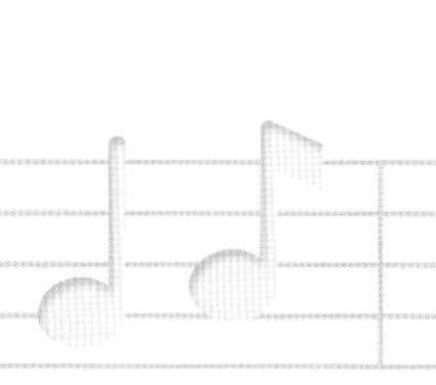

Lesson 3 Singing techniques

Music objective

Improve vocal quality; learn the rap section of the song.

Learning activity

- Full vocal warm-up and stretching voice further (QCA unit 1:1).
- Recapping verses and choruses (QCA unit 1:7).
- Learning rap section (QCA unit 1:8).

QCA learning objectives

Unit 1 Ongoing skills

'This unit highlights the musical skills that require regular practice and ongoing development throughout the key stage.'
'Singing songs with control and using the voice expressively.'

- Section 1 – Children should learn to use different voices and find their singing voice.

'Listening, memory and movement.'
Children should learn:

- Section 7 – to listen carefully and develop their aural memory.
- Section 8 – to develop physical response.

Scottish attainment targets

Using materials, techniques, skills and media (voice)

- Levels C/D – Sing confidently in unison producing a good clear vocal tone with awareness of dynamics, phrasing and expression.
- Levels D/E – Sing with a good sense of interpretation, sustaining enjoyment of singing during the transitionary period when the voice changes in range.

Expressing feelings, ideas, thought and solutions

- Level C – Create sound pictures which convey mood and atmosphere, displaying imagination.
- Level D – Invent music [rap] which incorporates simple melodic and rhythmic features and shows imagination and the ability to select appropriate sound sources.

Singing techniques

1 Start with a vocal warm-up, as in Lesson 1:

- Ask the children to stand in a circle and make sure they are standing in 'neutral' – with un-folded arms and legs shoulder-width apart. Ask them to imagine that their head is attached to a piece of string from above, which is pulling their head and shoulders up straight.
- Loosen up the body in whatever way is preferred (for example, rotating the head in a circle, doing large circles clockwise and anti-clockwise with the arms from the shoulder, circles with the hips, circles with the feet and knees, then shaking the whole leg away).
- Take a deep breath into the lower abdomen to the count of three through the nose, then continue to breathe in for a further three counts, bringing the breath into the upper chest. Then breathe out slowly to a count of 20. This ensures diaphragmatic, rather than shallow, breaths. Ask the children to put one hand on their stomach and the other on their upper chest, so they can feel them both rising and falling as they breathe.)
- Repeat, now doing a 'Sss' sound on the out-breath.
- Repeat doing a hum on the out-breath.

2 Continue with another vocal warm-up: sirens. Ask pupils to place their hands on their heads, lightly, and imitate the sound of a fire engine or the sound of a police siren. As the sound gets higher, the mouth should get wider. They should feel the 'buzzing' sensation coming from the top of the head. Ask the children to let their 'siren' sound higher and higher.

3 Listen to TRACK 30 on the CD. This is a more advanced vocal exercise, stretching the vocal range higher and lower, louder and softer. There is a gap for the children to copy this and sing it back.

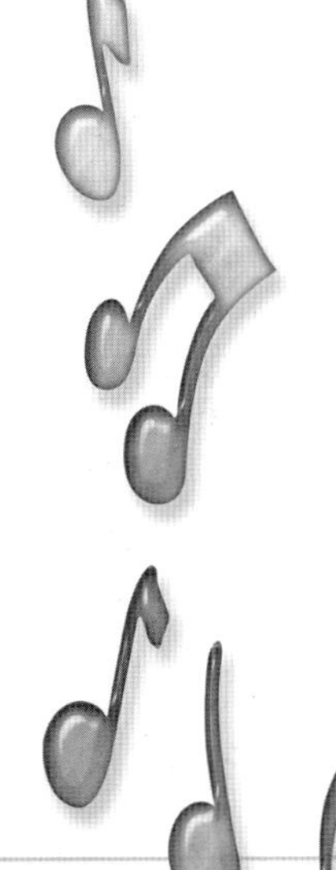

Lesson 3 Singing techniques

4 Follow the call-and-answer exercises on TRACK 31. Remember to take the sounds up and back in to the head and open mouths wide to get higher notes. Encourage the children to exaggerate the vowel shapes. Ask them to try smiling while they sing to see if it makes any difference.

5 Play TRACK 23 and ask the children to sing along. Ask if it is easier to sing after the advanced warm-up.

6 Play TRACK 27, which is the rap section. Help the children learn it by playing it through a number of times and encouraging them to join in. Ask them if they can remember the movements to go with the rapping.

7 Play TRACK 23 on the CD and have the children sing along. Ask them to think up some more animal noises that could be added on the end. Go round the group one by one, asking the children to share their animal sound with the rest of the class.

Chill out time!

Have the children sit down at their desks. Each child should lay their head on their arms with eyes closed, breathing slowly through their nose. Challenge them to keep silent for two minutes. Ask the children to think about nothing. If possible, play a tape of some different music to relax to. Music with 'high' string parts, as in Mozart, has a very calming effect on a group of children.

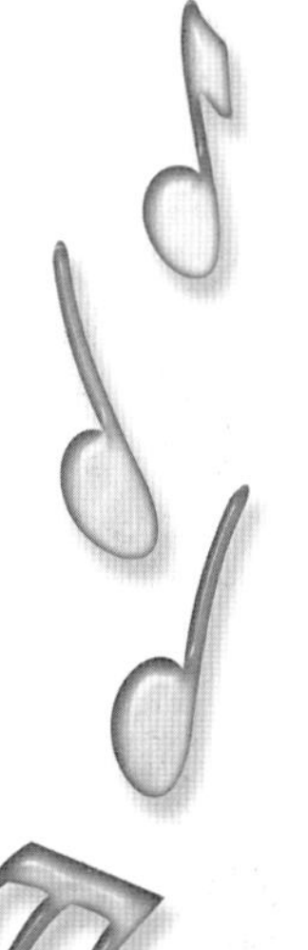

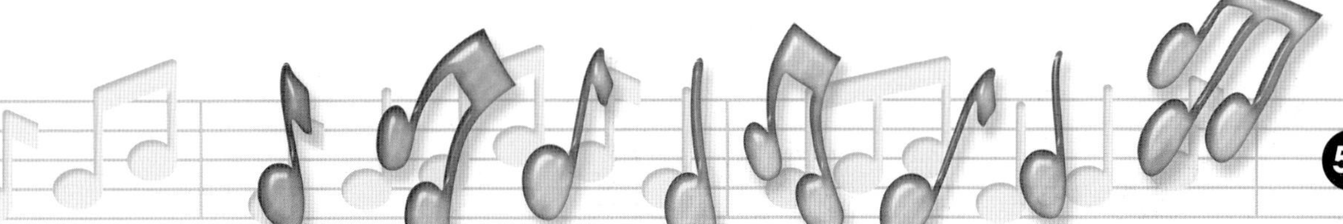

The rap

Note – You will be using the percussion trolley for this lesson.

Music objective

Learning the rap section in a song and writing their own section.

Learning activity

- Recapping verses, choruses and middle (QCA unit 1:1).
- Recapping rap section from the previous lesson (QCA unit 1:7).

QCA learning objectives

Unit 1 Ongoing skills

'This unit highlights the musical skills that require regular practice and ongoing development throughout the key stage.'
'Singing songs with control and using the voice expressively.'

- Section 1 – Children should learn to use different voices and find their singing voice.

'Listening, memory and movement.'
Children should learn:

- Section 7 – to listen carefully and develop their aural memory.

Scottish attainment targets

Using materials, techniques, skills and media (voice/investigating: exploring sound)

- Level D – Experiment and explore melodic, harmonic and rhythmic patterns.
- Level D – Sing together confidently in harmony and unison, demonstrating awareness of dynamics, phrasing and expression.

Evaluating and appreciating

- Level D – Discuss the effect of the use of particular instruments on the mood and character of music; give and accept constructive criticisms of performing and inventing.

Lesson 4 The rap

1 Tell the children that they are going to write a few lines about mammals.

2 Ask the children to list phrases to do with mammals that they can think of, or that they have heard already. For example: 'Mammals and me', 'Care for each other', 'Baby and mother', 'Sister and brother'. You can use the whiteboard as a 'rhyme board', allowing the children to freely call out rhyming words which you will scribble all over the board in roughly arranged groups of similar rhyming words.

3 Take the children through a warm-up, as in previous lessons. Have them form a circle and make the siren sounds (with their hands on their heads), and then repeat the 'Tarzan' cry (drumming the upper chest gently with fists). Next, tell the children to stamp forward after the count of three and shout 'ha', pulling back their elbows as they stamp. Repeat this with 'ho' and 'hee'.

4 Play the song through on TRACK 23 and sing along as a class.

5 Now play the rap section on TRACK 27 and encourage everyone to rap along. Without the music, try to come up with four more lines, using the rhyme board.

6 Tell the children to try the completed rap section, playing TRACK 27 and adding their new section at the end. If they have trouble writing the new lines, leave it out and continue the lesson.

7 Provide the children with the percussion instruments and recap on the pulse arrangement on TRACK 28 and rhythm arrangement on TRACK 29.

8 Play TRACK 24 for the children to play, sing and rap through the song.

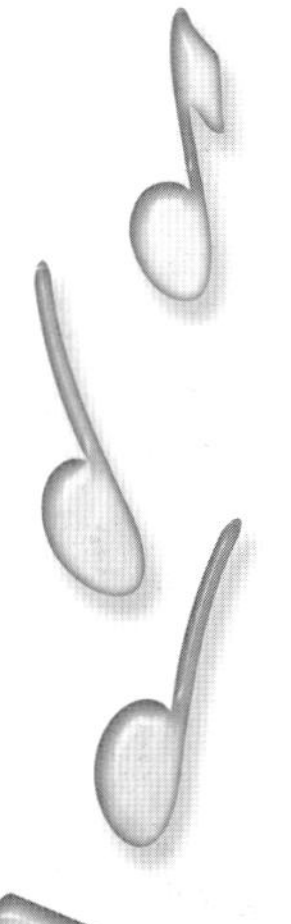

The rap

9 Now try singing along to TRACK 24, all the way through, using as many of the arm and leg movements they thought up before as possible.

10 Sit the children in a circle and once again ask them to make the sound of an animal; this time see if they can think of a simple movement to go with their sound. Go round the circle one by one asking the children to share their sound and movement. Reassure children that it's OK to have repeats or to have a sound but no movement. At the end, congratulate all the children for their creativity.

Chill out time!

Have the children sit down at their desks. Each child should lay their head on their arms with eyes closed, breathing slowly through their nose. Encourage them to listen to the sounds around them in complete silence for two minutes.

Lesson 5 Moods and feelings

Note – You will be using the instrument trolley for this lesson.

Music objective

Exploring musical processes.

Learning activity

- Composing music using a range of different sounds and musical ideas in response to a task (QCA units 1:1 and 3:5).
- Recapping the song (QCA unit 1:7).

QCA learning objectives

Unit 1 Ongoing skills

'This unit highlights the musical skills that require regular practice and ongoing development throughout the key stage.'

'Singing songs with control and using the voice expressively.'

- Section 1 – Children should learn to use different voices and find their singing voice.

'Listening, memory and movement.'

Children should learn:

- Section 7 – to listen carefully and develop their aural memory.

Unit 3 The long and the short of it – Exploring duration

'This unit develops children's ability to discriminate between longer and shorter sounds, and to use them to create interesting sequences of sound.'

'Can we work together to make extended sequences combining long and short sounds?'

- Section 5 – Children should learn how to use instruments to make sequences of long and short sounds.

Scottish attainment targets

Using materials, techniques, skills and media (voice/instruments)

- Level D – Sing together confidently in harmony and unison, demonstrating awareness of dynamics, phrasing and expression.
- Level C – Display two-handed co-ordination in playing.
- Level B – Play simple rhythmic parts, showing some control over speed and volume.

Using materials, techniques, skills and media (investigating: exploring sound)

- Levels D/E – Explore melodic, harmonic and rhythmic patterns and contrasts, electronic and acoustic effects and simple harmony.

Expressing feelings, ideas, thought and solutions (creating and designing)

- Level D – Invent music which incorporates simple melodic harmonic and rhythmic features, and shows imagination and some awareness of structure and contrasts.

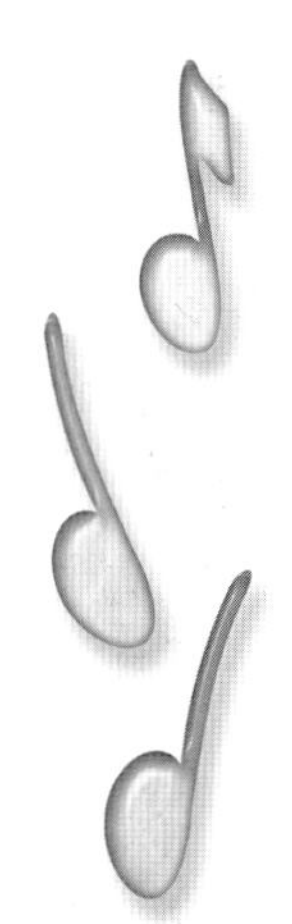

Mammals and me

Lesson 5 Moods and feelings

1 Carry out a vocal warm-up with the class as in Lesson 1.

2 In this lesson, we leave the song temporarily and explore music in another way. Ask the children to sit in a circle and remain quiet. Explain that they must listen to three pieces of music and answer questions about them.

3 Play TRACKS 32, 33 and 34 and listen to three musical sections: 'The Classy Cat', 'The Jazz Cat' and 'The Rap Cat'. Ask the children to identify which section matches each type of cat.

4 Split the class into three groups and give out any available un-tuned musical instruments.

5 Ask each group to explore one of the three areas: classy, rap or jazz. Don't tell the other groups which one they decide to interpret. Give them ten minutes to create the appropriate music.

6 Now each group should perform a piece of short composition to the other groups and the others should guess which cat is being portrayed.

7 Play TRACK 29 and recap the rhythm parts to the song.

8 Play TRACK 23 and sing and rap along as a class. The children could play percussion at a given section. Tell them to remember to include movements selected for the rap part.

Lesson 5 Moods and feelings

9 Practise the song again as a class with TRACK 23.

10 Play TRACK 24 (the backing track) and encourage the children to sing along, trying to get all the way to the end.

11 Split the class in half, and have each group try to sing the song and rap all the way through, performing to the other group. If the 'performance' breaks down, get the other children to applaud – it's not the completion that matters, it's the effort put in that counts.

Chill out time!

Have the children lie down and relax on the floor, closing their eyes and breathing slowly. Try to induce total silence. Ask the children to listen to the sounds around them. After a suitable amount of time, ask the children to sit up again, then go round the class one by one, asking each child to recount the different sounds they heard. Answers might include: the sound of someone breathing; the distant sound of cars or traffic; birds outside; voices from the classroom next door; someone in the room giggling.

Mammals and me

Lesson 6

The performance

Note – You will be using the percussion trolley for this lesson.

Music objective

Developing the ability to take part in a class performance with confidence, expression and control.

Learning activity

- Performing together (QCA units 1:1 and 1:3).
- Playing percussion parts (QCA unit 4:1 and 4:7).
- Doing a vocal warm-up (QCA unit 1:1).

QCA learning objectives

Unit 1 Ongoing skills

'This unit highlights the musical skills that require regular practice and ongoing development throughout the key stage.'
'Singing songs with control and using the voice expressively.'
Children should learn:

- Section 1 – to use different voices and find their singing voice.
- Section 3 – to sing with others.

Unit 4 Feel the pulse – Exploring pulse and rhythm

'This unit develops children's ability to recognise the difference between pulse and rhythm and to perform with a sense of pulse.'
'What is pulse?'

- Section 1 – Children should learn what is meant by pulse or steady beat.

'Bringing it all together: Can we use pulse and rhythm to make accompaniments?'

- Section 7 – Children should learn how to use pulse and rhythm to create an accompaniment for a chant or song.

Scottish attainment targets

Expressing feelings, ideas, thought and solutions (communicating and presenting)

- Levels C–E – Work co-operatively in a group when music making or inventing, showing a respect for the opinions of others. When and where appropriate, present and perform music to the teacher, another group, the rest of the class, or to a wider audience.

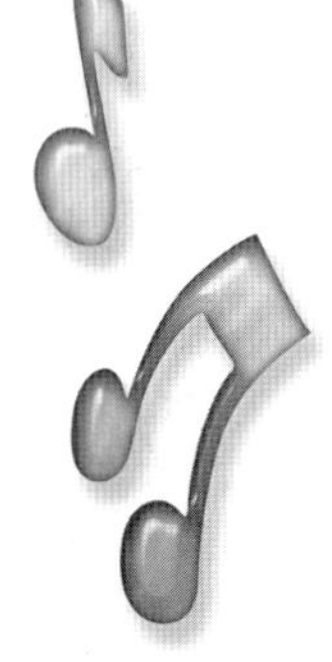

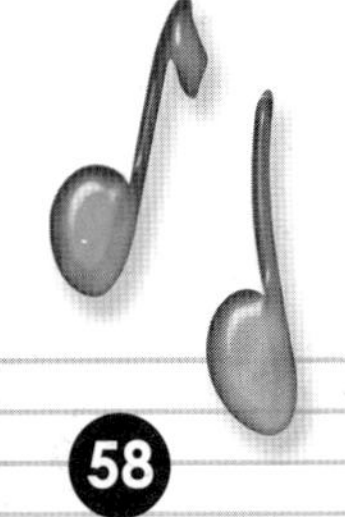

Lesson 6 The performance

1 This performance can be limited to the classroom. It can be later performed at a school assembly or included in a school play. Use TRACK 24 (the backing track) for the performance.

2 Take the children through a vocal warm-up, as in Lesson 1:

- Ask the children to stand in a circle and make sure they are standing in 'neutral' – with un-folded arms and legs shoulder-width apart. Ask them to imagine that their head is attached to a piece of string from above, which is pulling their head and shoulders up straight.
- Loosen up the body in whatever way is preferred (for example, rotating the head in a circle, doing large circles clockwise and anti-clockwise with the arms from the shoulder, circles with the hips, circles with the feet and knees, then shaking the whole leg away).
- Take a deep breath into the lower abdomen to the count of three through the nose, then continue to breathe in for a further three counts, bringing the breath into the upper chest. Then breathe out slowly to a count of 20. This ensures diaphragmatic, rather than shallow, breaths. Ask the children to put one hand on their stomach and the other on their upper chest, so they can feel them both rising and falling as they breathe.)
- Repeat, now doing a 'Sss' sound on the out-breath.
- Repeat doing a hum on the out-breath.

3 Practise the rap part first, using TRACK 27 on the CD.

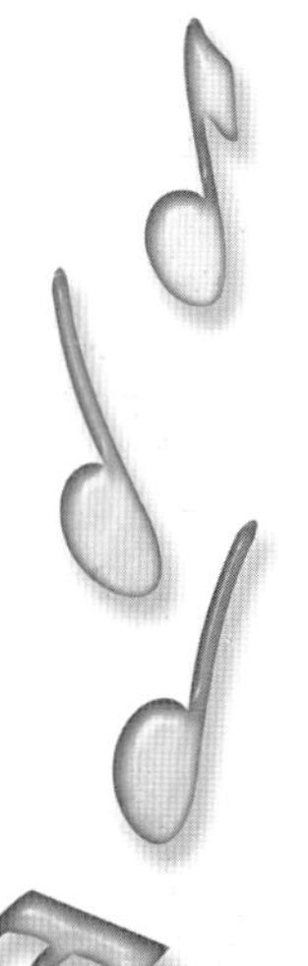

The performance

4 Get all percussion instruments ready and run through the percussion parts, playing TRACK 29 if necessary.

5 Arrange the children into their performing positions.

6 Children often do their best rendition the first time through, so if you are going to get the children to perform in front of others, try not to let them sing it all the way through, just refresh sections beforehand.

7 For fun, let half the class perform to the other half and then swap over, or boys to girls then girls to boys. The half listening are allowed to pull faces and try to 'put off' the performers but they must not make a sound. This leads to stifled laughter and a great deal of fun. Explain to the children the reason for this is so they may get used to performing in front of people without being 'put off'. It can lead to a strengthening in concentration.

8 Play TRACK 24 and have the children stand in a circle and perform the song, using the circular motion, and the arm and leg movements from the earlier lessons.

9 If the children have been able to manage it, split the verses up between them so that one half of the class sings verse one, the other half sings verse two, and then they all sing together on the chorus. Encourage them to make the choruses louder and louder. Perhaps the children could all sing the last chorus in a whisper, for an interesting effect, and see how quietly they can go.

Play some soft music in the background and have the children lie relaxed on the floor, stretched out with their eyes closed. Ask them to think about relaxing up from the ankles, legs, body, arms, neck to the head.

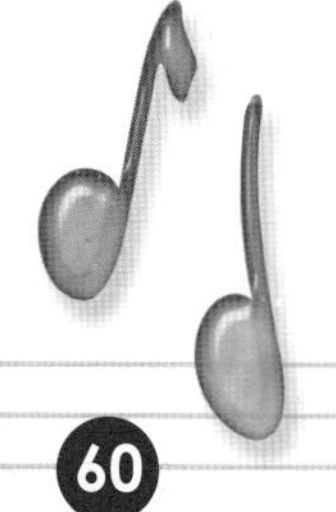

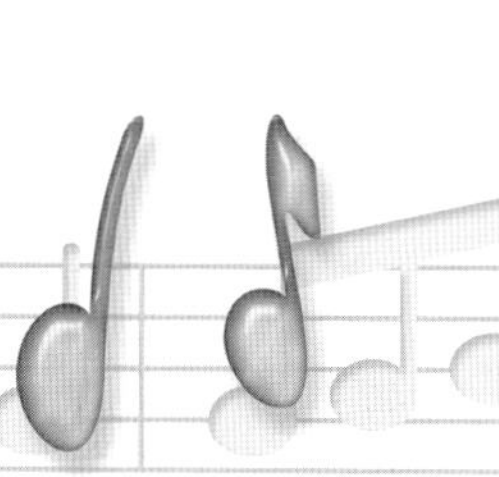

Mammals and Me

Chorus
Mammals and me
Mammals and me
Mammals and me
Mammals and me

Verse 1
We live in the land
We can live in the sea
Paw, fin or hand
And have little babies

Chorus
Mammals and me
Mammals and me
Mammals and me
Mammals and me

Verse 2
Some have big fins
Some have four legs
Me, I've got two
And we don't lay eggs

Chorus
Mammals and me
Mammals and me
Mammals and me
Mammals and me

Rap
Whales and dolphins in the sea
Sing and dance like you and me
Naughty monkey in a tree
Loves to climb like you and me

Rhythm break
Second rap

Chorus
Mammals and me
Mammals and me
Mammals and me
Mammals and me

Verse 1 repeat
We can live in the land
We can live in the sea
Paw, fin or hand
And have little babies

GOOD LUCK WITH YOUR PERFORMANCE!
(Note: This performance can take place in the classroom, in front of the whole school at assembly, or as part of a school play. Wherever you perform it, make sure you all have fun doing it!)

CARROTS
McCOURT&DONALDSON
♩=120
A C D7 A C
PLANT THAT SEED IN THE___ GROUND SUN - SHINE AND WA - TER
D7 A C D7
HELP IT TO GROW THEN THE GREEN SHOOTS START TO SHOW
A G E PLAY 3 TIMES A G E A
WATCH THOSE CA- RROTS GROW___ DOWN DOWN DEEP IN THE GROUND
A A A C D7
PUT THEM IN A SOUP OR PUT THEM IN A STEW
A C D7 A C
COOKED OR RAW IT'S UP TO___ YOU___ SCRAPE THEM GRATE THEM
D7 A G E PLAY 3 TIMES
CHOP THEM UP___ GO - NNA DIG MY CA- RROTS UP___ GO - NNA
A G E A A A
DIG MY CA - RROTS UP FROM THE GROUND
A C D7 PLAY 4 TIMES CHORDS SIM
SCOOP SCOOP SCOO - BY DOOP SCOO - BY DOO WA___ GO - NNA
A G E PLAY 3 TIMES A G E A
EAT MY CA- RROTS UP___ YUM YUM THEY TASTE REALLY SCRUM
2 A C D7 A C
VI - TA - MINS A C AND___ E___ I KNOW THEY ARE
D7 A C D7
GOOD FOR___ ME___ MAKE ME STRONG AND HELP ME TO GROW
A G E PLAY 3 TIMES
WATCH MY MUS - CLES___ GROW___
A G E A A FINE
GROW GROW FROM MY HEAD TO MY TOE___

NEESA

McCourt&Donaldson

$♩=50$

Voice

NEE-SA NEE-SA NEE - SA NEE-SA NEE-SA NEE - SA NEE-SA NEE-SA

6

NEE - SA GAI-WE-O GAI-WE-O

11

NEE-SA NEE-SA NEE - SA NEE-SA NEE-SA NEE - SA NEE-SA NEE-SA

16

NEE - SA NEE-SA NEE-SA NEE - SA GAI-WE-O

GAI-WE-O

21

NEE-SA NEE-SA NEE - SA NEE-SA NEE-SA NEE - SA NEE-SA NEE-SA

GAI-WE-O

26

NEE - SA NEE-SA NEE-SA NEE - SA GAI-WE-O

GAI-WE-O

30

FINE SPOKEN WORD 16 D.S. AL FINE

GAI-WE-O

16

MAMMALS AND ME
♩=120
DONALDSON&McCOURT
MAM-MALS AND ME
MAM-MALS AND ME MAM-MALS AND ME
MAM-ALS AND ME LIVE ON THE LAND WE CAN LIVE IN THE SEA
PAW, FIN OR HAND AND HAVE LIT-TLE BA-BIES
SOME HAVE BIG FINS SOME HAVE FOUR LEGS ME I'VE GOT
TWO AND WE DON'T LAY EGGS MAM-MALS AND ME
MAM-MALS AND ME MAM-MALS AND ME MAM-ALS AND ME
RAP SECTION
RHYTHM SIM.
16
RAP CONTINUES SIM.
MAM-MALS AND ME MAM-MALS AND ME
MAM-MALS AND ME MAM-ALS AND ME WE CAN
LIVE ON THE LAND WE CAN LIVE IN THE SEA
PAW, FIN OR HAND AND HAVE LIT-TLE BA-BIES

Healthy food

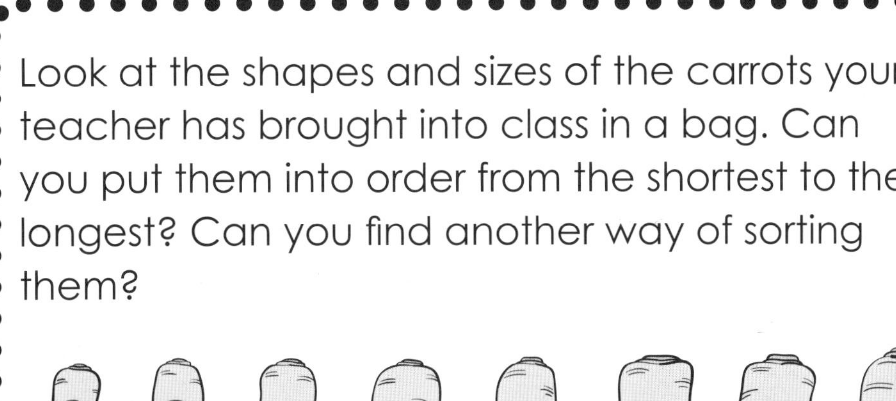

Look at the shapes and sizes of the carrots your teacher has brought into class in a bag. Can you put them into order from the shortest to the longest? Can you find another way of sorting them?

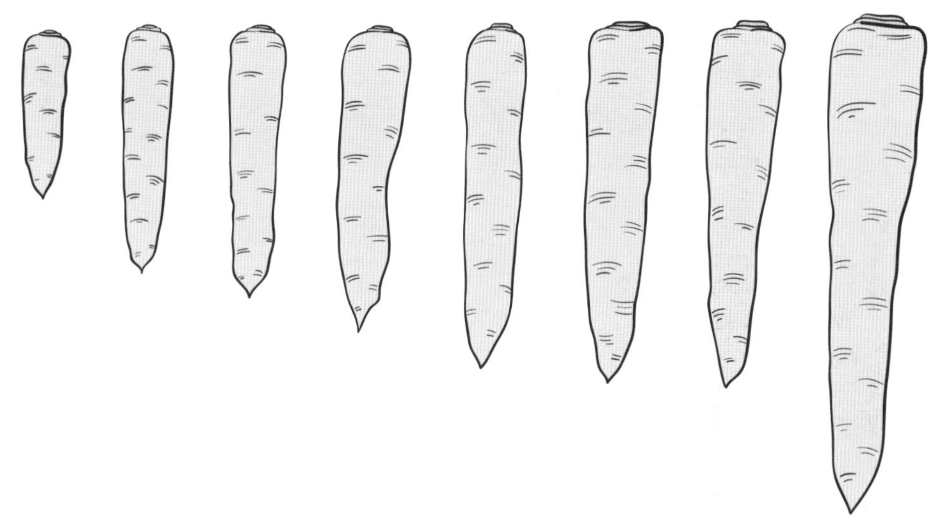

Activities

Healthy food

Coleslaw

Grate a carrot. Be careful to keep your fingers well away from the grater. Ask a grown-up to chop some white cabbage up very finely for you. Mix the cabbage and the carrots together with some mayonnaise. Yum!

What other foods do you eat with carrots in? Can you find out another healthy recipe using carrots? Write it down to share with the rest of your class.

Activities

Mammals and me

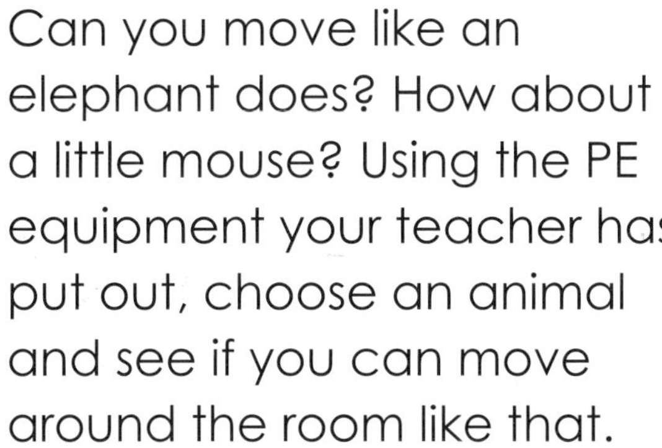

Can you move like an elephant does? How about a little mouse? Using the PE equipment your teacher has put out, choose an animal and see if you can move around the room like that.

Your teacher will put you into groups and will tell each group what kind of animal it's going to be. Work out how your animals would move together as a group – perhaps you're a pack, or a shoal, or a flock. Show the other children how your group moves and see if they can guess what animals you're being.

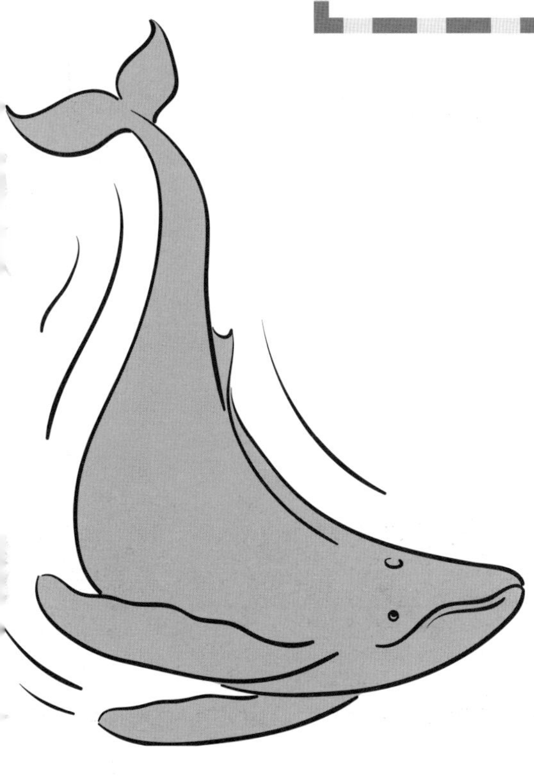

Activities

Mammals and me

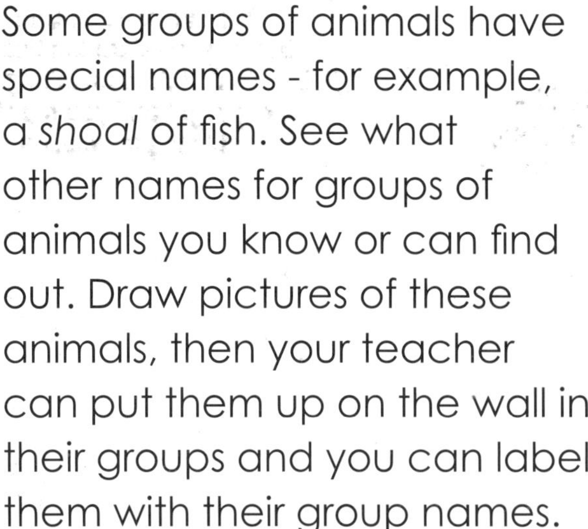

Some groups of animals have special names - for example, a *shoal* of fish. See what other names for groups of animals you know or can find out. Draw pictures of these animals, then your teacher can put them up on the wall in their groups and you can label them with their group names.

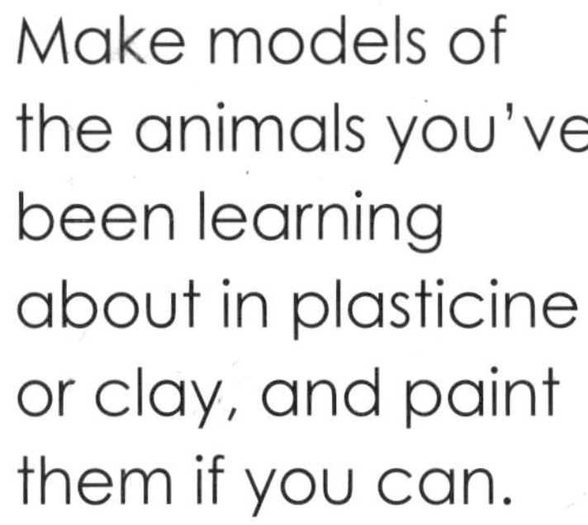

Make models of the animals you've been learning about in plasticine or clay, and paint them if you can.

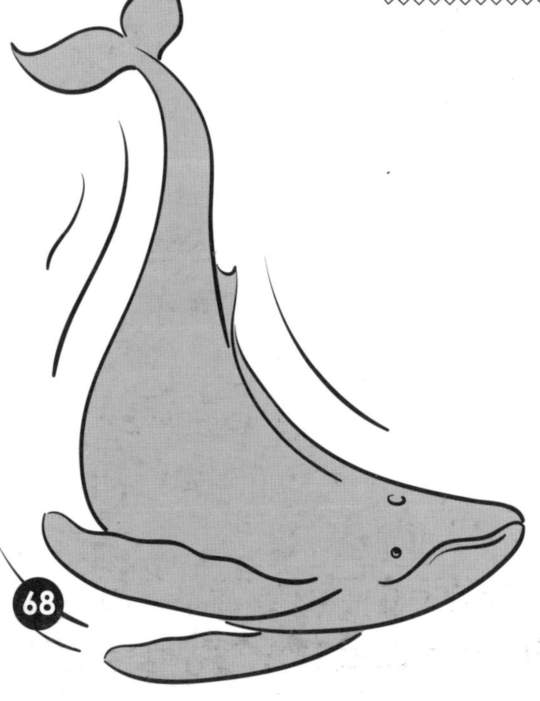